WILEY BOOKS IN THE CERTMIKE SERIES

CompTIA ITF+ CertMike: *Prepare. Practice. Pass the Test! Get Certified! Exam FC0-U61*
by Mike Chapple
(ISBN 9781119897811)

CompTIA A+ CertMike: *Prepare. Practice. Pass the Test! Get Certified! Core 1 Exam 220-1101*
by Mike Chapple and Mark Soper
(ISBN 9781119898092)

CompTIA A+ CertMike: *Prepare. Practice. Pass the Test! Get Certified! Core 2 Exam 220-1102*
by Mike Chapple and Mark Soper
(ISBN 9781119898122)

CompTIA Network+ CertMike: *Prepare. Practice. Pass the Test! Get Certified! Exam N10-008*
by Mike Chapple and Craig Zacker
(ISBN 9781119898153)

CompTIA® ITF+ CertMike

Prepare. Practice. Pass the Test! Get Certified!

CompTIA® ITF+ CertMike

Prepare. Practice. Pass the Test! Get Certified!
Exam FC0-U61

Mike Chapple

SYBEX®
A Wiley Brand

To all of my students at Notre Dame. The energy, enthusiasm, and experiences you bring to the classroom make me a better teacher and writer.

—Mike

ACKNOWLEDGMENTS

This book marks the start of a new test prep series called *CertMike: Prepare. Practice. Pass the Test! Get Certified!*, and I'd first like to thank the people who helped shape the vision for this series. The original idea was hatched over breakfast with two very supportive editors from the Wiley team: Ken Brown and Jim Minatel. I've worked with both Jim and Ken on many books over many years, and they're both insightful industry experts who know what it takes to produce a great book.

I'd also like to extend a special thank-you to my agent, Carole Jelen of Waterside Productions. Carole is also an experienced industry pro who can deftly navigate the murky waters of publishing. Carole is the one who pushed me to create my own series.

Of course, the creation of any book involves a tremendous amount of effort from many people other than the author. I truly appreciate the work of Adaobi Obi Tulton, the project editor. Adaobi and I have now worked together on many books, and she keeps the train on the tracks! I'd also like to thank Audrey O'Shea, the technical editor, who provided insightful advice and gave wonderful feedback throughout the book, and Archana Pragash, production editor, who guided me through layouts, formatting, and final cleanup to produce a great book. I would also like to thank the many behind-the-scenes contributors, including the graphics, production, and technical teams who make the book and companion materials into a finished product.

Finally, I would like to thank my family, who supported me through the late evenings, busy weekends, and long hours that a book like this requires to write, edit, and get to press.

About the Author

Mike Chapple, Ph.D., is author of the best-selling *CISSP (ISC)² Certified Information Systems Security Professional Official Study Guide* (Sybex, 2021) and the *CISSP (ISC)² Official Practice Tests* (Sybex, 2021). He is an information technology professional with two decades of experience in higher education, the private sector, and government.

Mike currently serves as Teaching Professor in the IT, Analytics, and Operations department at the University of Notre Dame's Mendoza College of Business, where he teaches undergraduate and graduate courses on cybersecurity, cloud computing, data management, and business analytics.

Before returning to Notre Dame, Mike served as executive vice president and chief information officer of the Brand Institute, a Miami-based marketing consultancy. Mike also spent four years in the information security research group at the National Security Agency and served as an active duty intelligence officer in the U.S. Air Force.

Mike has written more than 25 books. He earned both his B.S. and Ph.D. degrees from Notre Dame in computer science and engineering. Mike also holds an M.S. in computer science from the University of Idaho and an MBA from Auburn University. Mike holds the IT Fundamentals (ITF+), Cybersecurity Analyst+ (CySA+), Data+, Security+, Certified Information Security Manager (CISM), Certified Cloud Security Professional (CCSP), and Certified Information Systems Security Professional (CISSP) certifications.

Learn more about Mike and his other security certification materials at his website, CertMike.com.

About the Technical Editor

Audrey O'Shea holds CompTIA A+, ITF+, Network+, Security+, Project+, and other industry certifications. The former owner of a computer consulting company, she holds two degrees and a New York State teaching license. Audrey chose to become an educator to share her knowledge with the next wave of IT professionals. She has taught at the college level, in technical schools, and adult seminars with courses ranging from Electrical Theory and Practice for Energy Workers, to Microsoft Office, CompTIA A+, Introduction to Cybersecurity, and CISCO certification. Audrey is a teacher, author, consultant, and entrepreneur, and has helped many students learn what they need to know to pass their certification exams.

Audrey has authored two technical books: *A Geek Girl's Guide to Electronics and the Internet of Things* (Wiley, 2020) and *CompTIA A+ Complete Practice Tests*, 3rd Edition (Wiley, 2022). She has also served as technical editor on two other books leading to CompTIA certifications.

Audrey lives in upstate New York with her significant other and their fur babies. When she isn't behind a computer you can find her hiking in the Adirondack Mountains or kayaking on a lake somewhere.

CONTENTS

INTRODUCTION

If you're preparing to take the ITF+ (IT Fundamentals+) exam, you might find yourself overwhelmed with information. This exam covers a very broad range of topics, and it's possible to spend weeks studying each one of them. Fortunately, that's not necessary!

As part of the CertMike: Prepare. Practice. Pass the Test! Get Certified! series, this book is designed to help you focus on the specific knowledge that you'll need to pass the ITF+ exam. CompTIA publishes a detailed list of exam objectives, and this book is organized around those objectives. Each chapter clearly states the single objective that it covers and then, in a few pages, covers the material you need to know about that objective.

You'll find two important things at the end of each chapter: CertMike Exam Essentials and Practice Questions. The CertMike Exam Essentials distill the major points from the chapter into just a few bullet points. Reviewing these CertMike Exam Essentials is a great way to prepare yourself right before taking the exam.

I've also recorded an audio version of the CertMike Exam Essentials that you can access online at www.wiley.com/go/sybextestprep after registering and logging on. You can listen to the audio review when you're in the car, at the gym, or mowing the lawn!

Each chapter concludes with two practice questions that are designed to give you a taste of what it's like to take the exam. You'll find that they're written in the same style as the ITF+ exam questions and have very detailed explanations to help you understand the correct answer. Be sure to take your time and thoroughly study these questions.

Finally, the book's online test bank (www.wiley.com/go/sybextestprep) includes a full-length practice exam that you can use to assess your knowledge when you're ready to take the test. Good luck on the ITF+ exam!

> **NOTE**
>
> Don't just study the questions and answers! The questions on the actual exam will be different from the practice questions included in this book. The exam is designed to test your knowledge of a concept or objective, so use this book to learn the objectives behind the questions.

THE ITF+ EXAM

The ITF+ exam is designed to be a vendor-neutral certification for those seeking to enter the information technology field. CompTIA recommends this certification for three types of people:

- ▶ Students considering starting a career in information technology
- ▶ Professionals working in fields that require an understanding of information technology
- ▶ Sales, marketing, and operations professionals in IT-focused companies

The exam covers six major domains of knowledge:

1. IT Concepts and Terminology
2. Infrastructure
3. Applications and Software
4. Software Development Concepts
5. Database Fundamentals
6. Security

These six areas include a range of topics, from installing printers to securing networks, while focusing heavily on the basic knowledge expected of all IT professionals. That's why CompTIA recommends the ITF+ certification for those in any IT-related field.

The ITF+ exam uses only standard multiple-choice questions. Unlike other CompTIA exams, you won't find performance-based questions (PBQs) on the ITF+ exam. This exam is designed to be straightforward and not to trick you. If you know the material in this book, you will pass the exam.

The exam costs $130 in the United States, with roughly equivalent prices in other locations around the globe. More details about the ITF+ exam and how to take it can be found at www.comptia.org/certifications/it-fundamentals.

You'll have 50 minutes to take the exam and will be asked to answer up to 75 questions during that time period. Your exam will be scored on a scale ranging from 100 to 900, with a passing score of 650.

NOTE

CompTIA frequently does what is called *item seeding*, which is the practice of including unscored questions on exams. It does so to gather psychometric data, which is then used when developing new versions of the exam. Before you take the exam, you will be told that your exam may include these unscored questions. So, if you come across a question that does not appear to map to any of the exam objectives—or for that matter, does not appear to belong in the exam—it is likely a seeded question. You never really know whether or not a question is seeded, however, so always make your best effort to answer every question.

Taking the Exam

Once you are fully prepared to take the exam, you can visit the CompTIA website to purchase your exam voucher:

```
https://store.comptia.org
```

Currently, CompTIA offers two options for taking the exam: an in-person exam at a testing center and an at-home exam that you take on your own computer.

TIP

This book includes a coupon that you may use to save 10 percent on your CompTIA exam registration.

In-Person Exams

CompTIA partners with Pearson VUE's testing centers, so your next step will be to locate a testing center near you. In the United States, you can do this based on your address or your ZIP code, while non-U.S. test takers may find it easier to enter their city and country. You can search for a test center near you at the Pearson Vue website, where you will need to navigate to "Find a test center":

www.pearsonvue.com/comptia

Now that you know where you'd like to take the exam, simply set up a Pearson VUE testing account and schedule an exam on their site.

On the day of the test, take two forms of identification, and make sure to show up with plenty of time before the exam starts. Remember that you will not be able to take your notes, electronic devices (including smartphones and watches), or other materials in with you.

At-Home Exams

CompTIA began offering online exam proctoring in 2020 in response to the coronavirus pandemic. As of the time this book went to press, the at-home testing option was still available and appears likely to continue. Candidates using this approach will take the exam at their home or office and be proctored over a webcam by a remote proctor.

Due to the rapidly changing nature of the at-home testing experience, candidates wishing to pursue this option should check the CompTIA website for the latest details.

After the ITF+ Exam

Once you have taken the exam, you will be notified of your score immediately, so you'll know if you passed the test right away. You should keep track of your score report with your exam registration records and the email address you used to register for the exam.

After you earn the ITF+ certification, you're certified for life! Unlike many other CompTIA certifications that must be renewed on a periodic basis, the ITF+ certification is permanent and remains with you throughout your career.

Many people who earn the ITF+ credential use it as a stepping-stone to earning other certifications in their areas of interest. Those interested in technical support roles pursue the A+ certification, those interested in networking work toward the Network+ credential, and the Security+ certification is a gateway to a career in cybersecurity.

WHAT DOES THIS BOOK COVER?

This book covers everything you need to know to pass the ITF+ exam. It is organized into six parts, each corresponding to one of the six ITF+ domains.

Part I: Domain 1.0: IT Concepts and Terminology

Chapter 1: Notational Systems

Chapter 2: Data Types

Part V: Domain 5.0: Database Fundamentals

Chapter 30: Database Concepts

Chapter 31: Database Structures

Chapter 32: Database Interfaces

Part VI: Domain 6.0: Security

Chapter 33: Confidentiality, Integrity, and Availability

Chapter 34: Securing Devices

Chapter 35: Behavioral Security

Chapter 36: Authentication, Authorization, Accounting, and Nonrepudiation

Chapter 37: Password Best Practices

Chapter 38: Encryption

Chapter 39: Business Continuity and Disaster Recovery

CertMike: Prepare. Practice. Pass the Test! Get Certified! Series Elements

Each book in the CertMike Get Certified series uses a number of common elements to help you prepare. These include the following:

Exam Tips   Throughout each chapter, I've sprinkled practical exam tips that help focus your reading on topics that are particularly confusing or important to understand for the exam.

CertMike Exam Essentials   The exam essentials focus on major exam topics and critical knowledge that you should take into the test. The exam essentials focus on the exam objectives provided by CompTIA.

Practice Questions   Two questions at the end of each chapter help you assess your knowledge and if you are ready to take the exam based on your knowledge of that chapter's topics.

Practice Exam and Audio Review

This book comes with online study tools: a practice exam and audio review to help you prepare for the exam.

> **NOTE**
>
> Go to www.wiley.com/go/sybextestprep to register and gain access to the online study tools.

Practice Exam

The book includes a practice exam. You can test your knowledge of the ITF+ objectives that are covered in the chapters in their entirety or randomized. It's your choice!

Audio Review

I've recorded an audio review where I read each of the 39 sets of CertMike Exam Essentials. This review provides a helpful recap of the main topics covered on the exam, which you can listen to while you're commuting, working out, or relaxing.

> **NOTE**
>
> Like all exams, the ITF+ certification from CompTIA is updated periodically and may eventually be retired or replaced. At some point after CompTIA is no longer offering this exam, the old editions of our books and online tools will be retired. If you have purchased this book after the exam was retired, or are attempting to register in the Sybex online learning environment after the exam was retired, please know that we make no guarantees that this exam's online Sybex tools will be available once the exam is no longer available.

EXAM FC0-U61 EXAM OBJECTIVES

CompTIA goes to great lengths to ensure that its certification programs accurately reflect the IT industry's best practices. They do this by establishing committees for each of its exam programs. Each committee consists of a small group of IT professionals, training providers, and publishers who are responsible for establishing the exam's baseline competency level and who determine the appropriate target-audience level.

Once these factors are determined, CompTIA shares this information with a group of hand-selected subject matter experts (SMEs). These folks are the true brainpower behind the certification program. The SMEs review the committee's findings, refine them, and shape them into the objectives that follow this section. CompTIA calls this process a job-task analysis (JTA).

Finally, CompTIA conducts a survey to ensure that the objectives and weightings truly reflect job requirements. Only then can the SMEs go to work writing the hundreds of questions needed for the exam. Even so, they have to go back to the drawing board for further refinements in many cases before the exam is ready to go live in its final state. Rest assured that the content you're about to learn will serve you long after you take the exam.

CompTIA also publishes relative weightings for each of the exam's objectives. The following table lists the six ITF+ objective domains and the extent to which they are represented on the exam.

Domain	% of Exam
1.0 IT Concepts and Terminology	17%
2.0 Infrastructure	22%
3.0 Applications and Software	18%
4.0 Software Development Concepts	12%
5.0 Database Fundamentals	11%
6.0 Security	20%

FC0-U61 CERTIFICATION EXAM OBJECTIVE MAP

Objective	Chapter
1.0 IT Concepts and Terminology	
1.1 Compare and contrast notational systems	1
1.2 Compare and contrast fundamental data types and their characteristics	2
1.3 Illustrate the basics of computing and processing	3
1.4 Explain the value of data and information	4
1.5 Compare and contrast common units of measure	5
1.6 Explain the troubleshooting methodology	6
2.0 Infrastructure	
2.1 Classify common types of input/output device interfaces	7
2.2 Given a scenario, set up and install common peripheral devices to a laptop/PC	8

Objective	Chapter
5.3 Summarize methods used to interface with databases	32
6.0 Security	
6.1 Summarize confidentiality, integrity, and availability concerns	33
6.2 Explain methods to secure devices and best practices	34
6.3 Summarize behavioral security concepts	35
6.4 Compare and contrast authentication, authorization, accounting, and nonrepudiation concepts	36
6.5 Explain password best practices	37
6.6 Explain common uses of encryption	38
6.7 Explain business continuity concepts	39

> **NOTE**
>
> Exam objectives are subject to change at any time without prior notice and at CompTIA's discretion. Please visit CompTIA's website (www.comptia.org) for the most current listing of exam objectives.

HOW TO CONTACT THE PUBLISHER

If you believe you've found a mistake in this book, please bring it to our attention. At John Wiley & Sons, we understand how important it is to provide our customers with accurate content, but even with our best efforts an error may occur. In order to submit your possible errata, please email it to our Customer Service Team at wileysupport@wiley.com with the subject line "Possible Book Errata Submission."

Domain 1.0: IT Concepts and Terminology

IT Concepts and Terminology is the first domain of CompTIA's ITF+ exam. It provides the foundational knowledge that anyone in information technology needs to understand as they begin their careers. This domain has six objectives:

1.1 Compare and contrast notational systems

1.2 Compare and contrast fundamental data types and their characteristics

1.3 Illustrate the basics of computing and processing

1.4 Explain the value of data and information

1.5 Compare and contrast common units of measure

1.6 Explain the troubleshooting methodology

Questions from this domain make up 17% of the questions on the ITF+ exam, so you should expect to see approximately 13 questions on your test covering the material in this part.

CHAPTER 1

Notational Systems

Objective 1.1: Compare and contrast notational systems

Computers are designed to store and manipulate data in binary form, but that format isn't often convenient or appropriate for humans or software applications. *Notational systems* provide us with ways to use binary data storage technologies to represent numbers, text, and other data formats.

In this chapter, you'll learn everything you need to know about ITF+ objective 1.1, including the following topics:

▶ **Binary**
▶ **Hexadecimal**
▶ **Decimal**
▶ **Data representation**

STORING DATA

As we dive into the world of information technology, it's important to understand how computers store and work with data. Let's begin that discussion by talking about the basic units of storage in a computer system.

Binary Data

You've probably heard that computers work with *binary* data, or data that is stored as simply 0s and 1s. Everything that happens inside a computer system uses combinations of 0s and 1s. From the operating system and software that we run to our Microsoft Word documents or even a video file, everything is encoded in binary format. The reason for this is that computers can easily use this binary format to store data on disk, keep it in memory, or send it over a network.

The basic unit of binary storage in any computer system is the *bit*. A bit is a single binary digit that can be either 1 or 0. Those are the only two possible values for a bit. You can't put the number 2 or the letter Z in a bit. It can only be a 1 or a 0, as shown in Figure 1.1.

0
1

FIGURE 1.1 A single bit can only hold two values: 0 and 1.

When we store data on a magnetic hard drive, the computer divides the drive up into billions of tiny little spaces, each designed to store a single bit. If the value of the bit is 1, the computer places a magnetic charge in the location used by that bit. If the value of the bit is 0, the computer leaves no magnetic charge in that location.

When data is stored on a *solid-state drive (SSD)* or in memory, the process works the same way but using electricity instead of magnetism. If the value of a bit in memory is 1, a small electrical charge changes the value in that memory location to the "on" position. If the value of the bit is 0, the value in that position is set to the "off" position.

Now, computers may think in 0s and 1s, but that's not the way that we human beings think. We'd much prefer to think of our data in terms of letters and numbers! Computers store the data that we're more familiar with by combining multiple bits together.

If we have 2 bits of data, we can use them together to represent four different values, as shown in Figure 1.2.

0	0
0	1
1	0
1	1

FIGURE 1.2 Two bits can hold four possible values.

We could use the 2-bit values in Figure 1.2 to store whole numbers between 0 and 3. We simply assign each of the 2-bit binary possibilities a whole-number equivalent. Table 1.1 shows the standard conversion for these 2-bit values.

TABLE 1.1 Decimal conversion of 2-bit values

Binary Value	Decimal Value
00	0
01	1
10	2
11	3

If we have 3 bits of data, we can use them to store eight possible values: 000, 001, 010, 011, 100, 101, 110, and 111. These convert to decimal values ranging from 0 to 7, as shown in Table 1.2.

TABLE 1.2 Decimal conversion of 3-bit values

Binary Value	Decimal Value
000	0
001	1
010	2
011	3
100	4
101	5
110	6
111	7

Similarly, if we have 4 bits of data, we can store 16 possible values, and as we increase the number of bits, we increase the number of values. Once we get up to 8 bits, we find ourselves able to store 256 possible values, ranging from 0 to 255. That's an important number because we can store all of the possible characters and digits used by a computer system in this range.

This combination of 8 bits is known as a *byte*, and the byte is the second important unit of binary data storage. When you're thinking about text data, you can think of each character as being a single byte, made up of 8 bits.

Decimal Data

Whether or not you know it, you're already familiar with *decimal notation*. This is the numbering system that we use in our everyday lives, and it's based off multiples of the number 10.

In a decimal number, each digit can take on 10 possible values, ranging from 0 to 9, as shown in Figure 1.3.

0	5
1	6
2	7
3	8
4	9

FIGURE 1.3 **One decimal digit can hold 10 possible values.**

When we grow to two decimal digits, we can represent one hundred values, ranging from 0 to 99. Adding a third digit allows us to store numbers between 0 and 999. Every time that we add another digit, we increase the number of values we can store by 10.

Hexadecimal Data

Unless you've worked with computer memory before, you're probably not familiar with *hexadecimal notation*. In this notation, each value can store 16 possible values, ranging from 0 to 15. Now you're probably wondering how we can put a two-digit number like 10 or 15 into a single location. That's a good question!

We do this by using the values 0 through 9 to represent the numbers 0 through 9 but then using the values A through F to represent 10 through 15. Figure 1.4 shows the 16 possible values that may be stored in a single hexadecimal digit.

0	4	8	C
1	5	9	D
2	6	A	E
3	7	B	F

FIGURE 1.4 **A single hexadecimal digit can hold 16 possible values.**

Table 1.3 provides some examples of the same numbers expressed in decimal, binary, and hexadecimal forms.

TABLE 1.3 Binary, decimal, and hexadecimal equivalent values

Decimal Value	Binary Value	Hexadecimal Value
0	0	0
5	101	5
10	1010	A
123	1111011	7B

The math here gets a little complicated, but the good thing is that you won't be asked to convert these values on the exam. What you want to understand is that if you see a value consisting of 0s and 1s, that's binary. If you see values made up of the digits 0 through 9, that's decimal. And if you see the letters A through F mixed in with those digits, that's hexadecimal.

EXAM TIP

Expect to see exam questions that ask you to identify the best notational system or data representation for a given situation. If the question mentions anything about non-English characters, you'll probably want to use a Unicode data representation. If the question asks about values that can be encoded as 0 or 1, true or false, off or on, yes or no, or similar two-value options, that's a key indicator that binary data storage is appropriate.

CHARACTER ENCODING

We've discussed three notation systems: binary, decimal, and hexadecimal. Those are the different ways that we can represent numbers. But we often want to store and process text values instead of numbers when we're working with data. The way that we do this is to encode text characters as numbers.

You may remember when we first discussed binary data, I mentioned that computers typically work in units of bytes and that each byte consists of 8 bits. Bytes can store decimal numbers from 0 to 255, and we use 1 byte to store one character of text. We do this by using standard codes to describe how we encode each character as a number.

When we're using English or another language that uses our alphabet, we use a code called the American Standard Code for Information Interchange, or *ASCII*. This code describes what numeric value to use for each of the uppercase and lowercase letters, digits, punctuation, and other symbols commonly used in the English language. ASCII was originally designed as a 7-bit code, but modern computers use an extended version of ASCII that uses 8-bit bytes.

If you're working in languages other than English, you need to have more characters available to you. This requires the use of a different code. *Unicode* is a large character set capable of representing thousands of different characters using 8 or 16 bits of data.

CERTMIKE EXAM ESSENTIALS

▶ Binary data is the native format used by computer systems and is used to store values that can be represented as either 0 or 1. Decimal values are the base-10 numbers that we use in our everyday lives that use digits between 0 and 9. Hexadecimal values extend the number of possible values in a single digit to 16 by adding the values A–F as possibilities.

▶ ASCII data representations are used to store the characters of standard English text in binary form. Unicode data representations can store English characters as well as characters used in other languages.

Practice Question 1

A developer is working on a new software program that will store data in memory about many different characteristics of customers of a bank. Each of these characteristics is best represented as a "yes" or "no" value.

What notational system would *best* store this type of data?

A. Hexadecimal
B. Decimal
C. ASCII
D. Binary

Practice Question 2

Your company recently entered into a partnership with an organization based in Egypt and you are helping an executive receive documents that must be translated from Arabic into English. The documents contain Arabic characters, but those characters are not rendering properly on the screen.

What representational system is *best* used for this type of document?

A. ASCII
B. Binary
C. Unicode
D. Hexadecimal

Practice Question 1 Explanation

This question is asking us to identify the notational system that would *best* meet the described need. This is a very common format for CompTIA exam questions, and you should be prepared to evaluate all of the possible answer choices and find the one that is better than all the others.

Let's evaluate these choices one at a time:

1. First, we have the possibility of using hexadecimal values. It would indeed be possible to store "yes" and "no" as hexadecimal values by using the hexadecimal value of 0 to represent "no" and 1 to represent "yes." However, this is wasteful because a single hexadecimal digit can be used to store up to 15 possible values and we only need the ability to store two possible values. So this isn't a great option.

2. Next, we are presented with the choice of storing the values in decimal form. As with hexadecimal, we could encode "no" as the decimal value 0 and "yes" as the decimal value 1, but that would be wasteful, so it is not the best option.

3. We could use ASCII to store the text strings "yes" and "no" as well, but this requires us to use 3 bytes of storage to store a three-letter word. Again, this is a possibility, but it is not the best option.

4. The last option, binary, is the best one here. We can encode "yes" as the binary value 1 and "no" as the binary value 0 and use our data storage efficiently.

Correct Answer: D. Binary

Practice Question 2 Explanation

In this question, you're being asked to identify the best representational system to use when storing text data in a file. That allows us to narrow down our answer choices quickly. ASCII and Unicode are representational systems for text, whereas binary and hexadecimal are notational systems for storing data. We can, therefore, quickly eliminate binary and hexadecimal as answer choices.

When you take the ITF+ exam, watch for opportunities like this where you can immediately eliminate answer choices that are obviously wrong. This can help you focus your attention quickly and increase the odds that you will pick the correct answer.

Next, we must decide among the two remaining answers. ASCII only allows the storage of English characters, so it won't work very well in this scenario. We can, however, store the Arabic characters using a Unicode data representation, making Unicode our best option.

Remember, the use of non-English characters is a key indicator that Unicode is an appropriate choice!

Correct Answer: C. Unicode

CHAPTER 2

Data Types

Objective 1.2: Compare and contrast fundamental data types and their characteristics

While computers are designed to directly work with binary code, operating systems and applications are written with human users in mind. In the previous chapter, you learned how binary bits can be used to represent different decimal, hexadecimal, and text values. In this chapter, you'll discover the different types of data objects that you can use when creating software to run on a computer.

You'll learn everything you need to know about ITF+ objective 1.2, including the following topics:

▶ **Char**
▶ **Strings**
▶ **Numbers**
▶ **Boolean**

DATA TYPES

Each data object used by an application has an associated *data type* that tells the computer how to handle the data that it encounters. This is how we tell the difference between numeric values, character strings, and other types of data that we might have stored in memory or on disk.

> **EXAM TIP**
>
> Expect to see exam questions that ask you to identify the best data type to use in a given situation. When you face a question like this, you should first determine whether the data is numeric, text, or binary. If the data is numeric and a whole number, then choose integer values. If the data is numeric with a decimal, then choose floating-point values. If the data is text, choose char if it will be a single character or string if it will be more than one character. If the data requires only a single binary bit, such as a yes/no, on/off, or true/false value, use a Boolean data type.

Boolean Data

The most basic data type is the *Boolean* object. A Boolean data element consists of only a single bit, so it can only have two possible values—0 and 1. That might sound pretty limiting, but Boolean data types are widely used in computer systems to represent values that are either true or false. The value 0 represents false and the value 1 represents true.

When we're designing software, we often refer to these Boolean values as *flags* and use them for a wide variety of purposes. For example, if I'm storing data about products that I maintain in my store's inventory, I could have a flag called Taxable that represents whether sales tax should be charged when the product is sold or whether it is exempt from tax. Products that are taxable would have a 1 in the taxable field, making the taxable value TRUE, whereas products that are not taxable would have a 0, making the taxable value FALSE.

Numeric Data

We also commonly store numeric values in memory. They come in two basic forms: *integers* and *floating-point numbers*.

Integers

Integers are values that do not have decimal or fractional values. They are whole numbers, such as 1, 2, and 3. They may also take on negative values, such as –123.

Floats

Floating-point numbers, or floats, are numbers that do have decimal places associated with them. The precision of a floating-point number indicates how many decimal places may be used with that number. The more precision we use, the more memory a floating-point number consumes.

Examples of floating-point numbers include 1.2, 3.642, and 150.0. Note that it is possible to store numbers with no decimal content in a floating-point value, such as 150.0. However, it is more efficient to store this type of data in an integer, and software will treat floats and integers differently when performing some types of calculation.

Text Data

Finally, we often store text values in memory and on disk. A single character of text uses the *char* data type and, in the ASCII encoding system, consumes a single byte of memory.

Character strings consist of one or more characters strung together, such as in a word, sentence, or paragraph, and they consume 1 byte per character.

> **WARNING**
>
> ITF+ candidates often become confused about the appropriate data type to use for ZIP codes (the postal codes used in the United States). ZIP codes are 5- or 9-digit values that consist entirely of numbers. However, they should *always* be stored as character strings and not numeric values. The reason for this is that they are not used in computation, and because some ZIP codes start with the digit 0, numeric data types would truncate this digit, making the ZIP code invalid. For example, 07717 is the ZIP code for Avon-by-the-Sea, New Jersey. If this ZIP code were stored in an integer field, it would be truncated to 7717, which is not a valid ZIP code.

Tying It All Together

You should be prepared to answer questions where you are provided with a scenario and are asked to choose the best data type for that situation. Figure 2.1 shows a flowchart that you can use to make these decisions.

Table 2.1 provides an example of the types of information that a store might maintain about the products that it sells. Review this table and each of the data elements. What data type do you think should be used for each one?

T A B L E   2 . 1   Product information

Product Name	Price	Quantity	Taxable	Discounted
Bicycle	899.49	47	Yes	TRUE
Helmet	49.99	13	Yes	FALSE
Handlebars	62.99	85	No	FALSE
Seat	104.99	19	No	TRUE

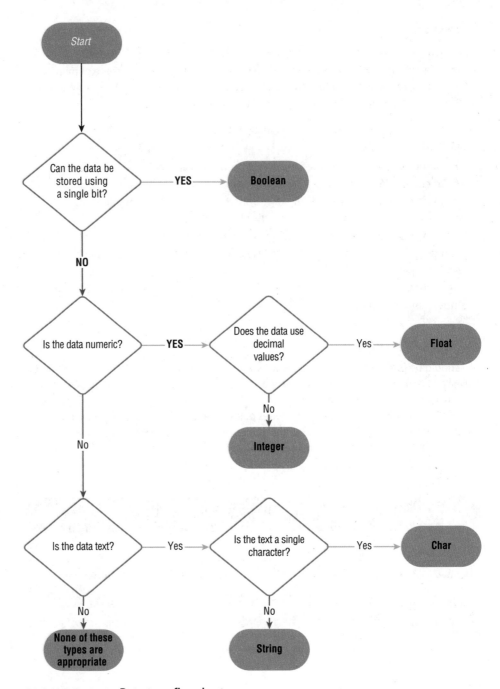

FIGURE 2.1 Data type flowchart

As you look through this table, consider each of the columns:

▶ Product Name is text data. The field contains words, which are multiple characters strung together, so it should be stored using a string data type.

▶ Price is monetary data. It contains numeric data that includes decimal values, so it should be stored using a floating-point data type.

▶ Quantity is also numeric data, but it contains only whole numbers, so it should be stored as an integer data type.

▶ Taxable is a Yes/No field, so it may be stored using a single binary bit, where 1 represents Yes and 0 represents No. Therefore, it should be stored as a Boolean value.

▶ Discounted is a TRUE/FALSE field and it may be treated the same way, encoding the value TRUE as 1 and the value FALSE as 0. It should also be stored as a Boolean value.

CERTMIKE EXAM ESSENTIALS

▶ Data that will be used in computations should be in numeric form. Numeric data may be either whole numbers, stored as integers, or decimal numbers, stored as floating-point values.

▶ Text data may be stored in character data types if it will be a single character or in character strings if the text will be multiple characters joined together, such as a word, sentence, or paragraph.

▶ Data elements that can be represented as a single binary digit (bit) should use the Boolean data type to conserve storage and memory.

Practice Question 1

You are creating a new software program for your organization that will track the number of times a customer visits your store. The program will contain a variable called visits that will maintain the tally.

What data type would be *best* suited for the visits variable?

A. Boolean
B. String
C. Integer
D. Float

Practice Question 2

You are working with a software developer who is creating a database that will track information about the guests who stay at a hotel. One of the variables that you wish to track is whether each guest is a member of the hotel loyalty program. You will track this in a variable called loyalty.

What data type would be **best** suited for the loyalty variable?

A. Boolean
B. String
C. Integer
D. Float

Practice Question 1 Explanation

In this question, we're asked to choose the most appropriate data type for a given situation. We can approach this using the flowchart method discussed in this chapter. Let's walk through that flowchart together.

First, we're asked if we can store the data in a single binary bit. This would allow us only two possible values, such as 0/1, true/false, or yes/no. The number of times a customer visits a store may take on many possible values, so we cannot store it in a bit and a Boolean data type is not appropriate.

Next, we're asked if the data is numeric. The number of times that a customer visits a store is numeric data, so we then ask the follow-up question of whether it uses decimal values. It wouldn't make sense for the number of customer visits to be a decimal number (what would 1.5 visits mean?), so a float is not appropriate. We then decide to use an integer value as the most appropriate data type.

The only other possible answer choice here is a string value, which is not appropriate because this data is numeric and we would very likely want to perform calculations on it, such as tallying the average number of visits per customer or the total number of visits per month.

Correct Answer: C. Integer

Practice Question 2 Explanation

This question also calls for the use of the flowchart shown in Figure 2.1. We begin the flowchart by asking the question: "Can this data be stored using a single bit?"

The variable will store data about whether a customer is a member of the loyalty program. There are only two possible answers to this question: yes and no. Therefore, it is possible to store this data in a single bit, so a Boolean data type would be the best choice.

You could also use any of the other data types listed to store this data. You could use character strings to store the words "yes" and "no." You could also use integers or floating-point numbers to store 0 and 1 values. However, these are not the best choices because those data types will use more storage than a single Boolean bit with no added value. That's why the flowchart directs us to use Boolean values whenever we can store data using only a single bit.

Correct Answer: A. Boolean

CHAPTER 3

Computing Basics

Objective 1.3: Illustrate the basics of computing and processing

Computers perform four basic operations on data : they accept input from users and devices, process data by performing calculations and other operations, store data obtained from input and processing, and provide output of their results.

In this chapter, you'll learn everything you need to know about ITF+ objective 1.3, including the following topics:

▶ **Input**
▶ **Processing**
▶ **Output**
▶ **Storage**

COMPUTER ACTIONS

Any computing device performs four basic operations: obtaining input, storing data, processing data, and providing output. This is true whether you're dealing with a laptop or desktop computer, a server, a smartphone, a tablet, or another specialized computing device.

Input

Input is when we provide information to the device to help us do our work. Input often comes from users, and we provide that input in a variety of ways. If we're using a laptop or desktop computer, we might provide input by typing on the keyboard or moving and clicking the mouse. On a tablet or smartphone, we're used to interacting by tapping or swiping on the screen or by using our voices.

Input doesn't have to come directly from a person. Computers can also receive input from other computers, from stored data, or even from sensors. For example, the thermostat in your home is a computer. It receives input from a built-in thermometer that tells it the current temperature in your home. It also receives input from residents when they change the temperature setting on the thermostat screen.

Storage

When a computer receives input, it can do two different things with that input: it can store the data directly or it might perform some processing on that data (discussed in the next section) and then store it.

Storage mechanisms allow computers to maintain data that they will need later. Computers can store data in two different ways. They might keep some data stored in memory, where the computer can quickly access it on a temporary basis, or they might write the data to a hard drive, cloud storage service, or other storage location where it may be kept more permanently.

Processing

Processing is when the computer analyzes data and performs operations on it. For example, if the computer calculates the total amount of a customer order by adding together the prices of individual products and computing taxes and discounts, that's an example of processing.

Computers can also process data in other ways. When a computer manipulates an image file, plays a video file stored on disk, or predicts the weather, all of those actions are examples of processing.

In most computer systems, processing is done by a special chip inside the computer called the *central processing unit (CPU)*. We'll cover CPUs and other ways of processing data in Chapter 9, "Internal Computing Components."

Output

For a computer to be useful to us, it needs some way to provide us with *output*. Output is simply the computer reporting back to us on the results of its processing.

Output can come in many forms. The simplest form of output is simply showing the results of processing data on the screen, where we can read it. We can also use a printer to create a paper record of output.

Output can also come in other forms. Instead of providing us with the output of its calculations for us to read, a computer might use output to provide instructions to another device on how it should perform.

Tying It All Together

Let's tie that all together by returning to the thermostat example from earlier.

Input

A thermostat is a computer that receives input from two different sources. You might provide input to the thermostat by telling it the temperature you'd like to have in your home. You might set your thermostat to 74 degrees Fahrenheit. The thermostat also receives input from its built-in thermometer, telling it the actual temperature in your home, which might be 77 degrees on a warm day.

Processing

The thermostat then performs some processing on that input. Basically, it asks the question, is the current temperature lower than the desired temperature, equal to the desired temperature, or above the desired temperature?

Storage

The thermostat might store the current temperature in memory so that it can later show you data on the temperature in your house over time.

Output

The thermostat provides some output in the form of instructions to other devices. If the current temperature is lower than your desired temperature, that means that your house is too cool and the thermostat tells the furnace to turn on and generate heat. If it's too warm in the house, the thermostat turns on the air conditioning to cool down the temperature.

These four actions—input, processing, storage, and output—are the basic activities carried out by any computing system. For example, think about the computer that you use most often. It likely has the following:

► Input devices, including a keyboard, mouse/trackpad, microphone, and video camera

► Processing capability in its CPU

► Storage capacity in memory and a hard disk drive (HDD) or solid-state drive (SSD)

► An output device, such as a display or printer

CERTMIKE EXAM ESSENTIALS

► Computers receive input from a variety of sources, including directly from users and from other devices.

► After receiving input, computers may perform processing on that input to perform computation or decision making. They may then store the original data and/or processed data in memory or on disk.

► Computers provide output in the form of data displayed to end users on monitors or printers as well as in the form of commands sent to other devices.

Practice Question 1

You are assisting a manager who is trying to print a PDF report saved on their laptop for distribution to their employees at a staff meeting in a few hours. The manager is frustrated because the printer keeps jamming, preventing them from printing the report.

What basic computing action is causing this problem?

A. Input
B. Processing
C. Output
D. Storage

Practice Question 2

You are working with a front desk technician at a hotel and troubleshooting an issue that guests are having with the hotel's check-in kiosks. The kiosks use a touchscreen to interact with guests. The touchscreens are correctly displaying information, but when users tap buttons on the screen, the device does not respond.

What basic computing action is causing this problem?

A. Input
B. Processing
C. Output
D. Storage

Practice Question 1 Explanation

This question asks us to evaluate the situation and decide whether it involves input, processing, storage, or output. Let's walk through each of the possibilities.

Input is when a user or system provides data to a computer. In this case, we don't need to gather any new data. The information the manager wants is already present in a PDF report.

Processing is when the computer performs computation or analysis on data. Again, we already have a PDF report that would contain the results of that analysis, so processing seems to be working fine.

Storage is when the computer saves data for later use. Once again, the report is already generated and saved on the device, so there is no storage issue.

The core issue here is that the printer is not creating the report. That's an output issue because the printer is an output device. The manager can't generate the report to provide to their team.

Correct Answer: C. Output

Practice Question 2 Explanation

This question also calls for the classification of this activity into one of the categories of input, processing, output, and storage. Once again, let's walk through each of the categories.

The use of a touchscreen makes this a very interesting question because touchscreens are both input *and* output devices. They accept input from users in the form of touches, and they provide output on the screen. With this knowledge that touchscreens perform input and output, we can quickly eliminate processing and storage as possible answers.

We don't seem to have an output problem here because the touchscreens are correctly displaying information. We do have an input problem because the devices are not responding when users attempt to input information by tapping buttons on the screen.

Correct Answer: A. Input

CHAPTER 4

Value of Data
Objective 1.4: Explain the value of data and information

In today's economy, information is often one of a business's most valuable assets. From product plans to customer records, every business has sensitive information and protecting that information is a crucial business concern. If that information falls into the wrong hands, it could damage the organization's reputation, injure its customers, or cause financial losses.

   In this chapter, you'll learn everything you need to know about ITF+ objective 1.4, including the following topics:

► **Data and information as assets**
► **Importance of investing in security**
► **Relationship of data to creating information**
► **Intellectual property**
► **Digital products**
► **Data-driven business decisions**

DATA AND INFORMATION

As an IT professional, you're responsible for protecting the information that your organization values. The first key step to that is recognizing that data and information are indeed assets that have value to your business, just like your vehicles, buildings, and other equipment.

Data

Let's talk a bit about the difference between data and information. *Data* is the raw facts that our systems and processes generate and collect on a regular basis. You can think of data as just bits of knowledge. For example, we might put a thermometer in our factory to monitor a piece of sensitive equipment. That thermometer might record a temperature reading every 10 minutes to determine the temperature inside the equipment.

The end result would be a spreadsheet or database table containing all of the temperature recordings over time, such as the one shown in Figure 4.1. Each of these temperature readings is one fact and all of this is data. We have a spreadsheet providing data about our temperature readings.

Time	Temperature
1/10/2022 0:00	107
1/10/2022 0:30	108
1/10/2022 1:00	101
1/10/2022 1:30	103
1/10/2022 2:00	107
1/10/2022 2:30	110
1/10/2022 3:00	101
1/10/2022 3:30	110
1/10/2022 4:00	101
1/10/2022 4:30	104
1/10/2022 5:00	102
1/10/2022 5:30	102
1/10/2022 6:00	110
1/10/2022 6:30	104
1/10/2022 7:00	110
1/10/2022 7:30	107
1/10/2022 8:00	109
1/10/2022 8:30	105
1/10/2022 9:00	104
1/10/2022 9:30	100

FIGURE 4.1 **A spreadsheet of temperature readings is only data.**

Information

Information is data that has been processed and analyzed. A system or person has put some effort into putting that data in the context of the business so that it is useful to us. The spreadsheet of temperature information in Figure 4.1 is all correct, but it isn't very useful to us. It's just a collection of data that isn't in any context.

Figure 4.2 shows what happens if we create a plot showing how the temperature of this equipment changes over time. Now we start to have some information.

Temperature vs. Time

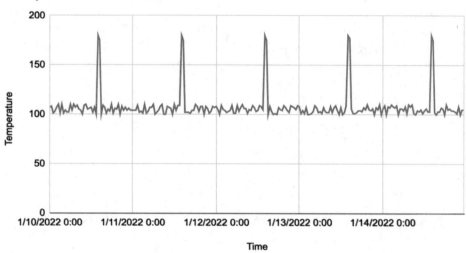

FIGURE 4.2   Plotting data over time is one way we can transform it into information.

Data-Driven Business Decisions

Looking at Figure 4.2 we can quickly see that the temperature in this machinery spikes to dangerously high levels every afternoon around 2 p.m., as shown in Figure 4.3.

That's information that we can act upon. We can tell the people responsible for this equipment that they need to figure out what is going on every afternoon that's causing this potentially dangerous situation.

That story is an example of a data-driven business decision. When we have the right information at our disposal, we can act upon it to improve our business. There are a few stages to this process:

1. We first capture and collect data that might have meaning to our business. Whether that's temperature data like our previous example, or data about our customers, products, or the operating environment, there are many different kinds of data that might be valuable to us.
2. Once we have that data, we can correlate it, performing analysis to help find the meaningful information that it contains.
3. With that information in hand, we can provide reports to business leaders, helping them make data-driven business decisions.

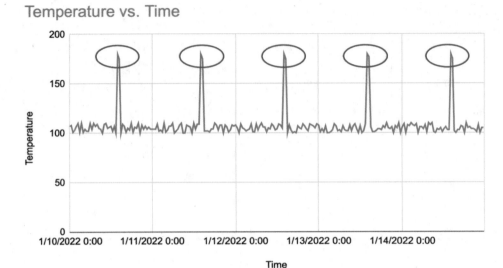

FIGURE 4.3 Information can drive action.

INTELLECTUAL PROPERTY

The information assets that an organization uses to create business value are a type of property that belongs to that business, just as real estate and physical items are examples of property. We use the term *intellectual property* to describe the information assets that belong to an organization.

The law provides businesses with three different ways that they can protect their intellectual property against theft or misuse: copyrights, trademarks, and patents. Each one of these legal tools provides different types of protection for different types of intellectual property.

Copyrights

Copyrights protect creative works against theft. Information protected by copyright includes books, web content, magazines, and other written works as well as art, music, and even computer software. Many organizations now spend much of their time creating digital products. Digital content may also be protected by a copyright.

Copyright protection is automatically granted to the creator of a work upon creation. Although copyright owners may choose to register their copyright with governmental authorities, this is not a legal requirement. In the United States, the Library of Congress administers the copyright program through the U.S. Copyright Office.

The length of copyright protection varies widely according to the country of registration, the type of work, and whether the author is an individual or a corporation. In all cases, it is a very long time. For example, if you create a new work today, the copyright protection for that work lasts for 70 years beyond your death. Once a copyright expires, work moves into the public domain and may be used freely by anyone without requiring licensing or permission.

Copyrights are denoted using the symbol shown in Figure 4.4.

FIGURE 4.4 Copyright symbol

Trademarks

Trademarks are used to protect the words and symbols used to identify products and services. Information protected by trademark includes brand names, logos, and slogans.

Owners of trademarks must register their marks with the government to achieve full protection. In the United States, this is handled through the United States Patent and Trademark Office, a division of the U.S. Department of Commerce.

Trademarks may last indefinitely, but their registration must be renewed every 10 years. Trademarks are only valid as long as they are being actively used. If an organization stops using a trademark in commerce, they are said to have abandoned the trademark after five years of non-use.

Trademarks are denoted using the superscript ™ symbol shown in Figure 4.5(a). Once they are granted registration status by the government, they may be denoted using the symbol shown in Figure 4.5(b).

(a)   (b)

FIGURE 4.5 Symbols used to denote (a) trademarks and (b) registered trademarks.

Patents

Patents protect inventions, providing the inventor with the exclusive use of their invention for a period of time. The purpose of patents is to stimulate invention by assuring inventors that others will not simply copy their ideas in the marketplace.

In order to be granted a patent, an inventor must demonstrate that their idea meets three criteria:

▶ It must be *novel*, meaning that it is a new idea that nobody has thought of in the past.

▶ It must be *useful*, meaning that it provides some benefit to someone and that it is actually possible to use the invention.

▶ It must be *non-obvious*, meaning that there was some inventive work involved.

Once granted, a patent generally lasts for 20 years beyond the filing date, but this may be extended if there are governmental delays in issuing the patent.

> **EXAM TIP**
>
> Expect to see at least one question on your exam asking you to decide what type of intellectual property protection would be best in a given situation: trademark, copyright, or patent. The exam objectives cover these protections directly, and those scenarios make for easy exam questions!

SECURING DATA

Information technology professionals are responsible for securing data of many different kinds. This includes the intellectual property that belongs to the organization as well as other sensitive information, such as the personal information of the company's customers and employees.

You'll learn much more about securing data in Part VI of this book, as security is an entire domain of the ITF+ exam.

> **CERTMIKE EXAM ESSENTIALS**
>
> ▶ Data consists of raw facts that may be transformed into information. Together, data and information are among a business's most valuable assets.
>
> ▶ Businesses may use data to make data-driven business decisions. To do this, they must first capture/collect data, then correlate that data with other sources, and finally provide reporting to decision makers.
>
> ▶ Organizations may protect their intellectual property through several mechanisms. Copyrights protect written works. Trademarks protect the words and symbols used to identify products. Patents protect inventions.

Practice Question 1

Your company publishes books that help IT professionals prepare for certification exams. You want to protect this intellectual property so that other organizations can't simply sell copies of it online.

What type of intellectual property protection is best suited for this situation?

A. Trade secret
B. Trademark
C. Copyright
D. Patent

Practice Question 2

Which of the following would best be described as information rather than data? (Select two.)

A. Receipt from a customer transaction
B. Arrival time of a bus
C. Average customer purchase size
D. Population of a country
E. Amount of rainfall in a city yesterday
F. Per capita income of a country

Practice Question 1 Explanation

As you prepare for the ITF+ exam, you should be familiar with the different types of intellectual property protection and how they apply in different situations. Let's walk through each of the options here.

Trademarks are used to protect company/product names and logos. They would not protect a creative work, such as the content of a book.

Patents are used to protect inventions and provide the inventor with the exclusive right to use that invention for a period of time. Books do not qualify as inventions, so patents are not appropriate in this situation.

Trade secrets may be used to protect many types of intellectual property, but it requires that the company keep the information secret. Books are intended for sale to the public and can't be maintained as trade secrets.

Copyrights are used to protect creative works and would be the most appropriate mechanism to protect the content of a book from unauthorized duplication.

Correct Answer: C. Copyright

Practice Question 2 Explanation

This question is asking us to select more than one correct answer. You'll likely see a few of these questions on the ITF+ exam. You should handle these questions by noting the number of correct answers and then walking through each option one by one to see if you think it is correct. If you find "extra" answers, remember that you're looking for the *best* answer choices.

Remember that data consists of raw facts while information has been processed and analyzed.

A receipt from a customer transaction is simply data—we haven't gathered any meaningful information from it. The average customer purchase size for a business is, however, analyzed information, so that would be a correct answer.

The arrival time of a bus and the amount of rainfall in a city yesterday are also just facts. They're data that has not been turned into information.

The population of a country is also just a fact and is data by itself, but when we use that data to compute the per capita income of a country, that becomes analyzed information.

Correct Answers: C. Average customer purchase size, F. Per capita income of a country

CHAPTER 5

Units of Measure

Objective 1.5: Compare and contrast common units of measure

Technologists throw around a lot of metrics and, as an IT professional, it's crucial that you understand the common measures used for storage, network throughput, and processing speed. You'll need to know how to compare these metrics and determine the largest, smallest, fastest, and slowest values.

In this chapter, you'll learn everything you need to know about ITF+ objective 1.5, including the following topics:

▶ **Storage unit**
▶ **Throughput unit**
▶ **Processing speed**

MEASURING DATA STORAGE

You've probably heard that computers work with binary data, meaning data that is stored as simply 0s and 1s. Everything that happens inside a computer system uses combinations of 0s and 1s. From the operating system and software that we run to our Word documents and photos, everything is encoded in binary format. Computers can easily use this binary format to store data on disk, keep it in memory, or send it over a network. Let's talk a little about how that actually works.

Bits

The basic unit of storage in any computer system is the *bit*. A bit is a single value that can be either 1 or 0. Those are the only two possible values for a bit. You can't put the number 2 or the letter Z in a bit. It can only be a 1 or a 0.

When we store data on a magnetic hard drive, the computer divides the drive up into billions of tiny little spaces, each designed to store a single bit. If the value of the bit is 1, the computer places a magnetic charge in the location used by that bit. If the value of the bit is 0, the computer leaves no magnetic charge in that location.

When data is stored on a solid-state hard drive or in memory, the process works the same way but using electricity instead of magnetism. If the value of a bit in memory is 1, there is a small electrical charge in that memory location. If the value of the bit is 0, there is no charge present.

Bytes

Computers may think in 0s and 1s, but that's not the way that we human beings think. We'd much prefer to think of our data in terms of letters and numbers! Computers store the data that we're more familiar with by combining multiple bits together.

If we have 2 bits of data, we can use them together to represent four different values, as shown in Table 5.1.

TABLE 5.1 Possible combinations of 2 bits

First Bit	Second Bit	Decimal Value
0	0	0
0	1	1
1	0	2
1	1	3

If both of the bits are 0, that represents the decimal value 0. If the first bit is 0 and the second bit is 1, that's a decimal value of 1. If the first bit is 1 and the second bit is 0, that's the decimal number 2, and if both bits are 1, that's the decimal number 3.

Each time that we add another bit to our data, we double the number of possible values that we can describe. Table 5.2 shows how we can use 3 bits of data to store eight possible values.

TABLE 5.2 Possible combinations of 3 bits

First Bit	Second Bit	Third Bit	Decimal Value
0	0	0	0
0	0	1	1
0	1	0	2
0	1	1	3
1	0	0	4
1	0	1	5
1	1	0	6
1	1	1	7

Similarly, if we have 4 bits of data, we can store 16 possible values. As we increase the number of bits, we increase the number of values exponentially. Once we get up to 8 bits, we find ourselves able to store 256 possible values, ranging from 0 to 255. That's an important number because we can store all of the possible characters and digits used by a computer system in this range.

This combination of 8 bits is known as a *byte*, and the byte is the second important unit of storage. When you're thinking about text data, you can think of each character as being a single byte, made up of 8 bits.

Multiples of Bytes

Many of the files that we store contains thousands, millions, billons, or even trillions of bytes! Instead of using extremely large numbers, we use larger units to help measure the size of stored data. You may already be familiar with this concept from the metric system; instead of referring to a distance as 1,000 meters, we can refer to that same distance as 1 kilometer. Data storage units use the same prefixes to denote multiples of bytes. Before you take the exam, you should be familiar with the standard multiples of bytes shown in Table 5.3.

EXAM TIP

You should be prepared to convert between these units. You may use the information in Table 5.3 and Table 5.4 to perform these conversions. For example, if you are presented with the fact that a file is 1.6 GB, you can use the table to convert that to 1,600 MB; 1,600,000 KB; or 1,600,000,000 bytes.

TABLE 5.3 **Data storage units**

Unit	Number of Bytes
Byte	1
Kilobyte (KB)	1,000
Megabyte (MB)	1,000,000
Gigabyte (GB)	1,000,000,000
Terabyte (TB)	1,000,000,000,000
Petabyte (PB)	1,000,000,000,000,000

MEASURING DATA THROUGHPUT

We use bytes to measure how much data we have stored in memory, on a hard disk, or in another location where data is at rest. When data isn't at rest, it is in motion, being sent over a network. Networks don't store data, so it doesn't make sense to describe network capacity in terms of how much data a network can store. Networks move data around, so we measure network capacity in terms of the speed at which a network can transfer data. This speed is a measure of how much data, measured in bits, a network can move in a unit of time, such as seconds. That gives us the measure that we commonly use for network throughput: *bits per second*, or bps.

Notice that when we write bps, we use a lowercase b. When we measured storage capacity in kilobytes, megabytes, and so on, we used a capital B. That's an important difference because the lowercase b represents bits whereas the uppercase B represents bytes. Remember that 1 byte is equal to 8 bits. So if you wanted to see how many bytes a network could move per second, you have to divide the number of bits per second by 8. After you perform that division by 8, you get the less commonly used unit of *bytes per second*, or Bps.

Networks transmit data using a variety of methods, but they all rely on sending pulses that represent 1s and 0s. When there is a signal present, that represents a 1, while the absence of a signal represents 0. Wired networks accomplish this by using copper wires to transmit pulses of electricity. Wireless networks use radio waves to transmit radio signal pulses, and fiber-optic networks use strands of glass or plastic to transmit pulses of light.

Multiples of bps

Modern networks are able to move data very quickly, so we don't actually measure their speed in bits per second. Instead, we use multiples similar to those that we used for data storage, as shown in Table 5.4. Remember, these units are in bits per second, not bytes per second!

TABLE 5.4 Data throughput units

Unit	Number of Bits per Second
bps	1
Kbps	1,000
Mbps	1,000,000
Gbps	1,000,000,000
Tbps	1,000,000,000,000

EXAM TIP

This material makes for easy exam question fodder. Expect to see at least one question asking you to compare values and/or units and select the largest or smallest value. When you see these questions, pay careful attention to the units and make sure that you're selecting a value that is appropriate for the question. If you're talking about storage, don't pick a throughput unit, and vice versa!

Your home Internet connection is probably measured in megabits per second, while your workplace's connection is likely measured in gigabits per second. You'd only see terabits per second on an extremely high-speed network inside a data center. We don't yet include petabits per second (Pbps) in this table, because there is not currently any network capable of transferring data at that speed.

NOTE

You'll often hear several different terms used to describe these measures of a network's capacity. Network speed, throughput, capacity, and bandwidth are all very similar terms. The difference between them is that network bandwidth and capacity refer to the amount of data that you are *supposed* to be able to send on a network, and network throughout and speed refer to the amount that you are actually able to send on that network. They are all measured using these units of bits per second.

MEASURING PROCESSOR SPEED

We also need to measure how fast a computer can process data. Basically, that's describing how quickly the computer can think.

In Chapter 9, "Internal Computing Components," we'll discuss how the computer's central processing unit (CPU) is the central brain of a computer that does its thinking. CPUs have internal clocks that time how quickly they can perform a single mathematical operation. Now this isn't a clock like you or I might have in our home that ticks every second. Computers think extremely fast and their internal clocks tick billions of times per second. We measure the speed of a CPU based on how fast that clock ticks, and we count those ticks using a unit called *hertz*, where each hertz is a single tick.

If you think about the clock that you have in your home, you know that it ticks one time per second. That clock is a one-hertz clock; one tick per second is one hertz.

We measure computer clocks in multiples of hertz. Early personal computers measured clock speed in *megahertz (MHz),* millions of ticks per second. Modern computer processors work in *gigahertz (GHz)*, billions of ticks per second. We call those each of those ticks of the computer's clock a *cycle*.

That wraps up the three basic ways that we measure the speed and capacity of data, networks, and computers. We measure data storage on disks and in memory using bits and bytes. We measure network speed in bits per second. And we measure computer processing speed in hertz.

CERTMIKE EXAM ESSENTIALS

▶ The most basic unit of storage is the bit, which represents a single 0 or 1. We more commonly use bytes, which consist of 8 bits, and multiples of bytes including KB, MB, GB, TB, and PB.

▶ Network throughput is measured in the number of bits per second (bps) that the network can carry. Network speeds are measured in Kbps, Mbps, Gbps, and Tbps.

▶ Processor speed is measured in the number of cycles per second (hertz) that the processor completes. We commonly measure processor speed in MHz and GHz.

Practice Question 1

You are selecting a new computer for a user and are evaluating the speed of different processors. Which one of the following would be the highest processor speed?

A. 3.2 MHz
B. 3.2 Mbps
C. 3.2 PB
D. 3.2 GHz

Practice Question 2

You are looking at four files stored on a filesystem and would like to delete the largest file to free up space for other needs. Which one of the following files is the largest?

A. 16,000 GB
B. 900,000 KB
C. 1,000 MB
D. 1 TB

Practice Question 1 Explanation

This question boils down to understanding the different units used to measure processor speed. The first piece of information that you should call to mind is the fact that processor speed is measured in multiples of hertz, or cycles per second. Based on this information, you can quickly eliminate two possible answer choices. 3.2 Mbps is a measure of network throughput, not one of processor speed. Similarly, 3.2 PB is a measure of data storage, not processor speed.

That leaves us with two possible answer choices: 3.2 MHz and 3.2 GHz. Both of these are indeed measures of processor speed, so we just need to know which unit is the largest of the two. 1 GHz is equal to 1,000 MHz, making 3.2 GHz the fastest processor speed listed here.

Correct Answer: D. 3.2 GHz

Practice Question 2 Explanation

This question is a little tricky because we're presented with file sizes in different units and asked to compare them. The best thing to do here is to first convert all of these file sizes to the same units. The smallest unit used in the question is kilobytes, so let's convert the four answer choices to KB.

That gives us:

▶ 16,000 GB = 16,000,000,000 KB

▶ 900,000 KB

▶ 1,000 MB = 1,000,000 KB

▶ 1 TB = 1,000,000,000 KB

With this information in hand, the comparison now becomes easy. 16,000,000,000 KB is the largest value, making our correct answer 16,000 GB.

If you face a question like this, where the units are all different and you have values with different numbers of zeros, the process we just outlined is the best approach. Convert all of the values to the same unit and then do the comparison.

You definitely should not just pick the largest unit. That's a common trap. Notice in this question that the answer choice with the largest unit (1 TB) was not the correct answer. There was another answer choice (16,000 GB) that is actually larger because 16,000 GB is 16 TB.

Correct Answer: A. 16,000 GB

CHAPTER 6

Troubleshooting Methodology

Objective 1.6: Explain the troubleshooting methodology

As an IT professional, you'll often be called upon to troubleshoot issues that are causing problems for users or teams. Troubleshooting can be challenging because you may be trying to diagnose a problem that nobody else can figure out. But, personally, I find troubleshooting exhilarating! It's an opportunity to figure out a mystery and show off your IT skills. And when you solve the problem, you get to be the hero of the hour!

In this chapter, you'll learn everything you need to know about ITF+ objective 1.6, including the following topics:

► **Identify the problem**
► **Research knowledge base/Internet, if applicable**
► **Establish a theory of probable cause**
► **Test the theory to determine the cause**
► **Establish a plan of action to resolve the problem and identify potential effects**
► **Implement the solution or escalate as necessary**
► **Verify full system functionality and, if applicable, implement preventive measures**
► **Document findings/lessons learned, actions, and outcomes**

TROUBLESHOOTING METHODOLOGY

Every troubleshooting situation is unique, but there are some basic steps that you can follow to conduct troubleshooting in an orderly manner that produces good results. CompTIA endorses the eight-step troubleshooting process shown in Figure 6.1. You should absolutely take the time to memorize the steps in this process.

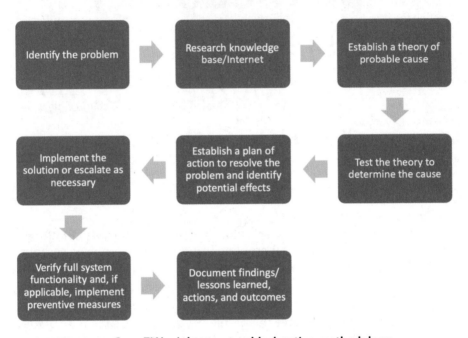

FIGURE 6.1 CompTIA's eight-step troubleshooting methodology

Let's examine the process in more detail. We'll explain what occurs during each step and also walk through an example.

> **EXAM TIP**
> It is vital that you memorize the steps of the troubleshooting methodology shown in Figure 6.1. You will almost certainly find one or more questions on the exam asking you to evaluate a situation and identify the current step that a technician is following or the next step that they should take.

Identify the Problem

The first thing that you need to do is identify the problem. Talk to the end user and figure out what issues they're experiencing and identify the symptoms. For example, they might tell you that their network connection is slow or that they can't access a certain website. Gather as much information as you can and try to duplicate the problem. You'll want to replicate the user's experience so that you can help find the resolution. It's also a good idea during this phase to determine if anything has recently changed on the user's system. When you question the user, be sure to ask them whether they've recently installed any new software, changed any components of their system, or made any other technology changes.

> **TIP**
>
> When you visit a user, you might often find yourself bombarded with multiple problems. They might call you about their slow network connection but then say "While you're here, there's something else I need your help with." It's certainly fine to help users with all of their issues, but it's a good practice to tackle one problem at a time. By approaching multiple problems individually, you're increasing your likelihood of success.

Imagine that you're a desktop support technician and you are called to the desk of a user who is having trouble using a browser to access the Internet. When you first arrive, you should work to identify the problem. Here are some actions you might take:

- ▶ **Gather information** from the user and the system. Find out what the user is experiencing and examine the system's settings. You might learn that the user is seeing an error page no matter what website they try to visit.
- ▶ **Duplicate the problem** by trying to visit some websites yourself from the user's computer. You might also try visiting websites from other computers on the same network to identify whether the problem exists on only one system or whether it is network-wide.
- ▶ **Question the user** about any things they've tried to do to resolve the problem themselves. Have they tried restarting the computer or reseating the network cable?
- ▶ **Identify any symptoms** that might exist. Is this affecting only web traffic, or does the system appear to be completely disconnected from the network?
- ▶ **Determine if anything has changed.** Ask the user when they last were able to use the web and whether they or anyone else has installed any software or altered any settings since that last known good state.

The identification stage is crucial to the remainder of the troubleshooting process, as it ensures that you have all the information you need to evaluate the situation.

Conduct Research

Once you've identified the problem, it's time to conduct some research. If it's not a simple problem, you can go back to your own workspace and consult the references available to you. And yes, Googling things is absolutely fine! I often solve my own problems by searching on the Internet, so don't feel shy about doing that. Googling an error message often leads you directly to a page full of possible solutions. You should also visit the website for the vendor of the hardware or software involved in the problem. Vendors often have *knowledge bases* that you can search for troubleshooting advice. Your own organization also likely has an internal knowledge base that documents common issues found within the organization. Whatever information sources you use, verify that they are providing you with current, reliable information.

In the case of the user who can't access websites, you might consult the organization's knowledge base and discover that website connectivity issues are often the result of misconfigured proxy servers, network outages, and incorrect domain names.

Establish a Theory

Next, establish a theory of the probable cause. That's a fancy way of saying that you should make an educated guess about what's wrong. You don't have to be correct the first time; you're just trying to identify what you think is the most likely cause of the problem. When you do this, you should question obvious assumptions and consider multiple problem-solving approaches to help you find the best idea. If you have other team members assisting you, it's okay to take a *divide-and-conquer* approach, letting different team members pursue different theories.

In the case of the user who can't access the web, you might establish a theory of probable cause that the user's proxy settings are not correctly configured to use the organization's proxy servers. That's only one of many possibilities, however, so you'll next test that theory to see if it is correct.

Test the Theory

Once you have a solid theory, you'll want to test that theory to see if it's correct. This will help you determine the root cause of the incident. If your theory holds up, then you can move forward with solving the problem. If your theory doesn't work out, just return to the previous step and start testing a new theory.

To test your proxy server theory, you might examine the user's proxy settings and see if they match the organization's standard settings that you discovered in the knowledge base. If the settings are not properly configured, that validates your theory that they are the cause of the user's trouble, and you can move on to establish a plan of action to correct the problem.

Establish a Plan of Action

After you determine the root cause of the incident, you can establish a plan of action to resolve the problem and identify any other effects that the problem may be having on this or other users. This may include altering system or network settings, installing or removing software, reconfiguring devices, replacing hardware, or performing many other possible steps.

If you discovered that the user's computer settings did not match the organization's standard proxy settings, you might then plan to reconfigure those settings to match the organization's standards. Before carrying out your plan, you should document the current settings so that you are able to undo any changes that you make if they are not successful.

Implement or Escalate

If you're able to fix the problem yourself, you can implement the solution, or if you need help from other IT professionals, you may escalate the problem as needed. You might go through an iterative process of implementing several possible solutions. If that's the case, it's a good idea to completely implement and test one change and then undo that change if it didn't work before moving on to the next possibility. Making multiple changes at the same time increases the likelihood of new issues.

After documenting the user's current proxy settings, you may then change the settings to match the organization's standard settings.

Verify Functionality

Once you've implemented your solution, verify that the full system is functioning normally, and if it makes sense, put measures in place to prevent the problem from recurring for this user or affecting other users. You should test the new settings completely to ensure that not only have you fixed the problem, but also that your solution did not cause new issues.

For example, after changing the user's proxy settings, you should then attempt to visit a variety of internal and external websites to ensure that the changes were effective. If the user's system is not working properly, you will need to establish a new theory and repeat the troubleshooting process.

Document Your Work

Finally, the resolution of the problem isn't the last step in the process. You still have one more task to complete. Document your findings, lessons learned, actions, and outcomes. Documenting troubleshooting efforts isn't a very exciting part of our work, but it's important because it creates a record for other IT team members to follow if they experience similar issues. You're saving them the work of going through all the same troubleshooting steps that you just followed!

This may be as simple as updating the current incident details in your organization's incident tracking system. On the other hand, if you discovered new information during your troubleshooting that wasn't included in the knowledge base, this is a good time to document that information so that the next technician who encounters the problem may benefit from your discovery.

CERTMIKE EXAM ESSENTIALS

The CompTIA troubleshooting process consists of eight steps:

▶ Identify the problem.

▶ Research knowledge base/Internet, if applicable.

▶ Establish a theory of probable cause.

▶ Test the theory to determine the cause.

▶ Establish a plan of action to resolve the problem and identify potential effects.

▶ Implement the solution or escalate as necessary.

▶ Verify full system functionality and, if applicable, implement preventive measures.

▶ Document findings/lessons learned, actions, and outcomes.

Practice Question 1

You are working with a user who was experiencing an issue with displaying computer-aided design (CAD) graphics on their computer. You replaced the user's monitor and performed some tests that showed that the problem is resolved and the user has full system functionality. What should you do next?

A. Document your findings.
B. Close the ticket.
C. Conduct additional testing.
D. Escalate to senior technicians.

Practice Question 2

You are helping a user troubleshoot a problem printing to a new all-in-one device that was recently installed. You have researched the problem on the Internet and in your organization's knowledge base, and that research is pointing you at several possible issues. You are working to identify which issue is the most likely culprit. What step are you taking in the troubleshooting process?

A. Verify full system functionality.
B. Identify the problem.
C. Implement the solution.
D. Establish a theory.

Practice Question 1 Explanation

This is a straightforward question that is asking you to identify where you are in the troubleshooting process and determine the appropriate next step. If you consult the troubleshooting methodology in Figure 6.1, you'll discover that verifying full system functionality is the seventh step in the process.

There is no need for you to conduct any additional testing or escalate to a senior technician, as you have resolved the problem successfully.

However, you are also not ready to close the ticket because you have not yet documented your findings. You should complete documentation of findings/lessons learned, actions, and outcomes before closing out the case.

Correct Answer: A. Document your findings

Practice Question 2 Explanation

This question is also testing your familiarity with the CompTIA troubleshooting methodology shown in Figure 6.1. In this case, you must determine where you are in the troubleshooting process.

The question indicates that you have already researched the problem. Researching the problem is step 2, so you know that the answer is not step 1, identify the problem, so you can eliminate that possibility.

You do not yet know which issue you are solving, so it would be premature to implement a solution (step 6) or verify full system functionality (step 7). The next thing that you need to do is establish a theory of the probable cause (step 3).

Correct Answer: D. Establish a theory

Domain 2.0: Infrastructure

Infrastructure is the second domain of CompTIA's ITF+ exam. It covers the core infrastructure components in any IT environment: servers, endpoints, peripherals, networking, and storage. This domain has eight objectives:

2.1 Classify common types of input/output device interfaces

2.2 Given a scenario, set up and install common peripheral devices to a laptop/PC

2.3 Explain the purpose of common internal computing components

2.4 Compare and contrast common Internet service types

2.5 Compare and contrast storage types

2.6 Compare and contrast common computing devices and their purposes

2.7 Explain basic networking concepts

2.8 Given a scenario, install, configure, and secure a basic wireless network

Questions from this domain make up 22% of the questions on the ITF+ exam, so you should expect to see approximately 17 questions on your test covering the material in this part.

CHAPTER 7

Input/Output Device Interfaces

Objective 2.1: Classify common types of input/output device interfaces

IT professionals are responsible for an almost overwhelming series of cables and connectors. As you work with users to connect their devices to networks, peripherals, and graphic displays, you'll need to know how to select the appropriate interface for a given situation and then use a cable with the correct connectors.

In this chapter, you'll learn everything you need to know about ITF+ objective 2.1, including the following topics:

▶ **Networking**
▶ **Peripheral devices**
▶ **Graphic devices**

NETWORK INTERFACES

The computers that we use are powerful, but they become even more powerful when they're connected to each other. That's the role of a *network*: connecting computer systems together, whether it's within an office or to the global Internet. Networks allow us to send email messages around the world, stream video, print to a printer down the hall, and perform many other important tasks.

We have two basic options for connecting computers, mobile devices, and other network-connected components to our networks: wired networks and wireless networks.

Wired Networks

Wired network connections function by connecting a cable called an Ethernet cable from a computer to a network jack in the wall, such as the one shown in Figure 7.1. Behind that wall plate there are more cables running back to switches and other network devices that make the network function.

FIGURE 7.1   Wall plate containing four network jacks

The Ethernet cables that we use for wired networks have plugs at the end that look like the one shown in Figure 7.2. This is called an *RJ-45* connector and it's an industry standard. RJ is an acronym for "Registered Jack" and the RJ-45 connector is the 45th standard in that series.

FIGURE 7.2   RJ-45 network connector

You'll sometimes hear the RJ-45 connector referred to as an 8-pin connector. That's because it has eight copper pins on the end. If you were to cut an Ethernet cable open, you'd find that there are actually eight copper wires inside. Each one of those wires connects to one of the pins on the connector.

You may also come across *RJ-11* connectors in your work. These connectors look similar to RJ-45 Ethernet connectors, but they're smaller, as you can see in Figure 7.3.

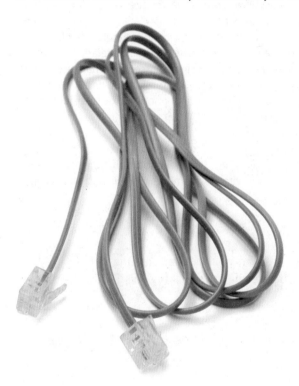

F I G U R E 7 . 3 **RJ-11 telephone connector**

RJ-11 connectors were used for landline telephones and older networks. They're quite similar to RJ-45 connectors except that they only have either four or six pins.

EXAM TIP

Don't be tricked if you see a question asking you about Voice over IP (VoIP) telephones. VoIP telephones connect to Ethernet networks, so they use RJ-45 connectors, not RJ-11 connectors.

Wireless Networks

Wired networks have the advantage of offering very high-speed connections, but they come with the major inconvenience of requiring physical cables between devices. For that reason, we often rely on *wireless networks* to make life more convenient.

Wi-Fi networks create powerful wireless LANs (WLANs) that allow us to use smartphones, laptops, and other networked devices anywhere in our home or office. We'll talk more about Wi-Fi networking in Chapter 16, "Wireless Networks."

You've probably also used a couple of other wireless networking technologies. *Bluetooth* networks are what we call *personal area networks (PANs)*. They're usually created by a computer or smartphone, and they're designed to support a single person. The main use of Bluetooth networks is to create wireless connections between a computer and its peripherals. Bluetooth allows us to use wireless headsets and connect our phones to our cars for hands-free access. The range of a Bluetooth network is around 30 feet, or 10 meters, and they use *radio frequency (RF)* communications.

Near-field communication (NFC) technology allows extremely short-range wireless connections. For two devices to communicate using NFC, they need to be no more than a few inches apart. NFC technology is often used for wireless payments and building access control systems.

> **EXAM TIP**
>
> Be sure that you know the uses and distances associated with the various wireless networking options and be prepared to select the one that's appropriate for a given scenario!

Bluetooth and NFC networks aren't general-purpose networks that connect many computers together, but they're very useful for short-range applications.

PERIPHERAL INTERFACES

Peripheral devices are the ancillary components, such as printers, scanners, keyboards, and mice, that we connect to computer systems. You'll learn more about the different types of peripherals in Chapter 8, "Installing Peripherals." For now, you need to know that there are many different kinds of connectors and cables used to connect peripheral devices to computer systems. As you get ready for the exam, you should be able to recognize each one of these connectors.

USB

The first set of connectors work with many different kinds of devices. The most common of these is the *Universal Serial Bus (USB)* connector. USB connectors come in three different variations: USB-A, USB-B, and USB-C. Those connectors each come in different sizes to make things more complicated.

Figure 7.4 shows you the common types of USB connectors that you might come across. You'll want to be able to recognize them so that you can select an appropriate cable for any situation that you face.

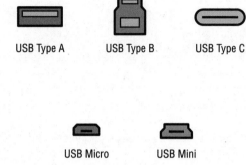

USB Type A   USB Type B   USB Type C

USB Micro   USB Mini

FIGURE 7.4 USB connectors

FireWire

The *FireWire* connector is a specialized connector that was designed by Apple and intended for use in many different applications, but it never really took off. Today, FireWire use is rare, but it is still listed on the IT Fundamentals exam objectives, so you should be able to recognize it. Figure 7.5 shows two common types of FireWire connector: FireWire 400 and FireWire 800.

FireWire 400   FireWire 800

FIGURE 7.5 FireWire connectors

Serial ATA

The *serial ATA (SATA)* connector is used to connect hard drives, optical drives, and other storage devices for high-speed data transfer. The SATA standard is typically used for devices that reside inside a computer system, whereas external storage devices can use the *external SATA (eSATA)* connector for the same purpose. Figure 7.6 shows the SATA and eSATA connectors.

SATA   eSATA

F I G U R E   7 . 6   **SATA and eSATA connectors**

NOTE

Some older devices may still use *infrared (IR)* communications, but this is rare in a modern computing environment.

GRAPHIC INTERFACES

We use a whole set of connectors to work specifically with video displays, projectors, and other graphics devices.

VGA

Older displays use *Video Graphics Array (VGA) connectors*, such as the one shown in Figure 7.7. They can only support very low-resolution displays that run at 640×480 resolution, so you won't find them in use on modern equipment, but you should be able to recognize VGA connectors on the exam.

F I G U R E   7 . 7   **VGA connector**

DVI

Digital Visual Interface (DVI) connectors, such as the ones shown in Figure 7.8, are also an older standard that you still may find out there. These connectors support high-definition video up to 1080p resolution.

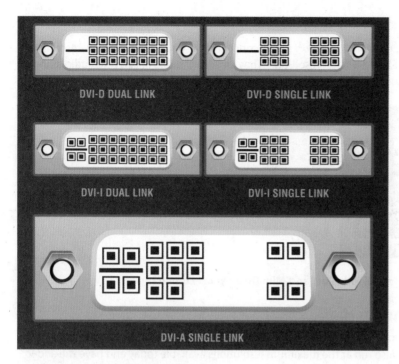

FIGURE 7.8 DVI connectors

EXAM TIP

The various connector types are an alphabet soup that can be very confusing! Be sure that you understand which connectors are used for video and which are used for other types of peripherals as you prepare for the ITF+ exam.

HDMI

High-Definition Multimedia Interface (HDMI) connectors are commonly used to connect home audio and video equipment and to connect computers to televisions and many monitors. The unique thing about HDMI is that it can carry both audio and video on the same wire. HDMI supports high-resolution video, up to 5K and beyond. You can see an example of an HDMI connector in Figure 7.9.

FIGURE 7.9 HDMI connector

DisplayPort

DisplayPort (DP) and *Mini DisplayPort (mDP)* connectors also support very high-resolution video, including 5K and greater resolution. They are also capable of carrying audio along with the video signal. Figure 7.10 shows these connectors.

FIGURE 7.10 **DisplayPort and Mini DisplayPort connectors**

USB and Thunderbolt

Modern monitors also may be connected to computers using USB-C connections. USB-C connections can also run at the maximum resolutions available today and have the added benefit of sending video, audio, and power over the same cable when used with the *Thunderbolt* standard.

Thunderbolt is a hardware interface standard designed by Intel that allows both data and power to be sent over a single wire. Thunderbolt uses some familiar connectors. The first two versions of Thunderbolt used Mini DisplayPort connectors whereas newer versions of Thunderbolt (Thunderbolt 3 and 4) use USB-C connectors.

CERTMIKE EXAM ESSENTIALS

▶ Users may connect to wired networks using Ethernet cables that follow the 8-pin RJ-45 standard. Old telephone cables used the 4-pin or 6-pin RJ-11 connector.

▶ Radio frequency connections include Wi-Fi, which provides wireless networking connections that cover a large area, such as a building or outdoor area. Bluetooth connections are used for peripherals with a range of approximately 30 feet. Near-field communication (NFC) connections are used for short-range connections, such as contactless payment.

▶ Peripherals may be connected to computers using USB, FireWire, eSATA, or wireless connections.

▶ Graphic displays may be connected to computers using VGA, DVI, HDMI, DisplayPort, Mini DisplayPort, USB-C, and Thunderbolt connections.

Practice Question 1

You are preparing to connect a user's desktop computer to a new monitor that they just purchased. Which one of the following connectors would not be a suitable option for this task?

A. HDMI
B. USB-C
C. SATA
D. DP

Practice Question 2

You are assisting a user with connecting a wireless headset to their laptop computer. Which one of the following connection types would be most appropriate for this scenario?

A. Bluetooth
B. USB-A
C. USB-C
D. NFC

Practice Question 1 Explanation

Many different types of connectors are used to connect displays to computers and other devices. These include High-Definition Multimedia Interface (HDMI) connectors and DisplayPort (DP) connectors, which are cable types used exclusively for audiovisual content.

Universal Serial Bus (USB) connectors are used for many different types of peripherals. The USB-C connector may be used to connect monitors and provide very high-resolution connections that combine video, audio, and power over a single cable.

Serial ATA (SATA) connectors are used to connect storage devices inside a computer and would not be used to connect a display.

Correct Answer: C. SATA

Practice Question 2 Explanation

Bluetooth is a wireless connection protocol that is specifically designed for connecting peripherals to devices with a range of approximately 30 feet. That makes it an ideal option for this scenario.

Near-field communication (NFC) connections have much shorter range than Bluetooth and are most commonly used for brief connections, such as those used to enter a building using a proximity card or to complete a payment using a contactless payment system.

While USB connections are very commonly used to connect peripherals, they require a cable, and this scenario specifically requested a wireless connection. Therefore, USB-A or USB-C connections would not be appropriate.

Correct Answer: A. Bluetooth

Installing Peripherals

Objective 2.2: Given a scenario, set up and install common peripheral devices to a laptop/PC

Users depend on a wide variety of peripherals to support their work with desktop computers, laptops, tablets, and other devices. From entering data with keyboards, mice, and scanners to generating paper documents with a printer, peripherals play an important role in making computers useful in an office environment.

In this chapter, you'll learn everything you need to know about ITF+ objective 2.2, including the following topics:

▶ Devices
▶ Installation types

PERIPHERAL TYPES

Peripherals are the devices that we connect to our computers that play a supporting role. We each use many different peripherals in our daily work. Let's explore some of the common peripherals you might find in an office environment.

Keyboards and Mice

Keyboards and mice are peripheral devices that allow you to provide input to a computer system. The keyboard allows you to enter text and numeric data, and the *mouse* allows you to move objects around and work within a graphical user interface. Keyboards and mice are pretty much mandatory for desktop computers. They're often built into laptops, but many laptop users prefer to have external keyboards and mice on their desks because these full-sized devices are easier to use than the smaller devices built into laptops. Figure 8.1 shows an example of a typical keyboard (on the left) and mouse (on the right).

FIGURE 8.1 Keyboard and mouse

Display

Displays are also pretty much mandatory for a computer to be useful to its users. The display is a device that allows the user to see what the computer is doing while they interact with the computer, such as the one shown in Figure 8.2. Servers generally don't have displays connected to them, but laptop and desktop computers must use displays to be useful to people. As with keyboards and mice, laptops also have built-in displays, but users often have larger monitors on their desks for when they're using their laptops in the office. Touchscreen displays are also quite popular because they allow users to interact directly with the display without using the keyboard or mouse.

ALL-IN-ONE (AIO) DEVICES

All-in-one (AIO) devices combine the monitor and computer into a single piece of hardware. These devices save space on a user's desk but have the disadvantage of requiring replacement of both the display and computer at the same time. Apple's iMac is a popular AIO device.

FIGURE 8.2 Typical computer display

Speakers

Speakers, such as those shown in Figure 8.3, produce sound and are also commonly connected to computer systems so that users may hear the sound created by or streamed through the computer. In busy office environments, users often prefer to use headphones instead of speakers for privacy and to avoid annoying their officemates.

FIGURE 8.3 Computer speakers

Printers and Scanners

Printers, such as the one shown in Figure 8.4, produce paper output and are either directly connected to an individual computer or connected to the network to serve many people.

FIGURE 8.4 **Typical desktop printer**

Scanners, such as the one shown in Figure 8.5, take paper and create digital documents in PDF form or using other image formats so that they may be stored electronically. Printing and scanning functionality is often combined in multifunction devices (MFDs).

FIGURE 8.5 **Typical desktop scanner**

Cameras

Cameras, such as the one shown in Figure 8.6, allow users to capture still images and video. They're pretty much essential today for participation in videoconferences. Laptops and smartphones usually have a built-in camera, whereas desktops require an external camera.

FIGURE 8.6 Camera used to capture still images and video

External Hard Drives

Users with large storage needs may use *external hard drives* in addition to the internal storage contained within their computer. These drives may be easily moved between computers.

> **EXAM TIP**
>
> As you prepare for the ITF+ exam, be sure to understand the purpose of each of these peripheral types and whether they are used for input, output, and/or storage. Keyboards, mice, cameras, and scanners are used for input. Printers, displays, and speakers are used for output. External hard drives are used for storage.

That's an overview of the most common types of peripheral devices used with modern computers. You'll find many more specialized devices in almost any business environment, and IT professionals spend a lot of their time configuring and troubleshooting peripherals.

INSTALLING AND CONFIGURING PERIPHERALS

IT professionals are often asked to install peripherals for use by individual employees or by the entire office. The process for installing and configuring these devices varies quite a bit and can be simple or quite challenging.

The simplest devices use a technology called *plug-and-play (PnP)* to make it easy for users to install them on their own. Just like the name implies, you simply plug these devices into the computer and the computer automatically configures them to work properly.

Other devices, particularly specialized or outdated devices, may require manual installation. The most important part of this is finding and installing a *driver* for that device and your operating system. The driver is a small piece of software that tells the operating system how to interact with the peripheral. You can usually find them on the peripheral manufacturer's website. Once you download the correct driver, you may select it when configuring the new peripheral through a computer's operating system.

Devices that are shared by an entire office, such as a large printer, typically don't connect to a single computer. Instead, they connect directly to the network and then may be managed over an IP network connection. These devices typically have web-based interfaces that allow administrators to configure, manage, and monitor the device remotely. You simply connect to the web-based interface using the web browser on a computer that is connected to the same network and then the device will guide you through the configuration process.

CERTMIKE EXAM ESSENTIALS

▶ Keyboards and mice provide users with the ability to provide input to a computer. Computers show users output on a display.

▶ Scanners allow users to create digital copies of paper records, whereas printers allow the creation of paper output from digital content.

▶ Plug-and-play (PnP) devices attempt to configure themselves automatically when connected to a computer system. Devices that do not support PnP often require specialized drivers.

Practice Question 1

You recently received a new external hard drive for your computer that attaches via a USB cable. On the hard drive's package, you read that it is a PnP device. What is the next step that you will need to take to install the drive?

A. Download and install a driver
B. Identify the drive's model number
C. Connect the USB cable
D. Configure the I/O settings

Practice Question 2

You are installing a large printer that will be shared by many people in your office. What is the most common way of connecting this type of device?

A. Ethernet cable
B. USB cable
C. FireWire cable
D. SATA

Practice Question 1 Explanation

The key to answering this question is noticing that the device uses plug-and-play (PnP) technology. This means that the device should configure itself automatically when it is connected to the computer. There should be no need to take any other steps, such as finding the device's model number, downloading or installing a driver, or performing any special configuration tasks. Instead, the PnP technology should automatically configure the device and make it ready for use as soon as it is connected to the computer with a USB cable.

Correct Answer: C. Connect the USB cable

Practice Question 2 Explanation

This question asks you to pull together a few pieces of information. You learned in this chapter that shared printers are most often connected directly to the network and accessed by users via the shared device's IP address. In Chapter 7, you learned that network connections are made using Ethernet cables. Therefore, the correct answer here is that you should use an Ethernet cable to connect the printer to the network, where it may be accessed by any user.

It is possible to connect a printer to a single computer using a USB cable, but this printer would then be available only to users of that computer, unless it is shared. If the user of that computer wanted to share the printer with others, they would need to leave their computer powered on all day and configure it as a print server. That is a much more cumbersome process than simply connecting the printer directly to the network.

Serial ATA (SATA) connections are used for storage devices, not printers.

Correct Answer: A. Ethernet cable

CHAPTER 9

Internal Computing Components

Objective 2.3: Explain the purpose of common internal computing components.

We've covered the ways that you get data into and out of a computer system and the use of peripherals. Now let's take a look inside the computer itself and learn about the internal components of a computer.

In this chapter, you'll learn everything you need to know about ITF+ objective 2.3, including the following topics:

▶ **Motherboard/system board**
▶ **Firmware/BIOS**
▶ **RAM**
▶ **CPU**
▶ **Storage**
▶ **GPU**
▶ **Cooling**
▶ **NIC**

CPU

The central processing unit (CPU) is the brain of the computer, and it performs most of the processing that happens inside the computer. Different computers have different types of CPUs, and those CPUs may be manufactured by different companies. Figure 9.1 shows an example of a CPU.

FIGURE 9.1 Central processing unit (CPU)

The typical Windows computer contains a processor manufactured by one of two companies: Intel or AMD. These two companies create most of the processors used by laptop and desktop computers, and you'll generally be fine with either option. If you have a specialized use case with unique needs for computing power, you'll want to analyze the specifications of the available processors, but generally speaking, Windows runs fine on both Intel and AMD processors.

Mac devices also use processors made by two different companies: Intel and Apple itself. Until 2020, Mac computers used the same Intel processors found in many Windows computers. In 2020, Apple released their own M1 processor, and they offer many of their products with either processor installed.

Mobile devices, such as smartphones and tablets, also have CPUs, but they use a different type of CPU. ARM processors are designed specifically for these devices, and they are specially designed to use as little power as possible, extending the battery life of mobile devices.

CPU Performance

When you're measuring a CPU, there are a few characteristics you should consider:

► **Clock speed** is measured in gigahertz (GHz), and the faster the clock, the faster the computer can process data.

▶ CPUs are also measured in terms of their number of **processing cores**. Each core is a separate processing unit within the same chip. Having multiple cores allows a computer to perform more than one task at the same time. Modern computers may have eight or more cores and supercomputers may have thousands or millions of cores.

▶ We also measure CPUs in terms of how much memory they can manage at the same time. We measure this by describing the **number of bits** that may be in a memory address. 32-bit processors were common in years past, and they could manage up to 4 gigabytes of memory. That was plenty a decade ago, but modern computers can support much more than that because they use 64-bit processors. A 64-bit processor can manage 16 exabytes of memory. That's far more than any computer we will be using any time soon, so expect 64-bit processors to stick around for a while!

MOTHERBOARD

Inside the computer, the CPU lives on the *motherboard*, also known as the system board. This is a printed circuit board that connects the CPU to memory, interfaces, and other system components. Figure 9.2 shows a photograph of a motherboard. The CPU is located under the tall fan that appears on the back center of the motherboard.

FIGURE 9.2 Motherboard

FIRMWARE

When a computer starts up, it uses a very small program that's stored on the motherboard that has the basic job of getting the system up and running and loading the real operating system from disk. This operating system is stored as *firmware*, a type of software that is permanently written onto chips so that it may be accessed before any other software is loaded from disk. The chips that store firmware are also known as *read-only memory (ROM)*.

There are two major options for the code stored in firmware:

▶ The *basic input/output system (BIOS)* is an older approach that has been largely phased out.
▶ The *Unified Extensible Firmware Interface (UEFI)* is a more modern approach that has largely replaced BIOS.

Modern computers are able to boot over the network, receiving software from a centralized server. This capability is known as the *Preboot Execution Environment (PXE)*.

MEMORY

The motherboard also contains slots where computer builders and technicians can insert memory chips known as dual in-line memory modules (DIMM). These memory chips contain the *random access memory (RAM)* that the computer uses to store software and data that it is actively using. The contents of memory are temporary and go away when the computer is turned off. This characteristic is known as *volatility*: volatile storage (such as RAM) is erased when the computer is turned off while nonvolatile storage (such as a hard drive) retains its contents when turned off. Figure 9.3 shows an example of a DIMM.

FIGURE 9.3 Dual in-line memory module (DIMM)

DISK DRIVES

Data that we want to keep around must be stored on more permanent, nonvolatile storage, and that's the role of disk drives. These drives may use magnetic media or solid-state storage. *Hard disk drives (HDDs)* are older and slower, but less expensive than *solid-state drives (SSDs)*, which are newer, faster, and more expensive than HDDs.

Figure 9.4 shows an example of a hard disk drive with its cover removed to reveal its inner workings.

Figure 9.5 shows an example of a smaller-form solid-state drive.

FIGURE 9.4 **Hard disk drive (HDD)**   **FIGURE 9.5** **Solid-state drive (SSD)**

NETWORK INTERFACE CARDS

Most computers also contain a *network interface card (NIC)*. The term NIC comes from the days that network interfaces were commonly add-on cards that were inserted into computers as they were built, such as the one shown in Figure 9.6. Today, add-on cards are still available that may be inserted directly into a computer or attached via a USB cable.

Modern NICs are often directly on the motherboard and provide the ability to connect to both wired and wireless networks. These NICs are known as *on-board* because they are "on the motherboard."

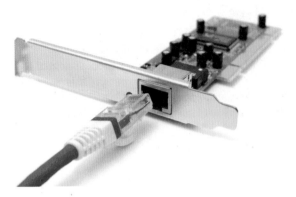

FIGURE 9.6   Network interface card (NIC)

GPU

Some computers also contain specialized *graphics processing units (GPUs)*. These powerful processors are designed to perform the intensive calculations required to render complex graphics on the screen. They're used by graphic designers, video editors, and gamers to speed up processing. GPUs are also quite useful for data science, analytics, and blockchain applications that require a lot of math. GPUs are expensive, however, so you won't find them in every computer. They're a cost that's only necessary for specialized applications. Figure 9.7 shows an example of a GPU.

FIGURE 9.7   Graphics processing unit (GPU)

POWER AND COOLING

The components of a computer system require a steady supply of power to operate. Specifically, they use a type of electric power called *direct current (DC)*. DC power is the type of power provided by batteries and is different from the *alternating current (AC)* power that is available in wall outlets. For this reason, computers must have *power supply units (PSUs)* that plug into the wall and convert the AC power supplied by electric utilities into the DC power used by computing components. Figure 9.8 shows a typical PSU that might be found in a desktop or server computer.

FIGURE 9.8   Computer power supply unit (PSU)

All of these components that we cram into a computer system generate a lot of heat. But computer components also don't like to be hot! Running electronic components in an overheated environment can result in errors and equipment failures, so computers and data centers contain cooling equipment that draws out the hot air and replaces it with cool air. Computers contain fans, and you can often hear those fans turn on when the computer is working hard. That whirring noise that you may hear is an actual fan inside the computer trying to cool it down. Data centers with many computers use massive air-conditioning systems to keep everything inside cool.

CERTMIKE EXAM ESSENTIALS

▶ Computers perform everyday processing using the central processing unit (CPU). Graphics processing units (GPUs) supplement CPU capacity for complex mathematics.

▶ The motherboard holds the CPU, in addition to random access memory (RAM), read-only memory (ROM), and other computing components.

▶ Long-term storage is provided by hard disk drives (HDDs) and solid-state drives (SSDs). SSDs are faster and more expensive than HDDs.

Practice Question 1

You are upgrading an old computer and find that it is not able to support high-speed networking. What component of the computer should you consider upgrading?

A. NIC
B. CPU
C. GPU
D. RAM

Practice Question 2

You are helping to configure a new computer that will be used by an executive and are selecting a long-term storage option for the executive's files. Which one of the following options will provide the fastest possible long-term storage?

A. RAM
B. ROM
C. SSD
D. HDD

Practice Question 1 Explanation

Any of the upgrades listed here may have the effect of speeding up the computer, but this question is asking specifically about networking speed. The computer component that controls networking is the network interface card (NIC), and you should consider upgrading that card to support higher-speed networking.

The central processing unit (CPU) is the main processing hub of the computer where it executes instructions, and the graphics processing unit (GPU) provides supplementary computing capability in support of graphics, data science, and other applications that require complex mathematics. Random access memory (RAM) is used to store programs and data being actively used by the computer.

Correct Answer: A. NIC

Practice Question 2 Explanation

As you approach this question, you can eliminate options by examining the requirements. First, you are looking for an option that will allow the executive to store files for long-term use. Random access memory (RAM) is temporary working memory for the computer and does not store data long-term. Therefore, it is not suitable for this purpose. Similarly, read-only memory (ROM) is not suitable because users cannot write data to ROM.

That leaves us with the two types of drives commonly used in a computer system—hard disk drives (HDDs) and solid-state drives (SSDs). Of these, SSDs are often faster than HDDs, making an SSD the best option here.

Correct Answer: C. SSD

CHAPTER 10

Internet Service Types

Objective 2.4: Compare and contrast common Internet service types

The internal networks built by organizations connect the computers and other devices in that organization to each other. They may serve a single building or a campus, or even connect together buildings in different geographic locations. However, these networks become most powerful when they are connected to the Internet, allowing access to any connected device around the world. Organizations connect their networks to the Internet by contracting with an Internet service provider (ISP), and those ISPs provide different types of service that should be familiar to all IT professionals.

In this chapter, you'll learn everything you need to know about the ITF+ objective 2.4, including the following topics:

► **Fiber optic**
► **Cable**
► **DSL**
► **Wireless**

SERVICE TYPES

We have some different technology options available to us for connecting our LANs to the global Internet. We purchase an Internet connection from an *Internet service provider (ISP)*, but the service may be delivered to us over a variety of types of connections.

These are important to understand because the type of connection that we have will determine the speed of our Internet connection.

All of the connections that we use today are known as *broadband* connections. These are always-on Internet connections that run at much greater speeds than the old dial-up modems that we used decades ago. However, not all broadband connections are equal. Some are much faster than others.

> **EXAM TIP**
>
> Questions related to this objective will likely be straightforward. You should expect to see a question where you are given a scenario and asked to identify the best possible service type for that scenario. When you see questions like this, remember that more than one option may be a possible solution and that you should evaluate which of those possibilities *best* meets the needs of the organization.

Dial-Up Modems

When we used dial-up modems, our computers placed telephone calls over standard copper telephone lines. When the computer on the other end answered, the computers transmitted data by making sounds, just as if you and I were speaking to each other on the telephone. This was incredibly slow and just didn't work that well for anything other than text.

I remember when I got my first dial-up modem in the 1980s and it had a speed of a whopping 300 bits per second. Now remember, it takes 8 bits to make a byte, right? And a byte is a single character. So that 300-bits-per-second modem would send and receive about 38 characters per second. At that speed, you could see the characters appearing on your screen one at a time. I could literally read faster than my computer could receive data!

Fortunately, we don't use these slow connections anymore. Today's Internet connection speeds are measured in megabits or gigabits per second. They're literally a million or even a billion times faster than my old modem!

Digital Subscriber Line (DSL)

One of the oldest technologies still in use today is the *digital subscriber line (DSL)* connection. DSL is the modern equivalent of that old dial-up modem, except it's much faster and offers an always-on connection. DSL connections do use a special DSL modem, but there's no "dialing up." The Internet is always there and ready for use. DSL works over copper telephone lines, and the technology it uses is able to achieve speeds measured in megabits per second. These days you'll still find DSL technology in some homes and small businesses, but it is not commonly used because it typically offers very low speeds, in the ballpark of 10 Mbps.

Cable

Cable television lines run through much of the developed world. These connections use the coaxial cable that you're probably used to seeing coming out of the back of a television or cable box. Just like DSL connections, cable Internet connections use a modem to convert the digital signals of a computer network to the analog signals that travel on copper wires. Cable modems can achieve very high speeds of 1 Gbps and beyond, with many different service offerings available suitable for homes or businesses.

Fiber Optic

The fastest connections available today come over *fiber-optic* cables. These cables are strands of glass that run between locations on a fiber-optic network. Fiber-optic networks use lasers to transmit data using pulses of light that can travel over the glass at extremely high speeds. The potential speed here is almost limitless. With perfect technology, you could theoretically send signals on fiber-optic cables at speeds approaching the speed of light! Internet service providers providing fiber-optic service today routinely offer multi-gigabit connections.

Wireless Connections

Sometimes a wired network connection just won't work for us. If we're moving around in a vehicle or on foot, we obviously can't drag a cable around with us. If we're in a remote location, there may not be any ISPs available to us. In those cases, we can use wireless connections to meet our needs.

Cellular

For mobile users, the best option is usually *cellular* service. Modern 5G wireless networks are capable of speeds up to 20 gigabits per second and are available in major metropolitan areas. Slower 4G networks are more widely available and offer speeds of around 14 megabits per second, which is still pretty respectable. This service is usually inexpensive and available through normal cellular providers.

Radio Frequency

Home users in remote locations may make use of fixed wireless services. These services are point-to-point services that use *radio frequency (RF)* communications. You'll need an antenna on your building that points directly at an antenna run by your ISP, so you'll need to be in an area where this service is provided.

Satellite

In very remote locations, *satellite* Internet connections provide service almost anywhere on the planet. For many years, satellite connections were very expensive and very slow, but that's changing. The new Starlink service offered by Elon Musk's company is deploying satellite service offering 100 megabit speed at a reasonable price.

Satellites are also used to provide *Global Positioning System (GPS)* service. While this is not an Internet connection type, it is a widely used service that can help devices pinpoint their exact location by using signals from multiple satellites.

CERTMIKE EXAM ESSENTIALS

► Fiber-optic connections offer the fastest possible Internet connections and should be the primary choice for high-bandwidth applications. However, fiber-optic connections are not available in all areas.

► Cable and DSL connection options offer slower, but reliable, wired connections in most populated areas.

► Wireless connections, such as cellular, satellite, and radio frequency (RF) service, are useful for supporting temporary locations and in areas where wired connectivity is not available.

Practice Question 1

You are helping your organization develop a connection to a new office location that is in a major metropolitan area. The users in that location will be working on computer-aided design (CAD) tasks that have very high bandwidth requirements. Which one of the following Internet service types provides the highest bandwidth?

A. Fiber optic
B. Satellite
C. DSL
D. Cable

Practice Question 2

You are supporting a team of scientists who will be traveling to a remote mountain area on a research expedition. They will need Internet service for emergency communications and to send back small quantities of research data during their trip. What type of connection would best meet their needs?

A. Cellular
B. Satellite
C. DSL
D. RF

Practice Question 1 Explanation

All of these connection types are possibilities for connecting an office located in an urban environment, but fiber-optic connections are the fastest possible connection type, so they would be the best option for an office that requires significant bandwidth.

Cable and DSL connections may also function in this environment, but they provide lower speeds than fiber. Satellite connections are also slower than fiber and may be difficult to implement in an urban area where the view of the sky may be obscured.

Correct Answer: A. Fiber optic

Practice Question 2 Explanation

Here we have a scenario where users are traveling in a remote location, making a wired connection impossible. Therefore, we can immediately rule out DSL as a possibility because DSL service requires wired telephone service to operate.

Cellular and radio frequency (RF) service are also not good options for this scenario. While they are wireless service types, they are only available near populated areas and it is extremely unlikely they will be available in a remote mountain area.

Satellite service is generally slow and expensive, but it is available almost anywhere on Earth. That makes it the best (and most likely only) option for this scenario.

Correct Answer: B. Satellite

CHAPTER 11

Storage
Objective 2.5: Compare and contrast storage types

As we wrap up our look at the inner workings of a computer, let's take a deeper dive into the different types of storage used by computer systems. We've already discussed how computers need different types of storage for different purposes. There are two major categories of storage: volatile storage and nonvolatile storage.

In this chapter, you'll learn everything you need to know about the ITF+ objective 2.5, including the following topics:

► **Volatile vs. nonvolatile**
► **Local storage types**
► **Local network storage types**
► **Cloud storage service**

VOLATILE STORAGE

Volatile storage is storage that is designed to be temporary. The most common example of volatile storage is the *random access memory (RAM)* that is on the computer's motherboard. RAM is very fast, but it's also relatively expensive. RAM contains all of the data that a computer is actively working with. However, it is volatile storage, so the contents of RAM are only there as long as the computer is turned on. If you turn the computer off, the contents of RAM are erased when you turn it back on again. A typical desktop or laptop computer might have 8–32 GB of RAM, but more powerful computers and servers may have hundreds of GB of RAM.

You learned more about the different types of RAM in Chapter 9, "Internal Computing Components."

NONVOLATILE STORAGE

Nonvolatile storage is just a fancy way to say permanent storage. Nonvolatile storage comes in many different forms, but the common characteristic they share is that once you write something to nonvolatile storage, it stays there until you delete it, even if you turn off the power.

We measure nonvolatile storage devices in two ways. First, we measure the total storage capacity of the device in bytes and the different multiples of bytes that you learned about in Chapter 5, "Units of Measure." It's common for a typical computer to have hard drives or solid-state drives that can store 500 GB, 1 TB, or more data. Second, we measure the speed at which storage devices can store and retrieve data. We measure this using a unit called *input/output operations per second (IOPS)*.

Magnetic Hard Drives

Some nonvolatile storage is local to a computer system. We've already talked about the use of *magnetic hard disk drives (HDD)*. Magnetic drives provide inexpensive storage that is relatively slow. Magnetic hard drives contain platters of magnetic material that spin around very quickly inside the computer where a head reads and writes magnetic charges to the disk. For this reason, magnetic hard drives are also commonly known as *spinning disk* drives. Figure 11.1 shows an example of a magnetic hard drive.

FIGURE 11.1 Magnetic hard disk drive (HDD)

Solid-State Drives

Solid-state drives (SSDs) are a modern replacement for magnetic drives. Instead of using spinning magnetic disks, they use stored electric charges and have no moving parts. This makes solid-state drives less likely to break and allows them to work more quickly than magnetic drives, but those benefits come with a cost: solid-state drives are more expensive than magnetic drives. Figure 11.2 shows an example of a solid-state drive.

FIGURE 11.2 Solid-state drive (SDD)

Flash drives use the same technology as solid-state drives but in a removable form. Flash drives are fairly inexpensive, but they have limited storage capacity when compared to solid-state drives. Figure 11.3 shows an example of a flash drive with a USB interface.

FIGURE 11.3 USB flash drive

Secure Digital (SD) cards are a proprietary format of flash drive and have the distinctive appearance shown in Figure 11.4. SD cards are primarily used as storage for cameras, tablet computers, and other portable devices due to their small size.

FIGURE 11.4 SD card

Optical Drives

Optical drives use lasers to etch data onto a removable disc that may be stored separately from the computer system. These optical discs, such as the one shown in Figure 11.5, come in a variety of forms:

▶ *Compact discs (CDs)* were the original optical storage media, allowing the storage of up to 680 MB of data on a single disc.
▶ *Digital video discs (DVDs)* increase the density of storage, allowing the storage of up to 17 GB of data on a single disc.
▶ *Blu-ray discs (BDs)* have the highest capacity of any optical format, allowing the storage of up to 128 GB of data on a single disc.

FIGURE 11.5 Optical disc

There are different types of each of these optical media:

▶ *Read-only* discs are recorded at the factory and users may not change the data stored on them.
▶ *Recordable* discs allow users to write data to them, but that data is then permanently stored on the disc and may not be erased or modified.
▶ *Rewritable* discs are erasable and may be reused after recording data on them.

Table 11.1 shows the common disc types.

T A B L E   1 1 . 1   Common disc types

	Compact Disc	Digital Video Disc	Blu-Ray Disc
Read-only	CD-ROM	DVD	BD-ROM
Recordable	CD-R	DVD-R	BD-R
Rewritable	CD-RW	DVD-RW	BD-RW

When optical drives read and write data to discs, they spin the disc rapidly in the drive and use a laser to read and write data. Therefore, optical drives, like HDDs, are examples of spinning disk media.

EXAM TIP

Make sure that you clearly understand the different types of storage media and how they might be used. As you prepare for the exam, know which storage media are optical, magnetic, and solid-state.

Enterprise Storage Services

Organizations generally don't want to manage large quantities of removable media or store data on drives attached to individual computers. Instead, they prefer to have centralized enterprise storage services that store data in a single location where it may be accessed by many different users.

Cloud Storage

Today, *cloud storage services* allow organizations to outsource storage, using services provided by a vendor who manages those storage resources and makes them available to users wherever they reside.

File Servers

Businesses that choose not to use cloud services may operate their own centralized storage services that meet the needs of their employees. They often do this by running a *file server*, which is just a computer with a lot of storage installed in it. The file server sits on the network and users may access it from their own computers.

Network attached storage (NAS) systems are self-contained file servers that plug directly into a network to provide users with access to shared storage space. Figure 11.6 shows an example of a NAS device.

FIGURE 11.6 Network attached storage (NAS) array

File servers and other enterprise storage services make use of technology called *Redundant Arrays of Inexpensive Disks (RAID)* to protect against disk failures. The general idea behind RAID technology is that the server or NAS array writes the same data to multiple disks so that if a single disk fails, the data may still be retrieved.

CERTMIKE EXAM ESSENTIALS

▶ Volatile storage, such as RAM, retains its contents only while a device is powered on. Nonvolatile storage such as HDDs, SSDs, and flash drives retains contents permanently, until the data is intentionally deleted or overwritten.

▶ Hard drives may be either magnetic hard disk drives (HDDs), which use spinning disks, or solid-state drives (SSDs), which have no moving parts.

▶ Optical media may be used to store data on removable disks. Common optical media formats include CDs, DVDs, and Blu-ray discs.

Practice Question 1

You are operating a computer system that will work in close proximity to a medical device that uses strong magnetic fields to image body parts. What type of storage is most likely to be damaged by the presence of these magnetic fields?

A. HDD

B. DVD

C. SSD

D. CD

Practice Question 2

Which one of the following storage options is an example of volatile storage?

A. NAS

B. Flash

C. BD-RW

D. RAM

Practice Question 1 Explanation

To answer this question, you need to know which storage media use magnetic fields to store data. Magnetic hard disk drives (HDDs) do this and would likely be damaged by the medical devices.

Solid-state drives (SSDs) use electricity, rather than magnetism, to store data and would be less likely to be damaged.

Compact discs (CDs) and digital video discs (DVDs) store data in optical form, which would not be damaged by the presence of a magnetic field.

Correct Answer: A. HDD

Practice Question 2 Explanation

Volatile storage is storage that loses its data when it is powered off. Random access memory (RAM) is temporary storage used by a computer to store data that is currently in use and it does lose its data when powered off. Therefore, RAM is an example of volatile storage.

Network attached storage (NAS), flash drives, and Blu-ray discs all retain data when power is removed. All three of these are examples of nonvolatile storage.

Correct Answer: D. RAM

CHAPTER 12

Computing Devices
Objective 2.6: Compare and contrast common computing devices and their purposes

We use many different types of computing devices to help us get our work done, organize our lives, and even entertain ourselves. From laptops to mobile phones, it's not uncommon these days for each one of us to have several devices that we use on a regular basis.

In this chapter, you'll learn everything you need to know about ITF+ objective 2.6, including the following topics:

▶ **Mobile phones**
▶ **Tablets**
▶ **Laptops**
▶ **Workstations**
▶ **Servers**
▶ **Gaming consoles**
▶ **IoT**

COMPUTING DEVICE TYPES

In Chapter 3, "Computing Basics," you learned about the four basic operations performed by any computing device: input, storage, processing, and output. No matter what type of device you use, it performs all of these functions and those functions are coordinated by an operating system.

The *operating system* is software that normally comes preinstalled on a new computer and coordinates everything else that the computer does. When you start an app, the operating system manages the input and output devices, memory, and storage used by that app and ensures that different apps running at the same time don't interfere with each other.

Let's talk a little about the different types of computing devices that you may encounter while working in the world of information technology.

Desktop Computers

The standard *desktop computer* was once the mainstay of any office environment. Everyone had a computer on their desk and the reality was that the computer took up most of that desk! When I first started working at the National Security Agency in the late 1990s, I had two different computers: one for classified work and another for unclassified work. Those computers were so large that they took up an entire desk themselves—I had to have a second desk where I could actually work!

Today, desktop computers, such as the one shown in Figure 12.1, take up much less space and they no longer dominate the office environment. Many people still have desktop computers because they are generally less expensive than more portable devices, but many users who travel or move around the office don't want to be tethered to their desks, so they choose other alternatives.

FIGURE 12.1 Desktop computer system

Workstations

Some users have special computing needs where they need enhanced graphics processing, computing power, or other capabilities. Instead of a normal desktop computer, they might use a specialized device called a *workstation* that provides high-performance computing at a user's desk. Video editors, graphic designers, and other people who work with computing-intensive applications use these devices.

Servers

There's one more type of nonportable computer that you should know about. *Servers* are powerful computers that carry out a dedicated function. Companies might use servers to share files internally, host a website, run a database, or perform many other functions. You'll learn more about server functions as you work your way through this book, but for now, just know that servers are powerful computers that typically reside in special data centers that are designed to house many servers in special racks, such as the ones shown in Figure 12.2.

FIGURE 12.2 Server racks in a data center

Mobile Devices

Today, more employees than ever find themselves working from locations other than the office. Whether they're traveling around the world meeting with customers or simply working from home, users and their managers prefer portable computing devices that can easily travel with users wherever they need to work.

Laptop Computers

Laptop computers (see Figure 12.3) are very similar to the desktop computers that used to sit in every cubicle and office but with the major benefit of being extremely portable. They package together all of the computer's components, including the display, keyboard, and trackpad, in a single device that can be easily moved from one location to another. Laptops also contain batteries, allowing them to be used for hours without connecting them to electricity. Today's laptop can be just as powerful as a modern desktop computer. The only disadvantage is that they typically cost more than regular computers, and laptop users generally prefer to also have a full-sized monitor at their desk, increasing the total cost of their computing environment.

FIGURE 12.3 Laptop computer

Smartphones

Most of us carry *smartphones* with us today, such as the one shown in Figure 12.4. These smartphones are also powerful computing devices. In fact, the smartphones we use today are far more powerful than the desktop computers that we used just a decade ago. Smartphones run their own specialized operating systems. iPhones run Apple's iOS operating system whereas most other devices run Google's Android operating system.

FIGURE 12.4 Smartphone

Tablets

Tablets fit in between smartphones and laptops in terms of both size and capabilities. Tablets, such as the one shown in Figure 12.5, have larger screens than a phone but lack the physical keyboard and processing power of a laptop device. Tablets are commonly used in environments where employees are walking around interacting with customers and need a device that is portable. They are also often used to power touchscreen kiosks, such as those found in a hotel lobby.

> **EXAM TIP**
>
> Be prepared for exam questions that describe the requirements of a user and ask you to select the device that's most appropriate for your needs. You should try to balance usability and cost. If a user can get by with a desktop computer or tablet, they may not need a more expensive laptop. However, if they travel frequently, a desktop computer probably isn't the right choice for their needs.

Convertible laptops, such as the one shown in Figure 12.6, may be flipped around and used as either touchscreen tablets or normal laptops.

FIGURE 12.5 Tablet computer

FIGURE 12.6 Convertible laptop being used as a tablet

Gaming Consoles

You won't generally find *gaming consoles* in an office environment, but they are common on home networks. Gaming consoles, such as the one shown in Figure 12.7, actually contain very powerful computers that are optimized to deliver the graphics and audio capabilities necessary to run modern games.

In any large organization, you'll likely find a mix of these different types of computing device. Many users will have several devices. I myself have a desktop computer that I use regularly in my office, a laptop that travels around with me, a smartphone that I keep in my pocket, and a tablet that I use occasionally for reading or watching videos. Today's IT professional needs to understand the many different device types available to users and help them select devices that best meet their needs.

FIGURE 12.7 Gaming console

INTERNET OF THINGS

It's not just laptops, desktops, and phones that contain computers these days. Virtually everything around us now contains an embedded computer and is connected to the Internet. These devices might automatically order groceries for our homes when we're running low, reduce our cooling and heating bills based on the weather forecast, or even manage our lawn sprinkler systems.

We use the term *Internet of Things (IoT)* to describe the way that we connect many everyday devices to the Internet. These devices commonly use wireless networking to make it easy to place them anywhere in our homes and connect back to web consoles or home automation systems that coordinate their activity.

Home IoT Devices

We can connect all sorts of different devices to an IoT network. Home appliances, such as refrigerators, stoves, and washing machines, can all connect to the Internet. Today's refrigerator can remind you to buy milk at the store or even have it delivered when you're running low. The washing machine might be able to reach out to your favorite e-commerce retailer and reorder detergent for you. It can also send you a text message to remind you to switch the load over to the dryer when it's finished.

Inside our homes, we also might have a smart thermostat, an Internet-connected security system with IP-enabled cameras, streaming media devices that connect to the Internet to deliver content, or even IoT cars that can obtain driving directions, report their maintenance status back to the dealer, or deliver entertainment content to passengers. Many IoT devices may be remotely controlled by smartphone apps.

Workplace IoT Devices

The Internet of Things also plays a role in the workplace, particularly in industrial settings. The many advances in technology that have sped up manufacturing, power plant monitoring, wastewater treatment, and other industrial processes require the use of computers. *Industrial control systems (ICSs)* are the devices and systems that control industrial production and operation. They include systems that monitor electrical, gas, water, and other utility infrastructure and production operations, as well as the systems that control sewage processing and control, irrigation, and other processes.

IoT devices also play a role in modern healthcare. Virtually every medical device in a hospital is now connected to a network to improve patient care, and patients may even bring home insulin pumps, blood pressure monitors, and other devices that can report a patient's medical status back to their physician.

The Internet of Things is an awesomely powerful technology that reaches into almost every area of our lives, allowing us to take advantage of the power of modern computing to live better lives. As IT professionals, we're responsible for connecting these devices to the network, managing them, and ensuring that they have proper security controls in place to protect sensitive information.

CERTMIKE EXAM ESSENTIALS

▶ Desktop computers and workstations serve the computing needs of users who remain at a single location as they work. Laptops, tablets, and smartphones serve the needs of traveling users.

▶ Servers reside in data centers and provide a variety of services to users on the local network and/or the Internet.

▶ The Internet of Things connects everyday devices in both the home and the workplace to the network.

Practice Question 1

You are helping a user select a new computing device. The user is a video editor who requires a significant amount of computing power and will be using the device at a video editing station. What type of device would best meet this need?

A. Workstation
B. Desktop computer
C. Laptop computer
D. Server

Practice Question 2

You are designing a check-in kiosk for a medical practice. You require the use of a touchscreen where users can register for their appointment. What type of computer would best meet this need?

A. Desktop
B. Laptop
C. Smartphone
D. Tablet

Practice Question 1 Explanation

We can take away a couple of important facts from this scenario. First, the user is working in a fixed location—at an editing station. There is no indication that they are mobile, so we can eliminate the need for a laptop computer.

Next, the user requires significant computing power. This would make us lean toward a more powerful computer than a desktop, such as a workstation or a server. However, since the user will be interacting with the computer directly, we would not want a server, which would reside in a data center. Therefore, a workstation is likely the best solution for this user.

Correct Answer: A. Workstation

Practice Question 2 Explanation

You should always select the computing device that best meets the requirements of a scenario while minimizing cost. In this case, there is a clear requirement for a touchscreen. All of these devices may be outfitted with a touchscreen, so they would all possibly meet the requirements.

Next, we should eliminate any options that wouldn't be user-friendly. A smartphone is likely too small to support a check-in kiosk, where users will want a larger screen, so we can eliminate that.

Then we can pick the device that is most cost-effective. Laptops and desktops are fully-featured computers, which is more than needed for a kiosk. A tablet would meet the needs in the most cost-effective manner.

Correct Answer: D. Tablet

CHAPTER 13

TCP/IP Networking
Objective 2.7: Explain basic networking concepts

The computers that we use are powerful, but they become even more powerful when they're connected to each other. That's the role of a network: connecting computer systems together, whether it's within an office or to the global Internet. Networks allow us to send email messages around the world, stream video, print to a printer down the hall, and perform many other important tasks.

In this chapter, you'll learn everything you need to know about the first portion of ITF+ objective 2.7, including the following topics:

▶ **Basics of network communication**
▶ **Device addresses**

The remaining portions of objective 2.7 are covered in Chapter 14 and Chapter 15.

NETWORK TYPES

The networks that we have in our homes and offices are called *local area networks (LANs)*. LANs connect devices together that are in the same building so that they can talk to each other and to servers, printers, and other devices located in the office.

LANs are then connected to *wide area networks (WANs)*. WANs connect together offices in different locations and also connect us to the Internet. When our LAN is connected to a WAN, it allows us to become part of the global Internet and communicate with anyone we'd like.

Wi-Fi networks create powerful wireless LANs that allow us to use smartphones, laptops, and other networked devices anywhere in our home or office. We'll talk more about Wi-Fi networking in Chapter 16, "Wireless Networks."

You've probably also used a couple of other wireless networking technologies. *Bluetooth* networks are what we call *personal area networks (PANs)*. They're usually created by a computer or smartphone, and they're designed to support a single person. The main use of Bluetooth networks is to create wireless connections between a computer and its peripherals. Bluetooth allows us to use wireless headsets and connect our phones to our cars for hands-free access. The range of a Bluetooth network is around 30 feet, or 10 meters.

Near-field communication (NFC) technology allows extremely short-range wireless connections. For two devices to communicate using NFC, they need to be no more than a few inches apart. NFC technology is often used for wireless payments and building access control systems.

Bluetooth and NFC networks aren't general-purpose networks that connect many computers together, but they're very useful for short-range applications.

TCP/IP NETWORKING

Now that you understand a little about the types of network connections, let's talk about how data flows on a network. To do that, we need to dive into a protocol that you've probably heard about but might not be familiar with yet. It's called *TCP/IP*. You might have heard people refer to TCP/IP networking because it's the protocol that runs the Internet and basically every local area network on the planet.

The acronym TCP/IP has two parts to it. *Transmission Control Protocol (TCP)* and *Internet Protocol (IP)*. Each of these protocols plays a vital role in making sure that data gets from point A to point B.

Internet Protocol

IP is responsible for routing information over the network. Even though we call it the Internet Protocol, IP is used both on the Internet and on your local area network.

IP assigns each computer on the network its own address, called an *IP address*. We'll talk more about those addresses later in this chapter. For now, just know that IP addresses uniquely identify computers on a network and they are the way that computers identify each other.

When data travels on a TCP/IP network, the Internet Protocol breaks it up into small pieces called *packets*. Each packet is a few kilobytes of data. If you're sending a large file consisting of many megabytes or gigabytes, it will be divided up into thousands of smaller packets that are sent over the network.

The reason that we break data up into packets like this is to make our networks more reliable. If we tried to stuff megabytes into a single transmission and that transmission failed for some reason, we'd have to do the whole thing over again. If we break that up into thousands of smaller packets and one of those packets fails, we only need to retransmit that single small packet.

Larger packets would also clog up our networks. Think about a city street. When we have lots of small cars moving through the streets, traffic flows pretty smoothly. Now imagine we had a miles-long freight train try to drive down a city street. That would clog up traffic for miles around and nobody else would be able to use the road until the train left the city. That would leave us with a lot of unhappy computer users!

The Internet Protocol's job is to manage all of this work. We can just send a large file and IP will handle breaking it up into packets and then putting those packets back together again on the other side.

Transmission Control Protocol

The next component of the TCP/IP suite is the Transmission Control Protocol. TCP is responsible for setting up connections between systems and tracking the packets that are sent. If a packet is lost or damaged along the way, it's TCP's job to request that the sender transmit a new packet to replace the one that didn't arrive correctly.

Internet Control Message Protocol

The *Internet Control Message Protocol (ICMP)* is the housekeeping protocol of the Internet. It is part of the TCP/IP suite and it's designed to allow networked devices and systems to communicate with each other about the operation of the network. For example, ICMP may be used to detect whether remote systems are live on the network, to discover the network path between two systems, and to report issues with network devices.

Now there's a lot of other stuff involved in getting TCP/IP up and running on a network, but fortunately, you won't need to know about those for the IT Fundamentals exam.

NETWORK ADDRESSING

We've talked a bit about network addressing already, but let's dive into it a little deeper. First, you need to know that each computer has two different addresses: the IP address that we already talked about and another address called a *media access control (MAC)* address.

IP Addresses

Just like telephones use phone numbers and postal mail uses street addresses, the Internet needs an addressing scheme to ensure that data reaches its intended destination. The addresses that are used by the Internet Protocol are known as IP addresses.

In most cases, IP addresses are written in what's known as the dotted quad notation of IPv4. This means that they are four numbers, separated by periods. Each number may range between 0 and 255. For example, you might have a computer that uses the IP address 10.15.100.240.

> **NOTE**
>
> The dotted quad notation is used by IPv4, the most common protocol in use today. IPv6, the next generation of addresses, uses eight groups of four hexadecimal digits. For example, fae0:2660:a0a1:2efe:c84b:4c44:3467:a1ed is an IPv6 address.

That number 255 might sound familiar to you from our discussion of the binary numbering system back in Chapter 1, "Notational Systems." Can you guess why each one of the pieces of an IP address may have values ranging from 0 to 255?

That's right! It's because each number is represented using 1 byte, or 8 binary bits. The entire IP address consists of 32 bits, or 4 bytes.

A system's IP address uniquely identifies it on a network. If the system is directly connected to the Internet, the IP address it uses must not be used by any other system in the world, just as your mobile phone number is not used elsewhere in the world.

Systems that are connected to private networks, such as the one in your home or office, may use private IP addresses that are reusable on other networks. Your router or firewall takes care of translating those addresses to public IP addresses when you communicate over the Internet.

There are two IP addresses involved in every network communication.

▶ The *source address* indicates the system sending information.

▶ The *destination address* indicates the system receiving information.

As two systems communicate back and forth, the source and destination addresses will swap places, depending on who sends each packet. For example, examine the communication between a user with IP address 10.12.0.1 and a web server with IP address 10.51.1.2.

When the user is sending data to the web server, the source address is the user's IP address and the destination server is the web server's IP address, as shown in Figure 13.1.

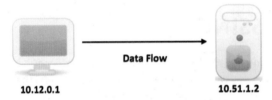

Source: 10.12.0.1
Destination: 10.51.1.2

FIGURE 13.1 Communication from a user to a web server

When the web server replies and sends data back to the user, the direction switches and the web server's IP address is the source address and the user's IP address becomes the destination address, as shown in Figure 13.2.

IP addresses may be assigned in two ways:

▶ You can assign an IP address **statically**. This means that you go into the system's settings and manually specify its IP address. You'll be responsible for ensuring that you choose a unique address that fits within the range for that network.

▶ You can assign an IP address **dynamically** by using the *Dynamic Host Configuration Protocol (DHCP)*. DHCP allows you to configure a pool of IP addresses and then DHCP will automatically assign those addresses to systems as they join the network. Typically, servers are configured with static IP addresses and end-user devices are configured with dynamically changing IP addresses.

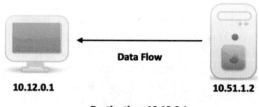

Data Flow

10.12.0.1   10.51.1.2

Destination: 10.12.0.1
Source: 10.51.1.2

FIGURE 13.2 Communication from a web server to a user

If a system is not configured with a static IP address, it reaches out on the network searching for a DHCP server that can supply it with a dynamic address. If the system is unable to find a DHCP server, it assigns itself an address using *Automatic Private IP Addressing (APIPA)*. APIPA addresses all begin with 169.254. If you see one of these addresses in use on your network, it means that something has likely gone wrong, as the system with that address was unable to obtain a valid IP address. In all but the smallest networks, addresses should be assigned by a DHCP server instead of being left to APIPA to assign.

Identifying Valid IPv4 Addresses

One of the things that you may be asked to do on the exam is to identify which IP addresses are valid for a host on a network. If you see a question like this, you should approach it using a process of elimination. Let's walk through a few simple rules that you can follow to eliminate invalid IP addresses.

No octet in an IP address should ever be larger than 255.   If you see a number greater than 255 in an IP address, that is not a valid address and you can immediately eliminate it as a possibility.

IP addresses starting with the number 127 are reserved for use as loopback addresses.   These addresses always reference the local system and are not valid as addresses on a network. The most common loopback address is 127.0.0.1, and when it's used in communications, it's the equivalent of telling a system to talk to itself. You should never see an address beginning with 127 as a host address for this reason.

The first number in an IP address should never be higher than 223.   While you can have values up to 255 in any octet, numbers higher than 223 in the first octet are reserved for special uses and shouldn't be assigned to systems. Addresses with first numbers between 224 and 239 are called *multicast addresses*, and they are used for sending messages to many systems at the same time and should never be assigned to an individual system. Addresses beginning with values between 240 and 255 are reserved for experimental use and, again, should not be found on individual systems.

MAC Addresses

I mentioned earlier that each computer on a network has two different addresses. The IP address is the one used to address network packets, and it's the one that we'll refer to most often. But computers also have media access control (MAC) addresses. MAC addresses are how computers communicate with their immediate neighbors on a network. Systems that are directly connected to each other use these addresses to transfer data. MAC addresses are assigned to a computer's network interface by the manufacturer and generally never change. IP addresses change frequently because they're usually assigned by the local network. If a computer moves from one network to another, its MAC address will remain the same but its IP address will change.

MAC addresses are written in hexadecimal notation, which you learned about in Chapter 1. This means that we can have MAC addresses consisting of the digits 0–9 and the letters A–F. Each MAC address is 12 hexadecimal digits. The first six digits identify the manufacturer of the device, and the next six digits are a unique identifier assigned by the manufacturer. MAC addresses are assigned to one device at the factory and should never be reused.

Here's an example of a MAC address:

```
14:9d:99:7f:3a:67
```

In this address, 14:9d:99 is the portion of the address that identifies the manufacturer of the device and 7f:3a:67 is the portion that uniquely identifies the device.

Address Lookup

As networks transmit data back and forth, computers and network devices often need to look up and translate between different types of addresses. They use special protocols to perform these lookups.

Domain Name System

Computers use IP addresses to communicate over the network. but those addresses are very difficult for people to remember. Just imagine if you had to memorize the IP address of every web server that you needed to access! The *Domain Name System (DNS)* allows people to use easily recognizable names in place of IP addresses.

DNS servers translate the names that you're more familiar with, such as www .certmike.com, into the IP addresses that computers use to communicate, such as 54.174.107.98. DNS is responsible for translating the *uniform resource locator (URL)* addresses that we commonly use for websites to the IP addresses associated with the servers supporting those sites.

NOTE

All of this terminology may be a little confusing. A domain name is a top-level name that may be registered by a company, organization, or individual. For example, `certmike.com` and `comptia.org` are both domain names. A URL is the address of a specific web page or other resource hosted on that domain. For example, `www.comptia.org/certifications/it-fundamentals` is a URL.

Every time you connect to a network, that network provides your computer with the IP address of a local *DNS server* that it can use to look up IP addresses. Then, whenever you type in the domain name of a website in your browser, your computer sends a request to the local DNS server asking it for the IP address associated with that name.

If the server knows the answer to your question, it simply responds to the request with the IP address, and then your web browser can go ahead and connect to the website using its IP address. If the local DNS server doesn't know the answer to your question, it contacts other DNS servers to determine the correct answer and then responds to you.

DNS is a hierarchical system, and organizations who own domain names designate DNS servers that are the responsible sources of information about their domain name. When a local DNS server needs to perform a lookup, it asks a series of questions that eventually lead it to the definitive answer from the DNS server that is responsible for a domain.

Address Resolution Protocol (ARP)

Network devices also often need to translate between the IP addresses used on the Internet and the MAC addresses used on local networks. That's the job of the *Address Resolution Protocol (ARP)*. You don't need to know much about ARP for the ITF+ exam. Just remember that it's used to look up the MAC address associated with an IP address.

EXAM TIP

Be sure that you are able to identify valid host IP addresses when you take the exam. Remember these three rules:

▶ No value in an IPv4 address should ever be higher than 255.

▶ The first value in an IPv4 address should never be 127.

▶ The first value in an IPv4 address should never be higher than 223.

CERTMIKE EXAM ESSENTIALS

▶ Wired networks use the Ethernet protocol and RJ-45 cable connectors to transmit data over copper wires. Wireless networks use the Wi-Fi standard to transmit data over radio waves.

▶ Each computer on a network has two different addresses: an IP address to identify it on the Internet and a MAC address to identify it on the local network.

▶ The Domain Name Service (DNS) translates URLs and other domain names to IP addresses. The Address Resolution Protocol (ARP) looks up the MAC address for an IP address.

Practice Question 1

You are assigning a host address to a new system on a network using a static IP address assignment. Which one of the following is a valid IP address?

A. 12.274.16.4

B. 127.19.6.200

C. 194.243.129.144

D. 240.1.15.2

Practice Question 2

Which one of the following characters should never appear in a MAC address?

A. 0

B. 9

C. .

D. F

Practice Question 1 Explanation

Let's walk through our three rules of valid IP addresses and handle this question by the process of elimination. We'll rule out any invalid IP addresses and then be left with the one valid address. First, no value in an IP address should ever be higher than 255. That eliminates our first option because it contains the value 274.

Second, the first value in a host address should never be 127. That eliminates the second option.

And finally, the first value in a host address should never be higher than 223. That eliminates the last option, which contains 243 as an octet value. That leaves us with one valid address: 194.243.129.144.

You should be prepared to answer questions like these when you take the IT Fundamentals exam. If you see a question like this, be sure to read it carefully. Depending on how it's phrased, it may be asking you to identify which one of a set of addresses is valid or which one of a set of addresses is invalid. Don't get tricked by assuming what the question is asking before you read the entire question.

Correct Answer: C. 194.243.129.144

Practice Question 2 Explanation

The underlying fact that you need to know to answer this question is that MAC addresses are written using hexadecimal notation. Hexadecimal notation allows the use of numeric digits and the alphabetic characters A, B, C, D, E, and F.

Looking at this question, the characters 0, 9, and F are all valid. The period should never be used in a MAC address. Periods are used to separate the octets of an IPv4 address. MAC addresses use colons (:) to separate different pieces of the address, as do IPv6 addresses.

Correct Answer: C.

CHAPTER 14

Application Protocols
Objective 2.7: Explain basic networking concepts

You've already learned about the roles that the Transmission Control Protocol (TCP) and the Internet Protocol (IP) play in routing traffic from one destination to another on the Internet. TCP and IP are used in combination with other protocols that are specific to the activity that the user is conducting.

In this chapter, you'll learn everything you need to know about the second portion of ITF+ objective 2.7, including the following topics:

▶ **Basic protocols**
- HTTP/S
- POP3
- IMAP
- SMTP

The remaining portions of objective 2.7 are covered in Chapter 13 and Chapter 15.

APPLICATION PROTOCOLS

There are different protocols for websites, email, file transfers, and other applications. As you prepare for the ITF+ exam, you'll need to be familiar with a few of these protocols.

EXAM TIP

There are two main types of questions that you should be prepared for related to application protocols. You should be able to identify the appropriate application protocol for use in a given situation, and you should be able to identify secure alternatives for insecure protocols.

Websites

The *Hypertext Transfer Protocol (HTTP)* is the protocol used for websites. When you load up your web browser and type in a URL, the web browser opens a TCP/IP connection to the web server that contains the content for that site. The server then uses HTTP to send you all the elements of the web page: text, graphics, ads, and anything else on the page. Your web browser then reassembles all of that content into a website that you can view.

There is one important catch to HTTP: it's not secure. When you connect to a website using HTTP, your information is unencrypted and anyone watching your network connection can see what you're doing online.

The fix for this is an updated version of HTTP that builds in security. The *Hypertext Transfer Protocol Secure (HTTPS)* adds encryption to web connections to prevent eavesdroppers from seeing what you're doing on a website.

You should also be familiar with two languages used for the content of web pages. Web developers write the code for a web page using the *Hypertext Markup Language (HTML)*. They may also create standard templates for websites using a format known as *Cascading Style Sheets (CSS)*.

Email

There are also a whole series of protocols used to support email messages. You'll need to be familiar with these for the exam as well.

Before we get into the specifics of email protocols, we need to first discuss how email works. If I send you an email message, my computer takes that message and sends it to my email server. When my email server gets the message, it looks to see whether you have an account on my mail server. If you do, it places the email in your inbox. If you don't, it looks up the correct email server for your address and transfers the message to that server where it is placed in your inbox. That transfer, sending the message from one server to another, uses a protocol called the *Simple Mail Transfer Protocol (SMTP)*.

When you go to check your email, your email client reaches out to your email server and requests your messages. That connection can take place using three different protocols:

> ▶ If you're using a web-based email client, such as Gmail, your connection takes place over the web, so it uses HTTPS for both sending and receiving messages.
> ▶ If you're using a traditional email client, such as Microsoft Outlook, your email client connects to the mail server and retrieves messages using either the *Post Office Protocol (POP3)* or the *Internet Message Access Protocol (IMAP)*.

POP3 and IMAP share a similar purpose, but they work in different ways. POP3 is an older protocol that takes new messages waiting for you on the server and downloads them to your computer. Once they're downloaded, they are deleted from the server and you won't be able to download them again. Your email lives only on your computer.

IMAP, on the other hand, uses a more modern approach where all of the emails remain on the server and your mail client just accesses them each time you connect. This allows you to access your email wherever you are, from any device. Traditional email clients use POP3 or IMAP only to receive messages. They use SMTP to send messages to your mail server for delivery.

All of these email protocols have both secure and insecure versions. The secure versions add encryption to the older, insecure versions of the protocol. These secure protocols include SMTP Secure (SMTPS), POP3 over TLS (Transport Layer Security), and IMAP Secure (IMAPS).

File Transfer

Finally, you should be familiar with a series of protocols that are used to transfer files between clients and servers. The original protocol used for this purpose is the *File Transfer Protocol (FTP)*. As with many older protocols, the FTP protocol does not include any security features. Two newer versions of the protocol, the *Secure File Transfer Protocol (SFTP)* and the *File Transfer Protocol Secure (SFTP)* add encryption to enhance the security of file transfers.

Make sure that you're familiar with all of these protocols and their purposes as you prepare for the ITF+ exam.

CERTMIKE EXAM ESSENTIALS

▶ Websites are written in the Hypertext Markup Language (HTML). The HTML files that make up a website are sent to users through the Hypertext Transfer Protocol (HTTP) and its secure alternative, the Hypertext Transfer Protocol Secure (HTTPS).

▶ Email is transferred from the sender to the mail server and between mail servers using the Simple Mail Transfer Protocol (SMTP). Users access their mail using HTTPS, the Internet Message Access Protocol (IMAP), or the Post Office Protocol (POP3). IMAP and POP3 have secure alternatives, known as IMAPS and POP3 over TLS, respectively.

▶ Files may be transferred between systems using the File Transfer Protocol (FTP). FTP is insecure and it is better to use the Secure File Transfer Protocol (SFTP) or the File Transfer Protocol Secure (FTPS).

Practice Question 1

You are helping a user who needs to send sensitive information to a website. What protocol would be most appropriate for this situation?

A. HTTP

B. FTP

C. HTTPS

D. SMTP

Practice Question 2

You create an email message and send it to your email server. Before it can reach its destination, the message must pass between several email servers. What protocol is most likely used for this communication between email servers?

A. IMAP

B. IMAPS

C. POP3

D. SMTP

Practice Question 1 Explanation

The first thing we should notice about this question is that the communication is between a user and a web server. This means that we should be using some version of the Hypertext Transfer Protocol (HTTP). For this reason, we can immediately eliminate the File Transfer Protocol (FTP), which is used to transfer files between systems, and the Simple Mail Transfer Protocol (SMTP), which is used for forwarding email messages.

Next, we should notice that the user is sending sensitive information. Sensitive information should always be sent using a secure protocol because those secure protocols encrypt data to protect it from prying eyes. Therefore, we should use the HTTP Secure (HTTPS) protocol for this communication instead of the insecure and unencrypted HTTP.

Correct Answer: C. HTTPS

Practice Question 2 Explanation

Messages are forwarded between mail servers using the Simple Mail Transfer Protocol (SMTP) or the secure version of that protocol (SMTPS). SMTPS is not an option here, so we should choose SMTP as the correct answer.

The other protocols listed here—the Internet Message Access Protocol (IMAP), IMAP Secure (IMAPS), and the Post Office Protocol (POP3)—are all used to transfer messages from the mail server to the intended recipient. They are not used to transfer messages between mail servers.

Correct Answer: D. SMTP

CHAPTER 15

Network Devices
Objective 2.7: Explain basic networking concepts

Networks are more than just cables. They also rely upon a series of specialized network devices that help the network carry data to its destination. These devices are the unsung heroes of modern information technology. They're often locked away in basements and closets, quietly playing a crucial role in keeping our networks running. In this chapter, we cover some of these devices and the roles that they play on our networks.

In this chapter, you'll learn everything you need to know about the third portion of ITF+ objective 2.7, including the following topics:

▶ **Devices**
- Modem
- Router
- Switch
- Access point
- Firewall

The remaining portions of objective 2.7 are covered in Chapter 13 and Chapter 14.

MODEMS

Modems provide a bridge between the analog and digital worlds, offering digital systems the ability to communicate over older transmission technologies. The word *modem* is an abbreviated form of two words that describe the functions of the device: modulator and demodulator. A modem converts a signal from digital form to an analog form, such as audio, electrical impulses, light pulses, or whatever is required by the transmission media. This is called *modulation*. On the other end of the connection, a modem converts that analog transmission back to digital form, a process called *demodulation*.

The earliest modems were used to connect computers to telephone lines that were designed to carry audio signals. They literally enabled computers to "speak" to each other over telephone lines.

Today, in home and small office environments, digital subscriber line (DSL) communications use modems to carry high-speed Internet over telephone lines, and cable modems such as the one shown in Figure 15.1 perform a similar task to allow the use of cable television infrastructure for data signals. You learned about these Internet service types in Chapter 10, "Internet Service Types."

FIGURE 15.1 Cable modem

SWITCHES

Switches are at the front lines of networking. In Chapter 13, "TCP/IP Networking," you learned that each of the network jacks in the wall of your office has cables running out of the back of it up into the ceiling. Those cables travel to a nearby technology closet, where they plug into a switch.

Switches, such as the ones shown in Figure 15.2, connect all of the devices on a local area network and make sure that the right data gets to the right device. They work using MAC addresses to send traffic that they receive to the correct port on the switch, traveling back through the appropriate wire to the computer at the other end of the right wall jack.

FIGURE 15.2 Network switches

EXAM TIP

Remember that switches are the devices that connect normal end-user devices to the network. In the case of a wired network connection, the cable connects from the device to the switch. Later in this chapter, you'll learn how wireless access points connect wireless devices to a switch over a wired connection between the access point and the switch.

ROUTERS

Routers are the core of the modern network. All of the switches in an organization connect back to a router that manages the traffic between an organization's switches and the Internet. I mentioned earlier that switches send traffic around the local network segment using MAC addresses. Routers carry traffic between those local networks and the Internet and do so using IP addresses.

SIMPLE NETWORK MANAGEMENT PROTOCOL (SNMP)

On large networks, it's clearly not practical to manage each device manually. Administrators would have to spend large portions of their time running around the network, either physically or virtually, adjusting configurations and collecting log entries. This is time-consuming work that is not particularly productive.

The *Simple Network Management Protocol (SNMP)* provides network administrators with a means to centrally configure and monitor network devices. SNMP automates many network administration tasks, performing the heavy lifting for administrators, who can then spend their time doing design work or higher-level monitoring.

FIREWALLS

Firewalls provide security for the network. They sit between two or more networks and monitor all the connection attempts that try to cross between those networks. Figure 15.3 shows an example of how a firewall might be used to separate three networks: an internal network, the Internet, and a special network known as the *demilitarized zone (DMZ)* that contains publicly accessible servers.

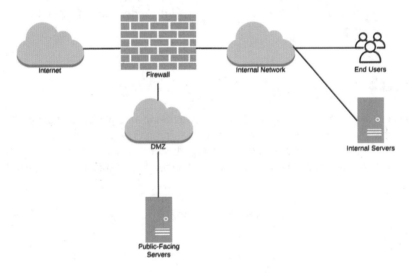

FIGURE 15.3 **Network firewall deployment**

Firewalls contain a set of rules describing the types of connections that are allowed to cross from one network to the other, and they strictly enforce that policy. Any connection attempts that aren't specifically allowed by a firewall rule are blocked from crossing the firewall. The most common example of a firewall is a border firewall that sits between an organization's internal network and the Internet. Any Internet connections that aren't covered by a firewall rule are automatically blocked, protecting the network from attack.

EXAM TIP

You won't need to know how to configure firewalls (or any other network device) on the ITF+ exam. When you review this material, you should focus on the roles of different network devices and be ready to answer questions about what type of network device would be used in a scenario.

ACCESS POINTS

Home and business networks use *wireless access points*, such as the larger of the two devices shown in Figure 15.4, to connect wireless devices to the building's wired network. These access points contain powerful antennas, transmitters, and receivers that allow them to broadcast Wi-Fi signals over large areas. They are also connected with a cable to a traditional wired network. Wireless devices in the area can then communicate with the access point to connect to other networks.

You'll learn more about wireless networking in Chapter 16, "Wireless Networks."

F I G U R E   1 5 . 4   Wireless access point

CERTMIKE EXAM ESSENTIALS

▶ Modems are used to convert between analog and digital signals. Today, they are commonly used for cable and DSL Internet connections.

▶ Routers and switches are the devices that form the backbone of the modern network. Networked devices connect to a switch via a network cable or to a wireless access point via a Wi-Fi connection. Switches connect to each other and to routers. Routers send traffic between switches on the internal network and the Internet.

▶ Firewalls are security devices that restrict the traffic that may enter and leave a network.

Practice Question 1

You are concerned about the ability of outside individuals to access your internal network and would like to use a network device to restrict this access. Which one of the following devices would best meet this need?

A. Firewall
B. Router
C. Switch
D. Access point

Practice Question 2

You are helping a user troubleshoot the network connection on their desktop computer. You examine the computer and it seems to be functioning normally. When you examine the network card, you determine that the cable is plugged in correctly but the link light is not on, indicating that there is a problem with the connection to the next network device. What type of network device should you check next?

A. Router
B. Access point
C. Switch
D. Firewall

Practice Question 1 Explanation

Looking at this question, you should be able to immediately eliminate two of the answer choices. Switches are components of an internal network. They are not connected to external networks and would not be used to control access into a network. Wireless access points are also internal network components used to connect wireless devices to the wired network. We can eliminate both of these options as possible answer choices.

That leaves us with two devices that do connect to external networks: firewalls and routers. The reality is that both firewalls and routers have the potential to fulfill this requirement. They both have filtering capabilities that can block unwanted external traffic. To answer this question correctly, focus on the word *best* that appears in the final sentence. We're not asking which device *can* meet this need—we're asking which can *best* meet this need. While routers do have limited filtering capability, they are not designed for this purpose. Firewalls, on the other hand, are designed specifically to restrict network traffic, making a firewall the best solution to this problem.

Correct Answer: A. Firewall

Practice Question 2 Explanation

There is a lot of detail in this question, but the most important fact that you can pick out to get started on your answer is that you are looking for the network device that is directly connected to a desktop computer. End-user computing devices connect to switches over a wired network connection or wireless access points over a Wi-Fi connection. They do not normally connect directly to a router or firewall.

Next, we notice in the question that the connection uses a network cable. This tells us that the connection is a wired connection and that it would use a switch, rather than an access point, because access points are only used on wireless networks.

Correct Answer: C. Switch

CHAPTER 16

Wireless Networks

Objective 2.8: Given a scenario, install, configure, and secure a basic wireless network

Wireless networking is everywhere. We use wireless networks to provide network access to our smartphones, tablets, and laptop computers and to a wide variety of other devices, including televisions, thermostats, and home automation systems. As the use of wireless networks continues to increase, the security of those networks becomes of critical importance.

In this chapter, you'll learn everything you need to know about ITF+ objective 2.8, including the following topics:

▶ **802.11a/b/g/n/ac**
▶ **Best practices**

WIRELESS NETWORKING

The most common wireless standard in use today is *Wi-Fi* technology. Wi-Fi is a set of standards created by the Institute of Electrical and Electronics Engineers (IEEE) and describes the technical details of how wireless devices communicate with each other and wireless access points. The use of a standard is absolutely essential because without a standard, wireless devices wouldn't speak the same language. Standardization is what allows any Wi-Fi device to work with any Wi-Fi network around the world.

Wi-Fi works by replacing the wires and cables of wired networks with radio transmitters and receivers. Every device that supports Wi-Fi contains a radio transceiver that is capable of communicating on one or more standard Wi-Fi bands. From smartphones to laptops and video game consoles to Internet-connected smoke detectors, each device contains a small chip and antenna used to transmit and receive Wi-Fi signals.

Most Wi-Fi networks are also connected to wired networks that are, in turn, connected to the Internet. This allows wireless devices to communicate with wired devices and systems located anywhere on the Internet.

Home and business networks use wireless access points to perform that connection. Enterprise networks may use sophisticated, ceiling-mounted access points, such as the one you saw in Figure 15.4. Small office/home office (SOHO) networks may use tabletop access points, such as the one shown in Figure 16.1. Both types of access points contain powerful antennas, transmitters, and receivers that allow them to broadcast Wi-Fi signals over large areas. They are also connected with a cable to a traditional wired network. Wireless devices in the area can then communicate with the access point to connect to other networks.

FIGURE 16.1 SOHO wireless access point

Wireless Networking Standards

The *IEEE 802.11* standard is the base standard for all Wi-Fi networks in use today. There are different versions of this standard that describe different versions of Wi-Fi networking and they're differentiated by the letter(s) that appear after 802.11. The two major differences among the standards are the maximum speed that each is able to achieve and the radio frequency ranges they use.

Frequency Ranges

Wireless networks using the 2.4 GHz frequency range are able to reach a longer distance than networks that use other frequencies, but they have slower speeds. Those running in the higher 5 GHz frequency range offer higher speeds but cover reduced distances. Choosing your frequency range requires thinking through this trade-off between speed and distance. If you want to use a 5 GHz network, you'll need to have more wireless access points because each access point covers a smaller area.

> **NOTE**
>
> When selecting wireless networking frequencies, be sure to consider device compatibility. You'll want to ensure that every device that must connect to your network is compatible with at least one of the frequencies that you offer.

802.11 Standards

The earliest version of Wi-Fi, 802.11, was released in 1997 and allowed communications up to 2 megabits per second (Mbps) using the 2.4 GHz frequency range. Two years later, the *802.11b* standard more than quintupled that speed to allow communication at 11 Mbps, also at 2.4 GHz. At the same time, the *802.11a* standard provided even faster 54 Mbps connectivity using 5 GHz band communications. However, 802.11a wasn't widely used because the 5 GHz equipment was much more expensive than 802.11b equipment.

802.11g, released in 2003, bumped up the maximum bandwidth to 54 Mbps at 2.4 GHz, while *802.11n* brought a tremendous boost in bandwidth to 600 Mbps in 2009 by using special antennas known as multiple input-multiple output (MIMO) antennas. 802.11n networks run at both 2.4 and 5.0 GHz. The *802.11ac* standard now allows communication at speeds over 1 Gbps using the 5.0 GHz band. Table 16.1 provides a summary of these facts.

> **EXAM TIP**
>
> Memorize the information in Table 16.1. This is absolutely crucial information for the exam. Yes, it's a boring list of numbers, but you shouldn't be surprised to find at least one question asking you about frequency ranges and/or speeds of different Wi-Fi standards on the ITF+ exam.

TABLE 16.1 Wireless standard frequencies and speed

Standard	Frequency range	Maximum speed
802.11	2.4 GHz	2 Mbps
802.11a	5.0 GHz	54 Mbps
802.11b	2.4 GHz	11 Mbps
802.11g	2.4 GHz	54 Mbps
802.11n	2.4 or 5.0 GHz	600 Mbps
802.11ac	5.0 GHz	1 Gbps

WIRELESS SIGNAL PROPAGATION

Wi-Fi signals are radio transmissions and, as such, they can be picked up by anyone with a suitable antenna and receiver. Unlike wired networks, wireless signals can travel out in many different directions. This introduces new security concerns as network administrators must carefully protect against eavesdropping attacks.

The radio waves that carry wireless network traffic are affected by many different factors as they travel across an area. Building materials, antenna placement, power levels, and many other characteristics can alter the flow, or propagation, of wireless signals. When conditions weaken radio signals, we call that situation *attenuation*. Attenuation limits the range of wireless networks.

Wireless Antennas

There are many different types of wireless antennas that may be used. While many organizations use the simple antennas built into wireless access points, other options are available. There are two basic categories of antennas:

▶ *Omnidirectional antennas* are the basic antennas used with wireless access points. They transmit radio waves in a donut-shaped pattern. The short, stubby, pole-like antennas attached to wireless access points are examples of omnidirectional antennas. The wireless access point in Figure 16.1 uses an omnidirectional antenna.

▶ *Directional antennas* allow network administrators to point a wireless signal in a specific direction, such as when creating a point-to-point network between buildings. This greatly increases the range of the network by focusing power in a single direction.

802.11ac networks include a new technology known as *beamforming*. With beamforming, the access point uses multiple antennas that look like simple omnidirectional antennas to detect the location of a device connecting to the access point and then steer the signal in the direction of the device. You can think of beamforming as a virtual directional antenna that can shift as needed based on device location.

Wireless Device Placement

Placing antennas and access points in a facility is a highly specialized area of networking. Many different characteristics of a building will affect wireless signal propagation, and engineers must take those into account to prevent dead spots while also ensuring that physically adjacent access points don't interfere with each other.

While it is possible to sketch out diagrams and place access points based on a theoretical design, the best way to place wireless access points is to conduct a *site survey* that uses specialized hardware and software to measure signal strength and provide optimal wireless signal coverage.

These surveys often produce a heat map that graphically illustrates areas of strong coverage and those that require improvement. They also may identify areas where electromagnetic interference is causing disruptions to your wireless network.

Interference

The Wi-Fi standard supports the use of different frequencies within the standard 2.4 and 5.0 GHz bands. The different frequencies available in each band are known as *wireless channels*. You can often improve your wireless coverage by adjusting the channels that you use in your building to avoid overlap with the channels used by other nearby businesses.

You also may find that other devices in the area, such as radio transmitters, baby monitors, and even microwave ovens can be sources of *electromagnetic interference (EMI)*. If you're experiencing wireless signal issues, it's helpful to track down and eliminate possible sources of electromagnetic interference while you troubleshoot.

Network engineers also have the ability to manipulate the power levels transmitted by each access point to tweak coverage and prevent interference. These power levels may be manually adjusted or automatically managed by wireless controllers.

WIRELESS SECURITY

One of the major responsibilities of IT professionals is to secure wireless networks to protect the traffic they carry from eavesdropping attacks and to protect the network from unauthorized access. There are a few best practices you can follow to protect your wireless network.

SSID

Each wireless network has a name that identifies it to users. This name is what you see on your phone or laptop when you're choosing the network you'd like to use. The technical term for this name is the *service set identifier (SSID)*. By default, wireless networks advertise themselves to potential users by broadcasting their SSID, telling everyone in the local area that the network is available and accepting connections. If you don't want to advertise your network, you can disable SSID broadcasting, hiding the network from users who don't already know that it is there.

> **EXAM TIP**
>
> If you find yourself facing a question asking you to troubleshoot connectivity between two devices on a wireless network, one of the possible issues is that the two devices may not be connected to the same wireless network. If the devices are connected to networks with different SSIDs, that's likely the issue.

Access Point Passwords

Your wireless access point also has an administrative password that allows you to connect to the device and configure the wireless network and its security settings. The access point may have come from the manufacturer with a default password already set that is printed in the user manual or on a label on the device itself. You should, as a matter of habit, immediately change these default passwords to strong passwords known only to you and other network administrators within your organization.

Wireless Access Control

You'll also need to decide what type of wireless network you'd like to run. *Open networks* are available to anyone who comes across them and would like to use them. Other networks use some type of authentication to limit access.

Preshared keys are the simplest kind of wireless authentication and are commonly used on SOHO Wi-Fi networks. In the preshared key approach, the network uses an encryption key to control access. Whenever a user wishes to connect a device to the network, they must enter the preshared key on the device. If you've ever been at an office or public place where there's a Wi-Fi password posted on the wall, that's an example of a preshared key. Preshared keys have major limitations that prevent them from being used on large networks:

▶ Changing the network encryption key is a tremendous burden. Each time the key changes, users must reconfigure all wireless devices to use the new key. This might not be bad on a home network supporting a handful of users, but it is impractical in most business environments.

▶ The use of a shared key prevents the identification of individual users and the restriction of access by user identity. For example, if a user leaves the organization, network administrators have no way to revoke that user's wireless network access short of changing the preshared key on all wireless devices in the organization.

A common way to approach wireless authentication is through the use of *enterprise authentication*. In this approach, the organization runs an authentication server that verifies user credentials and ensures that only authorized users access the network. In this approach, instead of entering a preshared key, users enter their individual username and password or provide other credentials to access the network.

The third approach to wireless authentication is the use of *captive portals*. You might not be familiar with the term *captive portal*, but you've certainly seen them in use in hotels, airports, coffee shops, and other public locations. Captive portals provide authentication on unencrypted wireless networks. When a user connects to a network using a captive portal, they are redirected to a web page that requires them to authenticate before gaining access to the network. This authentication may be as simple as accepting the terms of service, or it may require an account password or even a credit card payment to escape the captive portal and use the Internet.

WIRELESS ENCRYPTION

Network administrators may choose to add *encryption* to wireless networks to protect communications against eavesdropping. Wireless encryption is a best practice for network security. Encryption hides the true content of network traffic from those without the decryption key. It takes an insecure communications technology—radio waves—and makes it secure. You have several options for wireless encryption, the details of each are summarized in Table 16.2.

Wired Equivalent Privacy (WEP)

The original approach to solving this problem was a technology known as *Wired Equivalent Privacy (WEP)*. WEP was used for a long time, but it's now known to suffer from some serious security vulnerabilities. These issues are so significant that security professionals no longer consider WEP secure, and it should never be used on a modern network.

Wi-Fi Protected Access (WPA)

A newer technology called *Wi-Fi Protected Access (WPA)* replaced WEP back in 2003. This first version, just called WPA, used the *Temporal Key Integrity Protocol (TKIP)* to add security that WEP didn't have. TKIP changes the encryption key for each packet, preventing an attacker from discovering the key after monitoring the network for a long period of time. However, as happens with many security technologies, vulnerabilities in WPA have now come to light that also make it a poor choice for use on wireless networks.

Wi-Fi Protected Access v2 (WPA2)

In 2004, *WPA2* was released as an upgrade to WPA. Instead of simply trying to add security onto the old WEP standard, WPA2 uses an encryption protocol that is based on the *Advanced Encryption Standard (AES)*.This mode has a really long name—*Counter Mode Cipher Block Chaining Message Authentication Code Protocol*—but you just need to know it by the acronym CCMP. Security researchers have discovered some potential issues with WPA2, but it is still considered secure and is widely used.

Wi-Fi Protected Access v3 (WPA3)

As of 2020, new wireless devices are required to support the WPA3 standard. WPA3 also supports the CCMP protocol but it adds a new technology called *Simultaneous Authentication of Equals (SAE)*. SAE is a secure key exchange protocol based on the Diffie–Hellman technique to provide a secure initial setup of encrypted wireless communications.

> **EXAM TIP**
>
> You definitely need to know the different wireless encryption mechanisms when you take the exam. Table 16.2 provides a quick reference to help you remember the key facts.

TABLE 16.2 Wireless encryption options

Standard	Security status	Encryption algorithm	Encryption mode
Open	Insecure	None	None
WEP	Insecure	RC4	None
WPA	Insecure	RC4	TKIP
WPA2	Secure	AES	CCMP
WPA3	Secure	AES	CCMP and SAE

> **EXAM TIP**
>
> WPA3 is still fairly new and not widely used. Some of the ITF+ exam questions that you face may have been written before WPA3 was released. If you find a question that completely ignores the existence of WPA3, don't let that throw you off your game. Answer that question as if WPA3 doesn't exist!

If you ever find yourself in a situation where the network available to you is running an insecure encryption algorithm or is run by an untrusted source (such as a hotel or coffee shop), you can enhance the security of an insecure wireless network by using a *virtual private network (VPN)*. VPNs use encryption to create a secure connection back to a trusted network, such as the one in your office.

CERTMIKE EXAM ESSENTIALS

▶ Wireless networks vary in terms of the frequency ranges that they use and their maximum bandwidth. You should memorize the frequency ranges and speeds associated with each of the 802.11 standards.

▶ Enterprise authentication allows organizations to authenticate wireless users with their normal usernames and passwords. Preshared keys require the distribution of a common password.

▶ Wireless encryption protects information from eavesdropping while it is traveling over the wireless network. The strongest wireless encryption techniques are WPA2 and WPA3. WEP and WPA should no longer be used.

Practice Question 1

Your organization recently experienced an attack where an outside individual was able to eavesdrop on the wireless connections of network users. Which one of the following security enhancements would best protect against this type of attack?

A. Enabling WPA2

B. Enabling WEP

C. Changing SSIDs

D. Changing channels

Practice Question 2

Which one of the following wireless standards would allow you to achieve the highest speed connection using the 2.4 GHz frequency range?

A. 802.11ac

B. 802.11b

C. 802.11g

D. 802.11n

Practice Question 1 Explanation

This question is asking us to evaluate different changes that we could make to our wireless network. The key here is realizing that eavesdropping on a network connection is best defeated through the use of encryption technology. Two of the answer choices—WEP and WPA2—are options for adding encryption to a wireless network. WEP encryption is outdated and insecure, whereas WPA2 is a secure, robust encryption protocol.

You might look at this question and think that WPA3 is an even better choice. It definitely is! But it's simply not one of the options here, so we should go with adding WPA2 to the network.

Changing the SSID simply changes the name that the network broadcasts to the world, which would have minimal security impact. Changing the channel is a good option if you're experiencing interference on your wireless network, but it won't help with eavesdropping attacks because it's simple for the attacker to find the new channel.

Correct Answer: A. Enabling WPA2

Practice Question 2 Explanation

This question requires that you have the information from Table 16.1 memorized. Consulting that table helps you quickly identify the correct answer.

The fastest Wi-Fi network standard is 802.11ac, operating at speeds up to 1 Gbps. However, you also need to note that 802.11ac runs at 5.0 GHz, not 2.4 GHz, so it doesn't meet the requirements of the question. The fastest option for a 2.4 GHz Wi-Fi network is the 802.11n standard, operating at 600 Mbps.

The other Wi-Fi standards here operate at slower speeds. 802.11b runs at a maximum speed of 11 Mbps, and 802.11g runs at a maximum speed of 54 Mbps.

Correct Answer: D. 802.11n

Domain 3.0: Applications and Software

Applications and Software is the third domain of CompTIA's ITF+ exam. In this domain, you'll learn about the role of the operating system and how it mediates access between different types of applications and the computer's hardware. This domain has six objectives:

3.1 Explain the purpose of operating systems

3.2 Compare and contrast components of an operating system

3.3 Explain the purpose and proper use of software

3.4 Explain methods of application architecture and delivery models

3.5 Given a scenario, configure and use web browsers

3.6 Compare and contrast general application concepts and uses

Questions from this domain make up 18% of the questions on the ITF+ exam, so you should expect to see approximately 14 questions on your test covering the material in this part.

CHAPTER 17

Operating Systems
Objective 3.1: Explain the purpose of operating systems

The operating system is at the heart of the modern computer. Whether you use Microsoft Windows, Apple macOS, or a version of Linux, the operating system plays the same important role on every computer. It serves as an essential interface between you and the computer, translating your keystrokes to bits and bytes and displaying output on the screen. It's the interface between applications and hardware, providing software with the memory, storage, and network access that it needs to carry out its work.

In this chapter, you'll learn everything you need to know about ITF+ objective 3.1, including:

▶ **Interface between applications and hardware**
▶ **Disk management**
▶ **Process management/scheduling**
▶ **Application management**
▶ **Memory management**
▶ **Device management**
▶ **Access control/protection**
▶ **Types of OS**
▶ **One subtopic of this objective, hypervisors, is covered in Chapter 18, "Virtualization."**

OPERATING SYSTEM ROLES

The *operating system (OS)* serves as a layer of *abstraction*. This just means that it hides the details of the hardware from different software applications. The creators of a new web browser don't need to design that browser to work with every possible hardware configuration imaginable. Instead, they design it to work with common operating systems and then it's the operating system's job to serve as an interface for interactions between applications and the hardware.

Let's dive a little deeper into the many different roles handled by the operating system.

Disk Management

The operating system is responsible for *disk management*. As you learned in Chapter 11, "Storage," hard drives are just massive storage devices that contain billions of individual locations where you can store values of 0 and 1. There's no natural organization to a hard drive. You can think of it as an enormous empty warehouse.

The operating system brings order to the empty warehouse of a hard drive. Just like you'd create aisles and install shelving in a warehouse, the operating system builds a folder structure on disk that helps you organize your files. It also then has to remember where all of the bits making up each one of those files are stored on the disk. Then when you want to read that file from disk, the operating system finds the right bits and puts them back together in your file.

Memory Management

Memory works in a way that is very similar to disks. It's just a large storage location as well, and the operating system performs *memory management* tasks to organize the contents of that memory. It's also responsible for making sure that different applications only have access to the memory areas reserved for their use. It would be a big security issue if one application was able to access memory spaces reserved for another application.

Process Management and Scheduling

When you're using your computer, you're normally running many different pieces of software at the same time. You might be using a web browser, working on a Word document, and listening to music all at once. You also might have other software running in the background, synchronizing your files to the cloud, scanning for security issues, and performing many other tasks. Each instance of these applications that's actively running on a computer is called a *process*, and the operating system manages those processes to make sure that they each get their fair share of access to the CPU when they need to perform some processing.

Operating systems are also responsible for performing *task scheduling*. This allows administrators to configure a computer to execute an action at a specific time in the future, either once or on a repeating basis. For example, an administrator might configure a script to run once a day to generate a daily report of system activity.

Application Management

IT professionals sometimes need to intervene when a process goes haywire. If an application crashes and won't respond to user input, every operating system provides a mechanism to manually *kill* that process, ending the task and allowing the user to restart it and get things up and running again. This work of *application management* is another of the major roles of the operating system.

Device Management

In Chapter 8, "Installing Peripherals," you learned about some of the different peripheral devices that you might use with a computer. That's another one of the operating system's jobs: *device management*. The operating system is responsible for running the *drivers* that tell the computer how to interact with different devices, interpreting the data received from devices, and sending data to them as appropriate.

Access Control and Protection

Finally, the operating system also plays an important role in the world of cybersecurity. It performs access control and protection tasks. These include making sure that only authorized users gain access to a computer system and that those users can't access data that exceeds their assigned permissions.

> **EXAM TIP**
>
> Microsoft Windows uses *security identifiers (SIDs)* to perform access control tasks. Every user, system, group, and object in a Windows environment is assigned a unique identifier that may be used to track the identified item across the domain, even if the name later changes.

OPERATING SYSTEM TYPES

You should now have a good understanding of the role that the operating system plays in the world of computing. It's a critically important interface between users, software, and all the hardware components of a device. You also know that there are different operating system options out there, and you may have used some different operating systems yourself. Maybe you've used a mix of Microsoft Windows, Linux, and Apple operating systems. The next thing that you need to understand is that there are different types of operating systems for different uses.

Desktop Operating Systems

The one that you're probably the most familiar with are the desktop, laptop, and work-station operating systems that run on most of the computers that we interact with on a daily basis. The two most common workstation operating systems are Microsoft Windows and Apple's macOS. If you're using Apple laptop and desktop computers, you'll run macOS on them. If you're using any other brand of computer, you're most likely running Micro-soft Windows.

There are other operating systems for laptops and desktops, but they're just not all that common. For example, you can run variants of the Linux operating system on a laptop or desktop computer if you'd like, but most people choose not to do that because they want the convenience of being able to run consumer software that is usually only available for the Windows and Mac platforms.

Another operating system that we're seeing more frequently these days is Chrome OS and a free variant of Chrome OS called Chromium. These operating systems, built around Google's Chrome browser, are designed to run on very inexpensive minimal computers called *thin clients*. Chromebooks and other thin clients are meant to be a cheap way to get onto the web and use software-as-a-service applications. They're very popular in schools and other environments where you want inexpensive access to computing.

Mobile Operating Systems

Mobile operating systems run mobile devices, such as smartphones and tablets. In the mobile operating system space, there are three major players. Apple's iOS runs on iPhones, and iPadOS runs on iPads. Google's Android operating system supports a wide variety of mobile devices. Microsoft once made a mobile version of Windows but stopped support-ing Windows phones a few years back and now makes a version of the desktop Windows operating system that runs on tablets.

Server Operating Systems

Servers also need operating systems, and they run operating systems that are similar in function to those that support desktop and laptop computers, but they are engineered to support the file sharing, web hosting, and other functions specific to servers. The two major server operating systems are Microsoft Windows Server and the many different distributions of the Linux operating system.

Embedded Operating Systems

As we continue to develop the Internet of Things, many common household, office, and industrial devices are basically small computers with a specific purpose. These devices also need operating systems to be able to interact with users, communicate on the network, and carry out their intended function. The operating systems that run on these devices are called *embedded operating systems*. These embedded operating systems are very small and have limited functionality when compared with their desktop and server cousins because they're designed to run on hardware with limited memory and processing power. Many embedded operating systems are capable of being stored in *firmware* so that the IoT device doesn't require a hard drive.

You'll likely encounter all of these different types of operating systems during your career in information technology, so you should be familiar with the options available and the use cases they serve.

CERTMIKE EXAM ESSENTIALS

▶ Operating systems serve as an interface between applications and hardware, abstracting the details of the hardware from the application.

▶ The operating system serves in several roles: disk management, memory management, process management and scheduling, application management, device management, and access control.

▶ Different operating systems provide support for desktops, laptops, workstations, mobile devices, servers, and embedded devices.

Practice Question 1

You are assisting a manager who oversees a team of telephone sales representatives. The manager maintains a spreadsheet on their computer that tracks sales and would like to email a copy of that spreadsheet to the team every morning at 9 a.m. They would like to automate this to save time. What operating system role can best assist with this task?

A. Memory management
B. Disk management
C. Process management
D. Task scheduling

Practice Question 2

You are working with the floor supervisor in a factory to troubleshoot a series of sensors that help track the manufacturing process. These are small devices that gather information on temperature, humidity, and motion. What type of operating system do they most likely run?

A. Mobile operating system
B. Embedded operating system
C. Desktop operating system
D. Workstation operating system

Practice Question 1 Explanation

Automating this report would be an excellent way for the sales manager to save time. Any time you encounter a situation where someone is performing repetitive actions that require little thought or insight, you should consider the possibility of automating that work.

This type of automation may be accomplished by using task scheduling. You can work with the manager to design a script that creates and sends the required report and then schedule that task to run every morning at 9 a.m.

Memory management, disk management, and process management are all operating system roles, but they are concerned with managing the real-time operations of the computer, rather than scheduling automated tasks.

Correct Answer: D. Task scheduling

Practice Question 2 Explanation

This is a perfect example of an Internet of Things (IoT) deployment where many sensors are distributed throughout the factory to gather information that may be used for real-time or after-the-fact analysis. These small devices have simple tasks to perform and only need a very lightweight, power-efficient operating system. The best choice for this type of environment is an embedded operating system that may be stored in the device's firmware.

While it would be possible to create sensors that could run more robust operating systems, such as mobile, desktop, or server operating systems, the hardware required to do so would likely increase the cost and physical size of the sensor with no real added benefit.

Correct Answer: B. Embedded operating system

CHAPTER 18

Virtualization
Objective 3.1: Explain the purpose of operating systems

The world of enterprise computing has changed dramatically over the years, and the advent of virtualization is one of those transformative changes and is the driving force behind cloud computing infrastructure.

In this chapter, you'll learn everything you need to know about the last remaining subtopic of ITF+ objective 3.1:

▶ **Hypervisors**

The remainder of objective 3.1 was covered in Chapter 17, "Operating Systems."

VIRTUALIZATION

It was only a few decades ago that enterprise computing was confined to the world of the data center and its mainframe. Dozens of computing professionals carefully tended to this very valuable resource that served as the organization's electronic nerve center.

Then, in the 1980s and 1990s, the enterprise IT landscape shifted dramatically. We moved away from the world of monolithic mainframes to a new environment of client/server computing. This shift brought tremendous benefits. First, it put computing power right on the desktop, allowing users to perform many actions directly on their machines without requiring mainframe access. Centralized computing improved also, by allowing the use of dedicated servers for specific functions. It became much easier to maintain data centers with discrete servers than tend to a cranky mainframe.

Virtual Servers

Over the past decade, we've seen another shift in the computing landscape. The client/server model served us well, but it also resulted in wasted resources. Data center managers realized that most of the time, many of their servers were sitting idle waiting for a future burst in activity. That's not very efficient. Around that same time virtualization technology became available that allows many different *virtual servers* to make use of the same underlying hardware. This shared hardware platform makes it easy to shift memory, storage, and processing power to wherever it's needed at the time. *Virtualization* platforms like VMware and Microsoft Hyper-V make this possible.

Hypervisors

At a high level, virtualization platforms involve the use of a host machine that has physical hardware. That hardware then hosts several virtual guest machines that run operating systems of their own. The host machine runs special software known as a *hypervisor* to manage the guest virtual machines. The hypervisor basically tricks each guest into thinking that it is running on its own hardware when, in reality, the guest is running on the shared hardware of the host machine. The operating system on each guest machine has no idea that it is virtualized, so software on that guest machine can function in the same way as it would on a physical server.

There are two different types of hypervisors:

▶ In a *Type 1 hypervisor*, also known as a bare-metal hypervisor, the hypervisor runs directly on top of the hardware and then hosts guest operating systems on top of that. This is the most common form of virtualization found in data centers.

▶ In a *Type 2 hypervisor*, the physical machine actually runs an operating system of its own and the hypervisor runs as a program on top of that operating system. This type of virtualization is commonly used on personal computers. Common Type 2 hypervisors include VirtualBox and Parallels.

In an enterprise technology environment, you'll often encounter Type 1 hypervisors. If your organization runs its own data centers, those data centers will probably use a Type 1 hypervisor to run many different virtual machines on the same hardware. If you use *infrastructure-as-a-service (IaaS)* providers to run your servers, you'll also be using machines that run on a Type 1 hypervisor, but you won't see the hypervisor yourself. In the case of cloud services, the cloud service provider is responsible for managing the hypervisor.

CERTMIKE EXAM ESSENTIALS

▶ Virtualization technology allows multiple virtual servers to share the same physical hardware. When virtualization is used, a hypervisor is responsible for managing access to the physical hardware.

▶ Type 1 hypervisors are used in enterprise data centers. These "bare-metal" hypervisors run directly on physical hardware and do not require a host operating system.

▶ Type 2 hypervisors generally run on personal computers and require the presence of a host operating system. They are typically used to allow users to run software that requires a different operating system or to create a test or development environment.

Practice Question 1

You are assisting a user who prefers to normally use a MacBook but occasionally needs to run software that is only available for Windows. You want to meet this user's needs while keeping costs under control. What would be the best solution to this problem?

A. Deploy a Type 1 hypervisor
B. Deploy a Type 2 hypervisor
C. Switch the user to a Windows laptop
D. Provide the user with both Mac and Windows laptops

Practice Question 2

Your organization uses an IaaS provider for its computing infrastructure. In this scenario, who is responsible for managing the hypervisor?

A. Your organization is solely responsible.
B. The IaaS provider is solely responsible.
C. Your organization and the IaaS provider share responsibility.
D. Neither your organization nor the IaaS provider has responsibility.

Practice Question 1 Explanation

Any one of these solutions could provide the user with the ability to run the Windows program. However, most of the options fail to meet other requirements.

Switching the user from a MacBook to a Windows laptop does not meet the requirement that the user prefers to use a MacBook.

Providing the user with two separate laptops would meet the software requirements, but would be both inconvenient for the user (who would have to carry around two laptops!) and expensive for the organization.

Using a hypervisor to provide a virtualized Windows environment that the user may access is the best solution here. A Type 2 hypervisor is inexpensive and could run on the user's laptop. A Type 1 hypervisor requires specialized hardware that would run in a data center. Therefore, a Type 2 hypervisor is the best choice to meet this need.

Correct Answer: B. Deploy a Type 2 hypervisor

Practice Question 2 Explanation

This scenario requires you to call upon several pieces of information. First, you must know that an infrastructure-as-a-service (IaaS) provider offers its customers access to foundational computing resources, such as virtual servers. They do this using massive data centers. Therefore, they would use a Type 1 hypervisor to do this in an efficient manner.

In this scenario, there is a shared responsibility model for computing resources, but there is a clear division of responsibility. The customer has no access to the hypervisor, so the cloud service provider bears sole responsibility for managing the hypervisor. The customer takes over responsibility at the operating system level.

Correct Answer: B. The IaaS provider is solely responsible.

CHAPTER 19

Filesystems

Objective 3.2: Compare and contrast components of an operating system

Filesystems provide the operating system (and its users!) with a method to organize all of the data that is stored on disk to make it easy to find files and open them with the appropriate application. As you prepare for the ITF+ exam, you'll need to be familiar with the features of common filesystems.

In this chapter, you'll learn everything you need to know about the first set of subtopics for ITF+ objective 3.2:

▶ **Filesystems and features**
▶ **Features**
▶ **File management**

The remainder of objective 3.2 is covered in Chapter 20, "Services and Processes," and Chapter 21, "Drivers, Utilities, and Interfaces."

FILES AND FILESYSTEMS

Earlier in this course, you learned how computers store data on magnetic and solid-state drives using magnetic or electrical charges to represent values of 0 and 1. We also talked about how one of the operating system's jobs is to make sense of all those binary values and organize them into the files that we use every day. The *filesystem* is the technology that defines how that data is stored, and the operating system is responsible for managing the filesystem on a disk.

Files and Folders

The most important task performed by the filesystem is to remember where the bits comprising a file are stored on the disk and organizing those files into *folders* (also known as *directories*) that help us manage where our files are stored. These directories are hierarchical. That just means that we can put folders inside other folders to help us organize our files.

For example, Figure 19.1 shows a folder structure on a Mac. Inside the My Documents folder, there are subfolders for Math, Science, and History. Inside the Science folder is a Word document containing a report called Unravelling the Mystery.

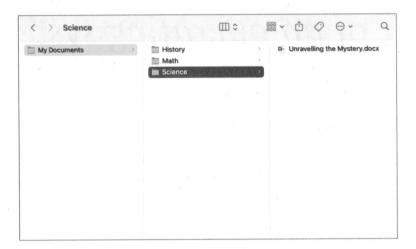

FIGURE 19.1 **Directory structure**

All filesystems provide you with the ability to organize files hierarchically. We can also set *permissions* on our files to control who can access them and whether they can read, write, edit, or execute each file. Figure 19.2 shows the detailed properties of that file. In the bottom section of that window, you'll notice a Sharing & Permissions section that details who has what access rights to the file. In this case, my account (mchapple) has read and write access to the file. This file is also set so that anyone in a group called staff or, in fact, everyone using this computer has the ability to read this file. If this file contained any sensitive information, I could change that setting to limit access to the file to just me.

Filenames and Extensions

Every file has both a name and an *extension*. The name is whatever the user chooses to name the file. The extension tells the operating system and users what type of file we have and what application to use to open that file. In Figure 19.2, we have a Microsoft Word document, so it has the extension .docx, which is the standard format for Word documents. So, the full name of this file on disk is Unravelling the Mystery.docx.

FIGURE 19.2 File permission settings

Other file types use different extensions. For example:

▶ Microsoft Excel spreadsheets are saved with the `.xlsx` extension.
▶ Adobe Acrobat documents are saved with the `.pdf` extension.
▶ Java archive files are saved with the `.jar` extension.
▶ Python programs are saved with the `.py` extension.

One of the roles of the operating system is to keep track of which programs should be used to open files with each extension.

Some operating systems use special reserved file extensions for *executable files*, files that should be run as applications instead of opened with another application. For example, Windows systems commonly use the `.exe` extension for executable files, instructing the operating system to treat the file as an application. Similarly, the Android mobile operating system uses the `.apk` extension for mobile apps stored as Android packages.

> **EXAM TIP**
> Filesystems associated with Macintosh and Linux/Unix systems do not depend on file extensions to determine whether a file is executable. Instead, they track a special attribute for each file that indicates whether it is an application.

When you name files on disk, you can generally use any name that you'd like. However, filesystems do restrict you from using some special characters in filenames because they cause undesirable results if the filesystem uses them for other purposes. These reserved characters include /, \, *, <, >, ", |, ?, and :. While every filesystem might not prohibit all of these characters, it's a good idea to avoid them just to be safe.

FILESYSTEM FEATURES

Let's talk now about some of the key features of filesystems. We've already talked about one of those core features: permissions and the role that they play in limiting access to files. We can set permissions on files to allow different users and groups of users the ability to read, write, delete, and modify files. There are several other key features that you'll need to understand for the ITF+ exam: compression, encryption, and journaling.

Compression

Compression is another feature provided by some filesystems that reduces the amount of space taken up on disk by a file. Many of our documents contain a lot of repetitive data. For example, Figure 19.3 shows the properties of a file containing the full text of William Shakespeare's play *Macbeth* in HTML format for viewing in a web browser. It takes up 196 kilobytes on the disk.

FIGURE 19.3 Uncompressed *Macbeth* script

Figure 19.4 shows a compressed version of the file. After compression, the file type changes from HTML text to a ZIP archive and the file shrinks to a much smaller size, 56 kilobytes. That's less than a third of the size of the original file, saving space on the disk. Compression works by replacing duplicate chunks of data in a document with smaller values. For example, the word *strange* appears 16 times in *Macbeth*. The compressed file only needs to store the full word one time and can then replace it with a smaller placeholder value everywhere else that it appears.

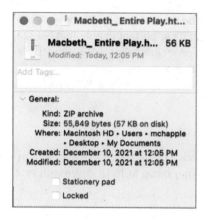

FIGURE 19.4 Compressed *Macbeth* script

Encryption

Encryption is an important security feature of filesystems. It is a technology that makes it impossible for someone to read a file unless they have the necessary decryption key. Many filesystems can apply encryption to files, folders, and entire disks automatically, making it easy for users to add security to their data. You'll learn more about encryption in Chapter 38, "Encryption."

Journaling

Some filesystems support a technique called *journaling*. In a journaling filesystem, the filesystem maintains a log of all the changes that it plans to make to disk to help protect against a power failure or any other interruption to the disk's normal operation. If access to the disk is interrupted during a write operation, the filesystem can use the journal to restore itself to a consistent state.

FILESYSTEM TYPES

Just like we have many different operating systems, we also have many different filesystems. Each operating system has a preferred filesystem, but many are able to read filesystems created by other operating systems.

NTFS

The *NTFS* filesystem used by Microsoft is the most popular filesystem for the Windows operating system. It provides compression, encryption, and journaling. NTFS works natively with Windows operating systems. It's possible to access NTFS filesystems from Mac and Linux systems, but doing so requires special configuration.

FAT32

The *FAT32* filesystem is an older filesystem that used to be the standard for Windows systems. It's still supported by many operating systems, but it's important to note that FAT32 does not provide any support for encryption, compression, or journaling. FAT32 limited file sizes to 4 GB, whereas NTFS allows files up to 16 exabytes in size.

The FAT32 filesystem draws its name from the *File Allocation Table (FAT)*, a data structure that Windows uses to track the location of files on disk.

ext4

Linux systems generally use a filesystem called *ext4*. This is a powerful filesystem that does support encryption, compression, and journaling. Files may be up to 16 TB in size with ext4 filesystems.

Apple Filesystems

Apple provides three different filesystems. The *Mac OS Extended* filesystem, called the *Hierarchical Filesystem (HFS)*, was a simplistic filesystem created in the 1990s. It did not support encryption, compression, or journaling and had a maximum file size limit of 2 GB.

HFS was upgraded over the years, and the newer *HFS+* now supports encryption, compression, and journaling. It also supports file sizes up to 16 exabytes.

The newer *Apple Filesystem (APFS)* was released in 2017 and is a higher-performance operating system designed to work very well on solid-state drives. It removed journaling to increase performance and replaced it with other crash protection technology. APFS supports encryption but does not provide native compression capabilities.

CERTMIKE EXAM ESSENTIALS

This chapter contained quite a bit of information about filesystems and their characteristics. Table 19.1 offers a summary that you can use to help you remember the different features supported by different filesystems and the major operating system used with each filesystem. You'll want to be able to remember these facts when you take the IT Fundamentals exam.

TABLE 19.1 Summary of filesystem characteristics

Filesystem	FAT32	NTFS	ext4	HFS	HFS+	APFS
Operating System	Windows	Windows	Linux	Mac	Mac	Mac
Encryption	No	Yes	Yes	No	Yes	Yes
Compression	No	Yes	Yes	No	Yes	No
Journaling	No	Yes	Yes	No	Yes	No
Maximum File Size	4 GB	16 EB	16 TB	2 GB	16 EB	16 EB

Practice Question 1

Which one of the following operating systems requires that specific file extensions be used to indicate that a file is executable?

A. macOS
B. Windows
C. Linux
D. Unix

Practice Question 2

You are assisting an end user with storing files on a MacBook computer. Which one of the following filesystems would you most likely find on this computer?

A. FAT
B. APFS
C. FAT32
D. ext4

Practice Question 1 Explanation

Of the operating systems covered by the ITF+ curriculum, only Windows and Android require the use of specific file extensions for executables. Windows commonly uses the .exe extension and Android uses the .apk extension.

Filesystems based on the Unix standard, including Linux, Unix, and macOS, do not require specific file extensions. A file with any name may be marked as executable in those operating systems.

Correct Answer: B. Windows

Practice Question 2 Explanation

The three filesystems commonly used on Apple Mac devices are the Apple Filesystem (APFS), the MacOS Extended (HFS) filesystem, and the HFS+ filesystem.

The FAT and FAT32 filesystems are most closely associated with Windows systems, whereas the ext4 filesystem is most closely associated with Linux systems.

Correct Answer: B. APFS

CHAPTER 20

Services and Processes

Objective 3.2: Compare and contrast components of an operating system

Operating systems also bear responsibility for executing applications and managing interactions between different pieces of software running on a computer. Each time an application executes, it runs as a process. Some processes are configured as services. These services have special privileges to execute in the background.

In this chapter, you'll learn everything you need to know about the second set of subtopics for ITF+ objective 3.2:

▶ Services
▶ Processes

The remainder of objective 3.2 is covered in Chapter 19, "Filesystems," and Chapter 21, "Drivers, Utilities, and Interfaces."

APPLICATIONS

You use a wide variety of software applications every day, ranging from productivity applications like word processors and spreadsheets to communications tools like web browsers.

Each of these applications is stored as one or more files on the hard drive, accessible to the operating system. Applications are stored in a special type of file known as an *executable* file, meaning that it is a program that the operating system should run, or execute, rather than a file containing data that you'd want to read.

As discussed in Chapter 19, some operating systems require that these executable files have specific extensions for the operating system to recognize that they are executable. On Windows systems, executable files often end with the `.exe` extension. On Android devices, executable files must be stored in Android packages with the `.apk` extension. Linux and Unix operating systems also have executable files, but they do not require any specific extensions for those files to execute. Instead, they allow users to set an attribute on a file indicating that it is executable.

PROCESSES

Every application that is running on a computer system runs as a *process*. A process is simply an instance of an executable application that is actively in use. Processes are stored in memory and have access to the CPU, memory, and disk to carry out their work. Some applications may use multiple processes to run more efficiently. For example, web browsers like Google Chrome use a separate process for each tab that you have open. This allows the browsers to load multiple web pages at the same time and keep separate resources allocated for each page.

Operating systems provide utilities that help you monitor the processes that are in active use at any time. Figure 20.1 shows the Activity Monitor utility running on a Mac. Each line in this tool represents a single process, and there are dozens of processes running this computer. You can see a bunch of processes associated with Google Chrome as well as processes for Microsoft Teams, Safari, Google Drive, and other applications running on my computer. You can also see the percentage of CPU time being used by each process and all processes combined. That's helpful information when you're troubleshooting performance issues.

Windows Task Manager provides you with similar information for a Windows system, as shown in Figure 20.2. Using these tools, you can not only monitor performance but also kill troublesome processes that are misbehaving and consuming more resources than expected.

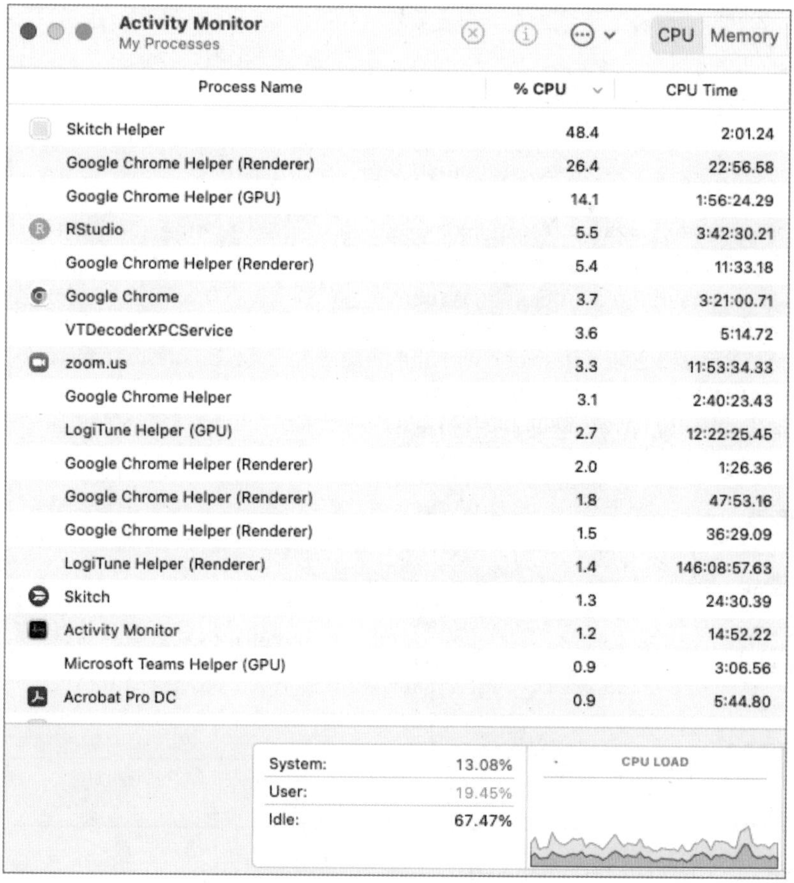

FIGURE 20.1   Activity Monitor on a Mac

SERVICES

In Figure 20.1, Activity Monitor shows many processes running on a normal user's Mac-Book. This computer is actually managing hundreds of active processes at the same time. If you look at the processes running on your computer, you'll see the same thing. You'll recognize some processes that are running the applications that you have open, but you'll also see some other processes that you don't recognize. These are services that are part of the operating system.

Services are processes that run in the background, mostly invisible to the end user. They manage networking, disk access, memory, and many of the other tasks performed by the operating system. If you didn't go looking for them, you'd never know that they were there! These processes do show up in operating system performance monitoring utilities because you can use the information about them that appears in those tools to help with trouble-shooting performance problems.

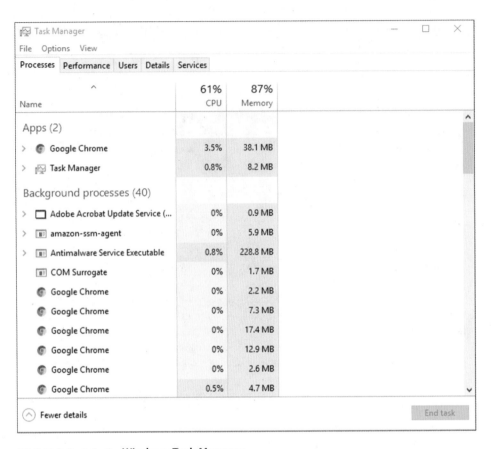

FIGURE 20.2 Windows Task Manager

CERTMIKE EXAM ESSENTIALS

▶ Applications are software programs stored on a computer in executable files. Executable files on Windows systems often have names ending with the `.exe` extension, whereas Android applications have names ending with `.apk`. Linux, Unix, and Mac operating systems do not require any specific file extension for executables.

▶ Each time an application executes on a computer, it creates one or more new processes. The process is the instance of that application.

▶ Some processes run automatically in the background to perform operating system and related tasks. These processes are called services, and they are normally invisible to end users.

Practice Question 1

You are working with a new desktop publishing application on a Windows system. The application is stored on your hard drive and you just double-clicked it to launch it. What term best describes what you created when you launched the application?

A. Service
B. File
C. Patch
D. Process

Practice Question 2

You would like to examine the different processes currently running on a Windows system. What utility would best assist you with this task?

A. Activity Monitor
B. Process Evaluator
C. Process Manager
D. Task Manager

Practice Question 1 Explanation

When you launch an application on a Windows system (or any other computer, for that matter), you create a new process on the system that is associated with that particular application launch. The process is created using an executable file, but the act of launching an application does not *create* a new file.

User applications run as processes that are visible to the user. Services are background processes that run invisibly and do not require any user intervention. Patches are updates to applications and the operating system that may be applied to fix bugs, correct security vulnerabilities, or add new features.

Correct Answer: D. Process

Practice Question 2 Explanation

Windows provides the Task Manager utility to allow users to view and manage the processes running on a Windows system. macOS provides the Activity Monitor utility for a similar purpose.

Process Evaluator and Process Manager are not the names of Windows or Mac utilities. They are simply made-up distractors designed to sound like the names of actual tools.

When you review the answer choices on the ITF+ exam, be careful to keep an eye out for sneaky tricks like the ones used in this question. If you read the question quickly, you might be tempted to answer Activity Monitor if you did not notice that the question asked about Windows systems.

Correct Answer: D. Task Manager

CHAPTER 21

Drivers, Utilities, and Interfaces

Objective 3.2: Compare and contrast components of an operating system

The operating system requires some internal components to help administrators manage the way it works and ensure compatibility with different hardware and applications. Drivers, utilities, and interfaces play an important role in the world of IT.

In this chapter, you'll learn everything you need to know about the third set of subtopics for ITF+ objective 3.2:

▶ **Drivers**
▶ **Utilities**
▶ **Interfaces**

The remainder of objective 3.2 is covered in Chapter 19, "Filesystems," and Chapter 20, "Services and Processes."

DRIVERS

Drivers are software components that tell the operating system how to interact with a particular piece of hardware. They are pieces of software that allow Windows, Mac, and Linux systems to all use the same printers, monitors, and other peripherals.

Your operating system comes preinstalled with hundreds or thousands of commonly used drivers. These drivers allow you to set up many pieces of hardware with plug-and-play technology, where the hardware can easily start working without much, if any, configuration on your part. It's the responsibility of each hardware manufacturer to create drivers for all the operating systems they wish to support and then make those drivers available to their customers.

In cases where you have a piece of hardware that doesn't just start working with plug-and-play functionality, you'll need to find the correct driver. Visit the website of that hardware's manufacturer and find the driver that matches the exact model of hardware that you're installing and your operating system version. It's important to have the correct operating system and model because your hardware may either behave strangely or not function at all if you use the wrong driver.

INTERFACES

The operating system also provides two different interfaces to users. You're already familiar with the *graphic user interfaces (GUIs)* that load when you start up your Windows or Mac system. GUIs are the most common way that people interact with computers. You can point-and-click with your mouse and access all of the operating system's functionality. Figure 21.1 shows an example of the GUI on a Mac system, and Figure 21.2 shows the GUI on a Windows system.

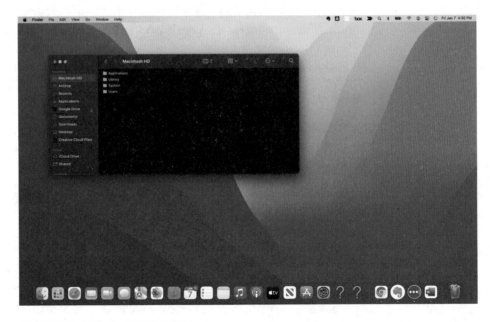

FIGURE 21.1 GUI on a Mac

FIGURE 21.2 GUI on a Windows system

Operating systems also provide another interface known as a console or command-line access. This is a text-based interface that allows you to type commands that you'd like the computer to execute. You can use this console access to launch applications, navigate the filesystem, or modify running processes. Using the console does require that you understand the commands used by the computer and it is technically complex, but skilled system administrators and power users often find the console a much easier way to quickly handle administrative tasks.

You access the console using different utilities. On a Mac you use an application called *Terminal* to type commands into the console. You can see an example of Terminal in Figure 21.3.

Windows systems provide two console utilities. The *Command Prompt*, the tool most commonly used by end users, is automatically installed on all Windows systems. It's shown in Figure 21.4.

PowerShell is an advanced shell with scripting capabilities that is a favorite of system administrators and others who want to access advanced capabilities of the operating system.

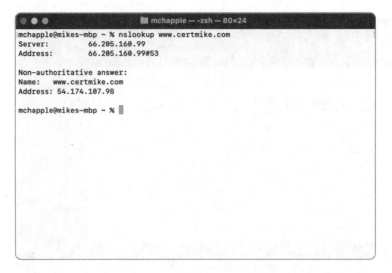

FIGURE 21.3 Terminal on a Mac

```
Microsoft Windows [Version 10.0.14393]
(c) 2016 Microsoft Corporation. All rights reserved.

C:\Users\mchapple>dir
 Volume in drive C is OS
 Volume Serial Number is C621-9DC9

 Directory of C:\Users\mchapple

12/10/2021  07:52 PM    <DIR>          .
12/10/2021  07:52 PM    <DIR>          ..
07/06/2021  02:32 PM       101,834,752 AdventureWorksDW2019 (1).bak
07/06/2021  02:31 PM       101,834,752 AdventureWorksDW2019.bak
01/07/2022  09:35 PM    <DIR>          Contacts
01/07/2022  09:35 PM    <DIR>          Desktop
01/07/2022  09:35 PM    <DIR>          Documents
01/07/2022  09:35 PM    <DIR>          Downloads
01/07/2022  09:35 PM    <DIR>          Favorites
01/07/2022  09:35 PM    <DIR>          Links
01/07/2022  09:35 PM    <DIR>          Music
01/07/2022  09:35 PM    <DIR>          Pictures
01/07/2022  09:35 PM    <DIR>          Saved Games
01/07/2022  09:35 PM    <DIR>          Searches
01/07/2022  09:35 PM    <DIR>          Videos
               2 File(s)    203,669,504 bytes
              13 Dir(s)  73,634,742,272 bytes free

C:\Users\mchapple>_
```

FIGURE 21.4 Command shell on a Windows system

UTILITIES

Operating systems also come with a number of *utilities* designed to help make using them easier. In Chapter 20, "Services and Processes," you saw Activity Monitor on the Mac and the Windows Task Manager.

You may also need to schedule tasks to run on a system at a specific time. You can use the Task Scheduler utility on Windows systems or the Automator utility on macOS for this purpose.

Those are some examples of utilities, but there are many others. Different utilities allow you to use accessibility features of the operating system designed for the vision and hearing impaired, manage disks, and fine-tune many other aspects of the operating system. They're very useful to learn as you deepen your understanding of operating systems.

CERTMIKE EXAM ESSENTIALS

▶ Drivers provide operating systems with the ability to interact with hardware from different vendors. Each driver is specific to a hardware device and operating system combination.

▶ Graphic user interfaces (GUIs) allow users to interact with a computer through a point-and-click interface. Console interfaces allow users to interact with the computer using text commands.

▶ Utilities perform a variety of tasks for the operating system, including disk management, process management, and accessibility.

Practice Question 1

You would like to enter commands into a Mac system using a text-based interface. What utility would assist you with this work?

A. PowerShell
B. Command Prompt
C. GUI
D. Terminal

Practice Question 2

You are having difficulty getting a new printer to work with a computer system in your office. You connected the printer via USB cable, but it does not appear to be working properly. Text prints in a garbled mess and printer options are not available. What component should you attempt to update?

A. Driver
B. Print Manager
C. Operating system
D. Application

Practice Question 1 Explanation

Mac systems provide two different user interfaces: a graphical user interface (GUI) and a text-based interface called Terminal. The GUI is a point-and-click interface, so it would not be appropriate for your situation. Terminal, however, is the perfect match to your needs.

The Command Prompt and PowerShell also provide text-based interfaces to a computer system, but they are designed for Windows systems and are not available on macOS.

Correct Answer: D. Terminal

Practice Question 2 Explanation

Since you are installing a new printer, it is unlikely that the issue is with the operating system or application. It is far more likely that this is an issue with the compatibility between this printer and the operating system. Therefore, the best solution would be to locate an updated print driver designed to work with this printer and operating system combination.

Correct Answer: A. Driver

CHAPTER 22

Software Types

Objective 3.3: Explain the purpose and proper use of software

Software is what makes computers powerful. We can use a wide variety of applications on our computers to transform them into the tools that we need to get our jobs done. Some of these applications are very common. Almost everyone uses web browsers, word processors, and spreadsheets to get their work done. Other software provides specialized technology for software developers, designers, and others requiring special tools for their needs.

In this chapter, you'll learn everything you need to know about ITF+ objective 3.3:

▶ **Productivity software**
▶ **Collaboration software**
▶ **Business software**

SOFTWARE

Over the past five chapters, you've read a lot about the operating system and how it helps you interact with the hardware in your computer. The operating system and its components are one example of *software*—a set of instructions that tell the computer what to do. There are also many other kinds of software that help us meet our needs for personal productivity, collaboration, and business. You'll need to know about each of these when you take the ITF+ exam.

Productivity Software

Productivity software is the common software that we all use to get our work done on a daily basis. Administrators typically install the same productivity software on every system they control because basically everyone needs it.

Word processing software, such as Microsoft Word, Google Docs, and Apple Pages, allows us to create and edit written documents and share them with one another. If you're creating text, whether it's a short note, a business report, or even an entire book, word processing software is the right tool for the job. Figure 22.1 shows a draft of this chapter being written in Microsoft Word.

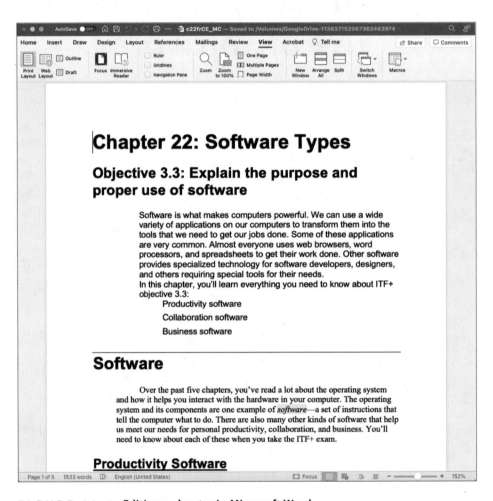

FIGURE 22.1 Editing a chapter in Microsoft Word

Spreadsheets, such as Microsoft Excel, Google Sheets, and Apple Numbers, allow us to easily create documents that are mostly made up of numbers organized into tables. We can use spreadsheets to quickly sort data and perform calculations. Spreadsheets also allow us to quickly create charts that display our numeric data visually. You can see an example of a Google Sheets spreadsheet being used to create a pie chart from a table of data in Figure 22.2.

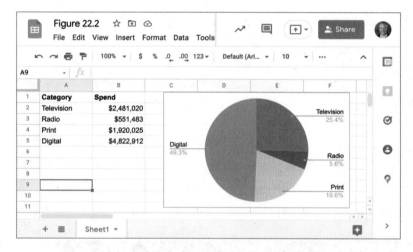

FIGURE 22.2 Creating a pie chart in Google Sheets

Presentation software, such as Microsoft PowerPoint, Google Slides, and Apple Keynote, provides us with the ability to quickly create visual slides that we can use to share information with others. We often display these presentations to our audience using large monitors or projectors. Figure 22.3 shows an example of a slide deck created in Keynote.

Web browsers, such as Google Chrome, Microsoft Edge, and Apple Safari, allow us to access the Internet, retrieving web pages from remote web servers and interacting with them. Figure 22.4 shows the use of Google Chrome to access the CompTIA website.

Visual diagramming software, such as Microsoft Visio and Lucid Software's Lucidchart, allows us to quickly create diagrams that we can then use in word processing documents, presentations, web pages, or other materials. Figure 22.5 shows the use of Lucidchart to create a network diagram.

EXAM TIP

You will almost certainly find at least one question on your ITF+ exam from this objective. There are quite a few different types of software listed here, so you should be familiar with each of them and, if you're given a scenario, be able to identify the appropriate type of software to meet a given need.

FIGURE 22.3 Editing a slide deck in Apple Keynote

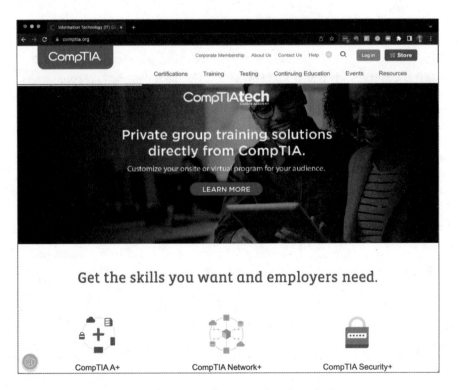

FIGURE 22.4 Accessing comptia.org using Google Chrome

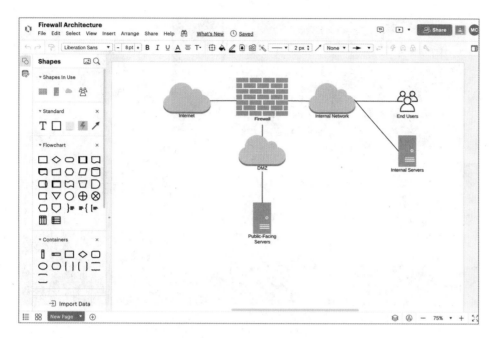

FIGURE 22.5 Creating a network diagram in Lucidchart

Collaboration Software

Collaboration software is the software that allows us to interact with our teammates, customers, and business partners on a regular basis.

Email clients are one of the most common pieces of collaboration software. While many of us access email through a web browser, programs like Microsoft Outlook allow us to manage our email using separate software.

Conferencing software, such as Zoom, Skype, and Microsoft Teams, allows us to have audio and videoconferences that can save on travel by taking the place of in-person meetings. Conferencing software also often has instant messaging features that allow us to exchange text messages with our colleagues without having a live meeting. Figure 22.6 shows a videoconference in progress using conferencing software.

Many organizations also use *online workspaces*, such as Microsoft Teams, to communicate with each other through message boards and shared documents. Figure 22.7 shows the Microsoft Teams workspace used to manage the files associated with the creation of a new book.

Business Software

The third software category, *business software*, is the software that we use to run and manage our businesses.

FIGURE 22.6 Conferencing software hosting a video meeting

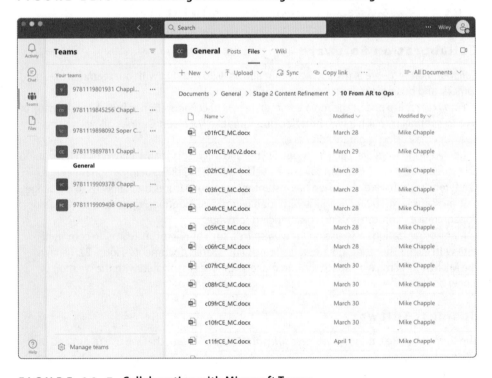

FIGURE 22.7 Collaborating with Microsoft Teams

In Part V of this book, "Database Fundamentals," you'll learn more about *databases* and the role they play in organizations. Specialized database software allows us to easily track and manage our data.

Project management software provides scheduling, task management, and other tools to help run complex projects. Options available in this space range from free online applications to complex enterprise project management packages.

Accounting software tracks an organization's finances, issues checks, and tracks customer invoices. Most businesses use some type of accounting software to monitor and manage their financial situation.

Organizations may also use specialized software for their line of business. For example, designers may use *computer-aided design (CAD)* software to create new products or even physical structures. Manufacturers may use *computer-aided manufacturing (CAM)* software to configure and run production lines.

And those are just a few examples of the many business-specific applications that we might find in use in our organizations. In fact, many organizations wind up creating their own software to meet specialized needs.

CERTMIKE EXAM ESSENTIALS

▶ Productivity software helps users complete day-to-day work. This category includes word processors, spreadsheets, presentation software, web browsers, and visual diagramming software.

▶ Collaboration software helps teams to work together and with business partners. This category includes email clients, conferencing software, and online workspaces.

▶ Business software manages and runs our businesses. This category includes databases, project management software, accounting software, computer-aided design (CAD), and computer-aided manufacturing (CAM) software.

Practice Question 1

You recently conducted a survey of your customers and would like to use a software package to create some quick charts of the results to share with your team. Which one of the following approaches would best meet your needs?

A. Spreadsheet
B. Database
C. Flat file
D. Accounting software

Practice Question 2

You lead a team that is working on a complex software migration effort where you have many different individuals following complicated schedules to complete their work. You would like to use a software package to manage all of this work and provide reporting on time use. Which one of the following software packages would best meet your needs?

A. Spreadsheet software
B. Presentation software
C. Visual diagramming software
D. Project management software

Practice Question 1 Explanation

This question is asking us to choose the best option from among several possibilities. Looking at the choices here, accounting software is clearly inappropriate because it is used to track an organization's finances and there is no financial data involved in this scenario.

Any of the other options could conceivably be used to store the data. However, storing the data in a flat file would not allow us to create charts, as a flat file simply contains data with no embellishment or formatting.

That leaves us with two options that would support the creation of charts—a spreadsheet or a database. Both of these software packages could meet the needs of this scenario, but notice that the scenario specifies that we would like to create some "quick charts." That leads us toward selecting a spreadsheet as the best option because we can load the data into a spreadsheet and quickly produce some charts in a matter of minutes. Using a database would require setting it up and configuring it. While that would give us a more permanent mechanism for storing the data in an organized and accessible form, it is overkill for this scenario.

Correct Answer: A. Spreadsheet

Practice Question 2 Explanation

This is another question where you are being asked to select the *best* option from among a set of feasible choices. You could definitely use a spreadsheet to track information about a project, and it's also possible that you could use the diagrams created by visual diagramming software as a project management tool. It's even conceivable that you would use a presentation to maintain information on a project's status. While any of these tools may be useful in managing a project, none is designed for the purpose.

Project management software, on the other hand, is specifically designed to meet this use case and includes features designed to assist with many different project management tasks. That makes it the best solution in this scenario.

Correct Answer: D. Project management software

CHAPTER 23

Application Architecture and Delivery

Objective 3.4: Explain methods of application architecture and delivery models

In some cases, organizations develop their own software to meet specialized business needs. We're going to discuss the software development process more in Part IV, "Software Development Concepts." For now, it's important that you have a thorough understanding of the ways that IT teams design these applications and deliver them to end users.

In this chapter, you'll learn everything you need to know about ITF+ objective 3.4:

▶ **Application delivery methods**
▶ **Application architecture models**

APPLICATION DELIVERY

When software developers create an application, they have several ways that they can deliver that application to end users. As you prepare for the ITF+ exam, you should be familiar with three major application delivery methods: locally installed applications, applications hosted on the local network, and applications hosted in the cloud.

Locally Installed Applications

Locally installed applications are applications that run entirely on the end user's computer. You likely use locally installed applications every day. When you open Microsoft Word, Apple Pages, or Adobe Photoshop, you're running software that exists completely on your computer. This has the benefit of not requiring any network access to run. The files that you create in locally installed applications are also saved on your local computer by default, and you'll need to be sure to back them up to protect against a disk failure.

Local Network–Hosted Applications

Applications may also be hosted on the local network. These applications are installed on a server that exists on your LAN and are available to users on that same LAN. You often access them through a web browser, so you can use any type of device to access them. If you use local network–hosted applications, you will need to have network access, but you won't need Internet access.

Sometimes users will need to access local network–hosted applications when they are away from the office. In those situations, organizations often offer a *virtual private network (VPN)* that allows remote users to securely connect back to the office network and access locally hosted network applications as well as other resources on the internal network.

Cloud-Hosted Applications

The final application delivery model is having cloud-hosted applications. These applications run on servers in the cloud and are usually managed by the vendor, who makes them available to customers using an approach called *software-as-a-service (SaaS)*. The SaaS model is easy for customers, because vendors maintain the software and the servers. It does require that application users have access to a network that is connected to the Internet.

> **EXAM TIP**
> The following table summarizes the information covered in this section. Make sure that you memorize this table before attempting the ITF+ exam!
>
> | | Locally Installed Applications | Local Network–Hosted Applications | Cloud-Hosted Applications |
> | --- | --- | --- | --- |
> | **Installation Location** | Local computer | Local server | Cloud server |
> | **Network Access Required?** | No | Yes | Yes |
> | **Internet Access Required?** | No | No | Yes |

APPLICATION ARCHITECTURE

In addition to understanding where applications may be installed, you should also understand the different architecture models that are used to deploy applications. These models
describe how many different servers are involved in presenting an application to end users.
We do this by talking about the number of tiers that make up the application.

One-Tier Applications

We've already discussed two of the simplest cases. The first of these is when you install an
application on the local computer and there aren't any servers involved. The entire application exists on that local user's computer, including the storage of data, the application's
processing power, and the presentation of an interface to the end user. This simple case
with no servers involved is called a *one-tier application*.

Two-Tier Applications

When we move into the world of client-server computing, we add tiers to our applications.
For example, consider a simple website. The company hosting the website operates a web
server that contains all of the web content and answers user requests. This web server is
the first tier of the application. The user accesses the website using a web browser, and
that browser is responsible for presenting the data to the end user. That web browser on
the user's local system is the second tier, so this is an example of a *two-tier application*.
Figure 23.1 shows an example of a two-tier application.

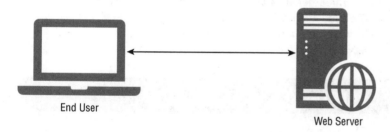

End User

Web Server

FIGURE 23.1 **Two-tier applications involve the client and one server.**

EXAM TIP

When you're counting the number of tiers in an application, remember that
the end user's computer always counts as the first tier. You can't just count the
number of servers involved. That's a common error made on the ITF+ exam!

Three-Tier Applications

Some applications are more complex and require additional servers. Imagine, for example, that the website we run is designed to receive and process orders from end users. Those orders will need to be stored in a database, and the web server will need to interact with the database to retrieve order information, add information about new orders, and perform other tasks. This is a *three-tier architecture* (see Figure 23.2) because we have the web browser handling the presentation of data to the end user, the web server handling the application side of things, and the database storing the data required by the web server.

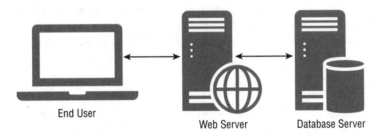

End User   Web Server   Database Server

F I G U R E   2 3 . 2   Three-tier applications involve the client and two tiers of servers.

n-Tier Applications

We can also move beyond three-tier architectures and have as many tiers as necessary to efficiently and effectively meet our requirements. The general term *n-tier architecture* describes this approach. In this case, *n* can be any value we require because we can have as many layers of servers as we need to get the job done.

CERTMIKE EXAM ESSENTIALS

▶ Locally installed applications run on the user's own computer and do not require any network access. Local network–hosted applications run on a local server and require network access but not Internet access. Cloud-hosted applications run on cloud servers and require both network access and Internet access.

▶ Applications that do not involve any servers and run exclusively on the end user's computer are also known as one-tier applications.

▶ Applications that make use of servers have more than one tier. A web server that uses the client-server model is a two-tier application. A dynamic web application that uses both a web server and a database server is a three-tier application.

Practice Question 1

You are working with a team of developers and infrastructure specialists who are designing a new application. This application will use a web server to answer user requests, and the web server will access information stored in a database server. What term best describes this application architecture?

A. One-tier application

B. Two-tier application

C. Three-tier application

D. Four-tier application

Practice Question 2

You are designing an application that will help salespeople produce estimates for new projects. The salespeople using the application often travel to remote locations where they do not have any network access. What delivery model would be best suited for this application?

A. Three-tier application

B. Local network–hosted application

C. Locally installed application

D. Cloud-hosted application

Practice Question 1 Explanation

This application uses two tiers of servers: a web server and a database server. However, the client system that accesses the web server also counts as a tier. Therefore, this is a three-tier application. The database-driven web application is a classic example of a three-tier application architecture.

Correct Answer: C. Three-tier application

Practice Question 2 Explanation

The key to answering this question correctly is recognizing that the application must work in cases where the user has no network access. This means that we cannot use an application that relies on servers hosted either on the local network or in the cloud, because the salesperson will not be able to access those servers when they do not have network access. Three-tier applications, by their nature, must use servers and will be either cloud hosted or local network hosted.

Therefore, the best approach here would be to use a locally installed application that runs entirely on the salesperson's computer. This application would be available regardless of the user's network access.

Correct Answer: C. Locally installed application

CHAPTER 24

Web Browsers

Objective 3.5: Given a scenario, configure and use web browsers

These days, the applications that we use most frequently are our web browsers. Whether we're accessing data in the cloud for work, watching streaming media, or just surfing the web, the web browser is our portal to the Internet.

In this chapter, you'll learn everything you need to know about ITF+ objective 3.5:

- ▶ Caching/clearing cache
- ▶ Deactivate client-side scripting
- ▶ Browser add-ons/extensions
- ▶ Private browsing
- ▶ Proxy settings
- ▶ Certificates
- ▶ Pop-up blockers
- ▶ Script blockers
- ▶ Compatible browser for application(s)

HOW THE WEB WORKS

Web browsers are the software that we use to access websites. They understand the *Hypertext Transfer Protocol (HTTP)* and help us view web pages. They reach out to the web servers containing the information we'd like to view and then open an HTTP, or a secure HTTPS, connection to that server and transfer the web content to our computer, where the browser displays it to us.

Figure 24.1 shows how this process works. When an end user wants to visit a website, they open a web browser on their computer and type the URL of that site into the address bar in their browser. The browser then determines the appropriate web server that hosts the web page the user wants to view and sends an HTTP GET request to that web server. The web server processes the request, determines what content the user should see, and sends the web page back to the user. The web content returned to the user is written in the *hypertext markup language (HTML)* and the user's web browser reads this HTML and converts it into the web page that the user sees in their browser.

FIGURE 24.1   Retrieving a web page

If this process looks familiar to you, this is an example of a two-tier application, as discussed in Chapter 23, "Application Architecture and Delivery." The end user's system is one tier and the web server is the second tier.

For the most part, modern web applications should work with all modern browsers. However, you may encounter a web application that doesn't work in a particular browser. If you see strange behavior on the web, a good troubleshooting step is to try opening the site in a different browser and see if that makes a difference. Web applications that commonly experience browser compatibility issues often advertise a list of browsers that will work properly with their sites.

CONFIGURING WEB BROWSERS

Because we use web browsers so frequently, it's important that IT professionals understand how to configure and use them. Let's talk about a few of the important settings that you can modify on a web browser.

EXAM TIP

The examples in this chapter show the configuration process for Google Chrome, but other browsers are similar. You won't be asked to actually configure these settings using any specific browser on the ITF+ exam, but you should be familiar with the various types of settings that you might alter.

Web Caches

Web browsers *cache* content. That means that they keep copies of content that we've viewed previously to make loading pages in the future move more quickly. That cache is saved on disk, and it does contain information about the web pages we've visited. If you want to delete that information, you can manually clear your cache.

In Google Chrome, you do so by clicking the icon with three dots in the upper-right corner of the browser, selecting More Tools, and then clicking Clear Browsing Data. You'll then get the pop-up window shown in Figure 24.2 asking you what you'd like to clear. Let's look more carefully at these settings.

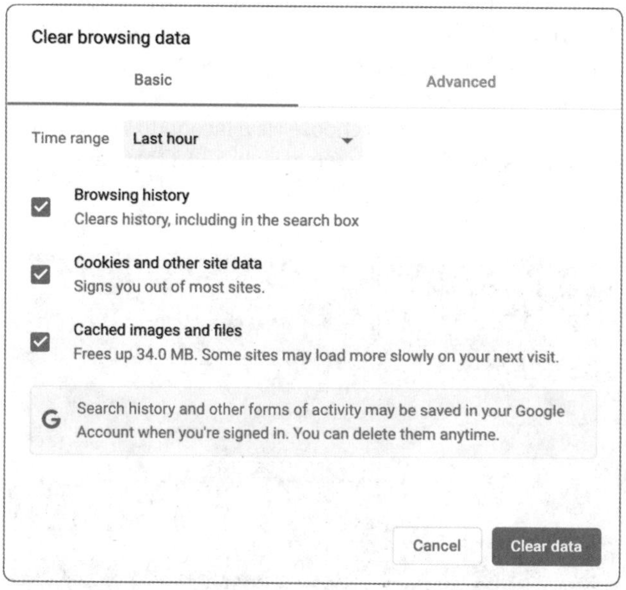

FIGURE 24.2 Clearing browsing data in Chrome

The first thing you can do is specify the time range from which you'd like to clear data. The default is just to clear information for the sites that you've visited in the last hour, but you can change that to whatever period of time you'd like or all time.

After you specify the time period that you'd like to clear, you next specify the types of data that you'd like to clear. Your first option is to clear your browsing history. This is the list of sites that you've visited that autocomplete as you're typing URLs into the browser window. If you visited a site that you don't want other people to see when you start typing a URL, this is the setting to clear.

You can also specify to clear cookies and other site data. This is the authentication information that's saved on your computer for later use. If you've ever logged into a website and then came back later and were still logged in, that's because the website left a cookie on your browser that identifies you. If you clear your cookies, you'll be logged out of all of those websites.

And then the last thing you can clear are cached images and files. This deletes all of the saved files in your cache. It removes that information from your computer so that other users can't see it, and it's also a useful step when you're troubleshooting issues with a website.

Private Browsing

Speaking of visiting websites confidentially, browsers also offer *private browsing* modes. When you're using private mode, your browser won't save information about the sites that you visit in your browsing history or cache. It's important to understand that this doesn't mean the website won't know who you are—the site will still see your IP address. It just means that information about the site won't be saved on your computer.

In Chrome, private browsing is called incognito mode and you activate it by opening up an incognito window. Just select the File menu and then choose New Incognito Window to activate it. Chrome will open the new browser window shown in Figure 24.3 that advises you that you are in incognito mode.

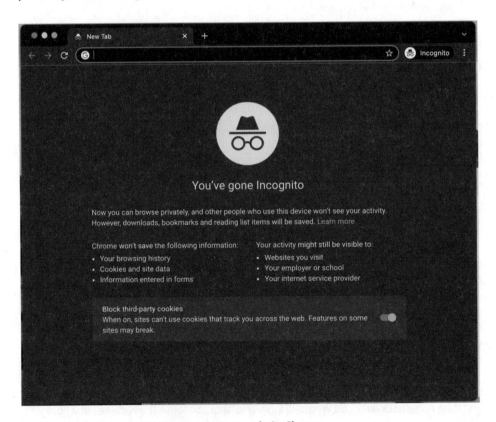

FIGURE 24.3 Activating incognito mode in Chrome

Deactivate Client-Side Scripting

You can make your browser more secure by deactivating *client-side scripting*. This stops websites from running small programs called scripts on your computer. These scripts are most often written in a language called JavaScript, and disabling them helps protect your system from some security threats, but doing so will also disable some functionality on websites that use scripting.

To set up a script blocker and disable JavaScript, go to the Settings menu in Chrome, choose Security and Privacy, click Site Settings, and then click JavaScript. You'll then see the menu shown in Figure 24.4, which allows you to choose a general setting of whether websites can run JavaScript on your computer and then to make exceptions to that setting for specific sites.

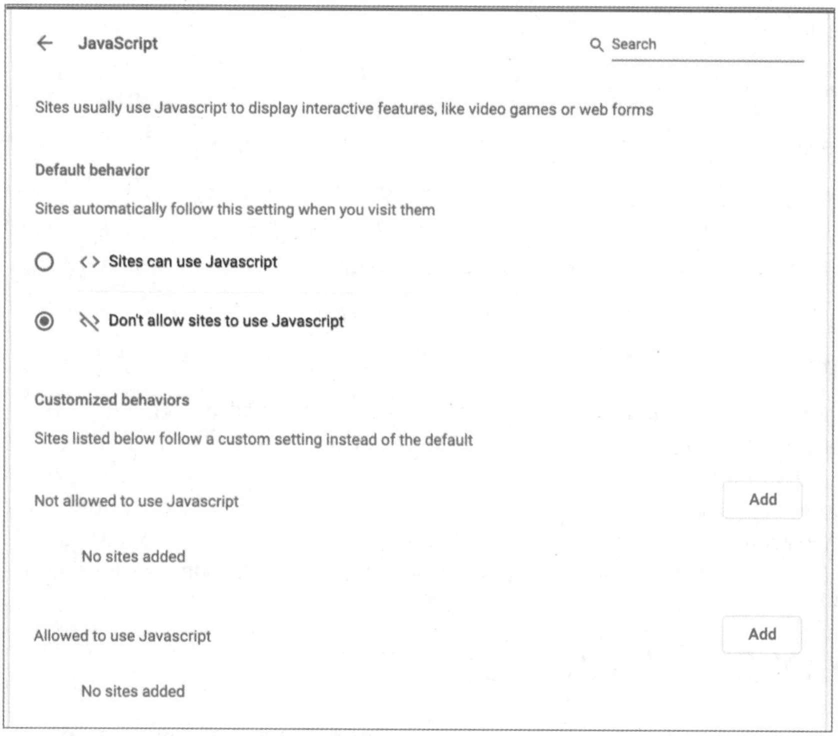

FIGURE 24.4 Deactivating client-side scripting in Chrome

Browser Add-Ons

Browser add-ons, or browser extensions, are extra software that you download to run in your web browser. Extensions help you with scheduling meetings, managing files, and performing many other tasks.

In Chrome, you can click the puzzle piece icon to access information about the extensions you're currently using. You'll see the pop-up window shown in Figure 24.5. In this window, you can add and remove extensions and also enable and disable them without removing them permanently.

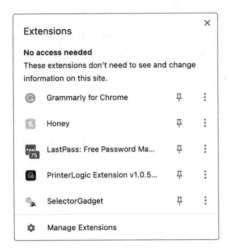

FIGURE 24.5 **Managing browser extensions in Chrome**

Pop-ups

Many websites open pop-up windows that contain information or advertisements, and users often find these pop-ups annoying. Because of this, web browsers allow you to disable pop-up windows.

In Chrome's Settings, go to Security and Privacy, click Site Settings, and then choose Pop-ups And Redirects. Just like with script blocking, you can use the settings shown in Figure 24.6 to either allow or block pop-ups for all sites or set exceptions for specific sites.

PROXY SERVERS

Some organizations use *proxy servers* to help users access the web. These servers might help improve web performance and also enforce security policies about the websites that you visit. If your organization uses a proxy server, you'll need to configure your computer to use that proxy server in order to access the Internet. This is an operating system setting, and it requires knowing the IP address and port for your proxy server.

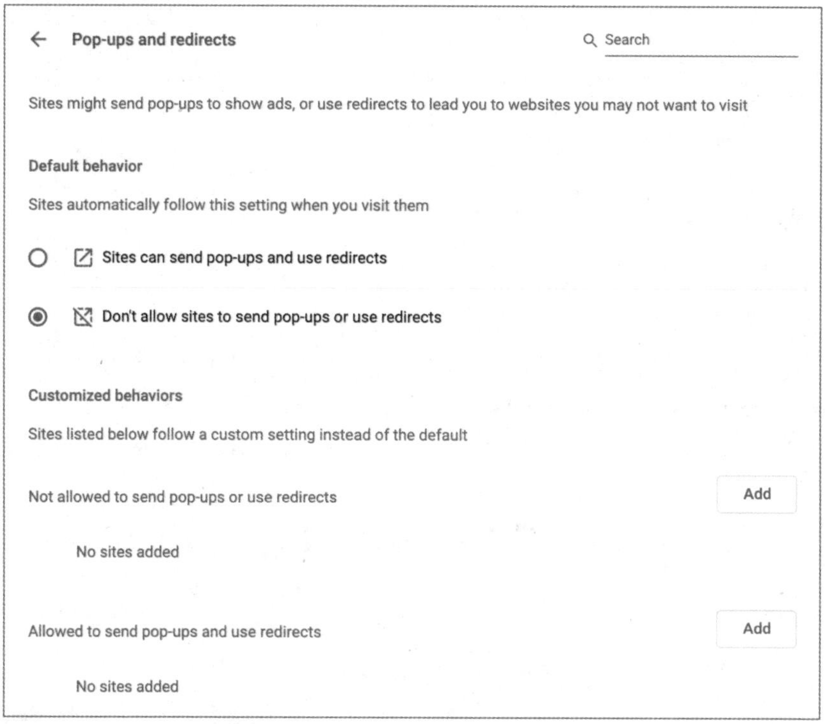

FIGURE 24.6 Disabling pop-ups and redirects in Chrome

For example, if you wanted to proxy all HTTP requests on a Mac, you'd go into the proxy settings on your Mac, specify that you'd like to use an HTTP web proxy, and then provide the IP address and port number for the proxy server, as shown in Figure 24.7. You can also set up an HTTPS proxy for encrypted connections.

These proxy settings can be the source of some problems for end users. If a user is on a network that requires the use of a proxy server and doesn't have that proxy server configured, they won't be able to access the Internet until they set it up. Similarly, if a user has a proxy server configured on their computer but then travels to a network where that proxy server is not available, they will need to disable their proxy settings before they will be able to access the Internet.

EXAM TIP

Some organizations may configure browsers to use proxies only for external websites, allowing users to directly access internal sites. If a user experiences difficulty accessing external sites but is able to view pages on the intranet, check the proxy settings for issues.

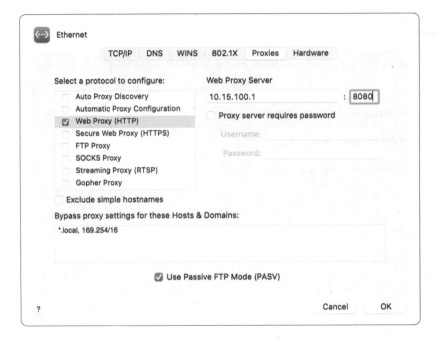

FIGURE 24.7 Configuring a proxy server on a Mac

Also, one of the ways that proxies improve performance is by maintaining their own caches of web content that are shared between users. If a user is seeing old web content that seems to be outdated but clearing the browser cache doesn't work, the problem might be that they are using a proxy server that has the old content cached.

DIGITAL CERTIFICATES

Earlier in this chapter, we discussed how web browsers use the HTTPS protocol to securely transfer web pages. Using HTTPS protects against eavesdroppers who might try to view web traffic by protecting it with encryption. This encryption depends on websites having a valid *digital certificate*.

Figure 24.8 shows the digital certificate for my website, www.certmike.com. This certificate is marked as valid by my web browser, and I can be confident that this website is secure.

On the other hand, if I visit the website https://wrong.host.badssl.com, I see the error message shown in Figure 24.9. This site has an invalid digital certificate. I see a warning message telling me that the certificate is invalid for this site and that I shouldn't continue accessing it because my communications with the web server will be insecure.

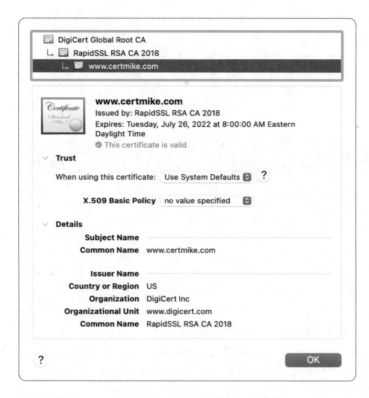

FIGURE 24.8 Valid certificate for CertMike.com

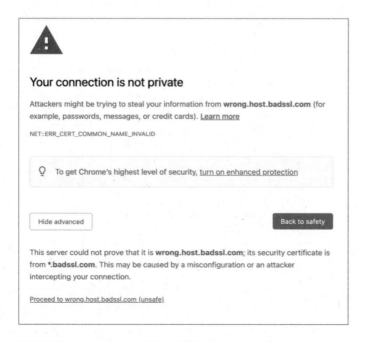

FIGURE 24.9 Invalid certificate warning for wrong.host.badssl.com

NOTE

If you see a message warning you that a certificate is expired and it has not yet reached its expiration date, check the date and time on your system. If your date is set incorrectly, you may see a lot of these errors!

CERTMIKE EXAM ESSENTIALS

▶ Users access websites by using web browsers that reach out to web servers using HTTP to retrieve web pages written in HTML.

▶ Users and administrators may configure a variety of security and privacy settings to customize their web browsing experience. These include clearing caches, enabling private browsing, deactivating client-side scripting, managing browser add-ons, and disabling pop-ups.

▶ Proxy servers retrieve websites on behalf of end users. If a proxy is misconfigured, the user will likely not be able to view any websites.

▶ Digital certificates enable encryption for websites, allowing them to transfer data using the secure HTTPS protocol instead of the unencrypted HTTP protocol.

Practice Question 1

You are helping a user troubleshoot their web browser. When they visit your company's internal portal, everything works fine. However, they are unable to access any external websites. What should be the first setting that you check?

A. Proxy configuration
B. Private browsing mode
C. Client-side scripting
D. Pop-up blocker

Practice Question 2

You visit a website that you normally use to transfer secure files and receive a message telling you that the site is not secure. Where is the likely issue in this situation?

A. Browser settings
B. Digital certificate
C. VPN
D. Incognito mode

Practice Question 1 Explanation

The scenario described here appears to be a proxy misconfiguration. The organization may require the use of a proxy for external websites but allow users to access internal websites directly without using the proxy. You should check the user's proxy settings and make sure that they are configured correctly.

Private browsing mode hides a user's identity from websites that they visit. It would not affect the user's ability to visit any external website.

Disabling client-side scripting or pop-ups may interfere with the correct functioning of some websites, but not all sites use these features. The fact that the user can't visit *any* external website indicates that neither of these is likely the issue at hand.

Correct Answer: A. Proxy configuration

Practice Question 2 Explanation

When your web browser displays an error message indicating that a site is not secure, this usually indicates an issue with the site's digital certificate. The certificate may be improperly used, fake, or expired. When you see these warnings you should not continue visiting the site unless you are comfortable with the information you send to that site being viewed by others.

This error message indicates a problem with the server and not an issue on the end user's system. Therefore, it is unlikely that you need to modify browser settings, activate or deactivate incognito mode, or use a VPN to resolve the issue.

Correct Answer: B. Digital certificate

CHAPTER 25

Application Concepts and Uses

Objective 3.6: Compare and contrast general application concepts and uses

IT professionals often find themselves responsible for installing and managing applications on systems throughout their organization. Let's take some time to talk about the key software management concepts that you'll need to understand for the exam.

In this chapter, you'll learn everything you need to know about ITF+ objective 3.6:

▶ **Single-platform software**
▶ **Cross-platform software**
▶ **Licensing**
▶ **Software installation best practices**

SOFTWARE COMPATIBILITY

Not all software is designed to work on all systems. You may have encountered this already in your career. Some software packages have versions that are designed to work on all major operating systems, whereas others are available only on a single operating system. For example, the Microsoft Office suite is compatible with both Windows and Mac platforms. It's an example of what we call a *cross-platform application*.

Apple's Keynote, Pages, and Numbers software are designed only to work on macOS. They're examples of *single-platform software*. When you use single-platform software, you run into compatibility concerns because if users in your organization are running different operating systems and can't all use the same applications, they may have difficulty working together.

When you download software, you'll want to make sure that you have the correct version for your operating system. If you're downloading Windows software, you'll need to choose the correct architecture as well. You'll find that some software has an extension that ends in x86. This means that it was designed to work on older 32-bit versions of Windows. It will still run on modern 64-bit versions of Windows, but it will have slower performance than if you obtain a native 64-bit version.

SOFTWARE INSTALLATION BEST PRACTICES

When you're installing software on a system, there are a few pieces of advice that you should keep in mind. Following these best practices will help you avoid issues that might cause trouble down the road.

- ▶ **Read the instructions** carefully for any software that you're installing. It's tempting to want to just dive right in and start installing things and you may do that on your personal computer, but that approach is risky in a business environment where a mistake that takes a computer out of commission can disrupt the organization.
- ▶ **Watch out for advanced options and configuration settings.** Take the time to understand how the software will be used and work with the end users to configure those settings to best meet their needs.
- ▶ **Read the license agreements for any software that you're installing.** Make sure you understand the details of the license and that you're complying with any obligations that you may have. This is true whether you're reviewing an *end-user license agreement (EULA)* that applies only to a single user or an enterprise license agreement that applies to the entire organization.

SOFTWARE LICENSING

Different types of licenses are available that describe the conditions of using the software:

- ▶ Software that we purchase from vendors is considered *proprietary software*. The vendor owns the software and charges for its use.
- ▶ Other software is developed by a community of developers and released as *open source software* that is free for use under the conditions of an open source license agreement. One of the major advantages of open source software is

that any developer is free to take an open source package, modify it to meet their own needs, and then even release that modified software as an open source application.

When you have proprietary software, there are also different types of licensing arrangements that describe how many people may use the software:

▶ A *single-user license* allows you to install the software on a computer for a single user to work with.

▶ A group-use or *site license* covers many people. It may be the entire organization, a specific team, or a set of named people who may all have access to the software.

▶ *Concurrent licenses* also allow multiple people to use the software. The difference is in how those people are counted. For a site license, the license counts the number of people who may have the software installed. A concurrent license counts the number of people who may be using the software at the same time.

Software may be licensed as a one-time purchase where you pay a single up-front fee for use of the software and then a small maintenance fee to receive support and updates. Or it may be licensed under a subscription model, where instead of paying a large up-front fee, you pay a monthly or annual fee for each user. Cloud services generally tend to use this subscription model.

When you purchase software licenses, you're often given access to a serial number or *product key*. This is basically the password for installing the software under the license, and it is tied to your organization. You want to keep track of that key and protect it. If someone gains access to your license key, they may be able to activate software under your license and use up some of your purchased capacity!

CERTMIKE EXAM ESSENTIALS

▶ Cross-platform software is designed to work on a variety of operating systems. Single-platform software works only on a single operating system.

▶ Proprietary software is sold by vendors and may only be used under a purchased license. Open-source software is developed by a community and is free for use or modification by anyone.

▶ Single-user licenses allow a single named individual to use a software package. Site licenses allow anyone in an organization to use the software. Concurrent licenses also allow anyone in the organization to use the software but limit the number of people who may use it simultaneously.

Practice Question 1

You recently purchased a new data visualization software package that will be used by business analysts in your organization. The license allows anyone in the organization to use the software as long as they are using a corporate-owned computer. What term best describes this type of license?

A. Site license

B. Open source license

C. Concurrent license

D. Single-user license

Practice Question 2

Your organization uses a combination of Windows and Mac systems for end-user computing. Users may select the system that they prefer. You are considering adopting a new collaboration software suite that will allow users to communicate, and you would like everyone in the organization to be able to use the software. What type of software should you select?

A. Open source software

B. Proprietary software

C. Single-platform software

D. Cross-platform software

Practice Question 1 Explanation

This is an example of a site license—a license that allows unrestricted use of a software package throughout an organization. The rule that the software may only be installed on corporate-owned devices is a common site license rule to prevent personal use of the software.

The software is not open source because open source software is not purchased. Rather, it is free for use or modification by anyone.

Concurrent licenses restrict the number of users that may use the software at any one time, whereas single-user licenses are for a named individual's use only. Neither of these restrictions appears on this license.

Correct Answer: A. Site license

Practice Question 2 Explanation

You should select a cross-platform software package that is available for both Windows and Mac systems. Otherwise, if you choose a single-platform package, some users will not be able to run the software and will be left out of the collaboration.

Open source software is software that is licensed for free use by anyone, whereas proprietary software must be licensed from the vendor for use by an individual or company. The requirements in this scenario do not specify whether cost is a factor, so either one of these approaches may be used.

Correct Answer: D. Cross-platform software

Domain 4.0: Software Development Concepts

Software Development is the fourth domain of CompTIA's ITF+ exam. In it, you'll learn the basics of programming, including the use of different programming languages and the basic structure of code. This domain has three objectives:

4.1 Compare and contrast programming language categories

4.2 Given a scenario, use programming organizational techniques and interpret logic

4.3 Explain the purpose and use of programming concepts

Questions from this domain make up 12% of the questions on the ITF+ exam, so you should expect to see approximately 9 questions on your test covering the material in this part.

CHAPTER 26

Programming Languages

Objective 4.1: Compare and contrast programming language categories

Software developers write code in programming languages to create software that meets an organization's business objectives. These programming languages each have different commands and formatting and focus on different types of development.

In this chapter, you'll learn everything you need to know about ITF+ objective 4.1:

▶ **Interpreted**
▶ **Compiled programming languages**
▶ **Query languages**
▶ **Assembly language**

PROGRAMMING LANGUAGE CATEGORIES

Computers execute code in different ways depending on the type of *programming language* used. They may either interpret the code directly or first compile it into a format that can be executed.

In either case, programmers develop applications by writing instructions in a language that looks somewhat similar to English. Figure 26.1 shows an example of code written in the R programming language, which is commonly used for statistical and machine learning applications. Don't worry about the content of the code. At this point, I just want you to have an idea what code looks like.

> **EXAM TIP**
>
> You won't find any questions on the exam that require you to know how to write code in any specific language. The questions you encounter will either test you on general concepts or ask you to read pseudocode that is written in a generic way.

```r
library(tidyverse)
library(stringr)
library(lubridate)

# Read in the dataset
disability <- read_csv("ssadisability.csv")
head(disability)

# Convert it to a long dataset
disability <- disability %>%
  gather(month, applications, -Fiscal_Year)
head(disability)

# Separate the month from the filing type
disability <- disability %>%
  separate(month, c("month", "format"), "_")
head(disability)

# Look at the month values
unique(disability$month)
```

FIGURE 26.1 Code written in the R programming language

The difference between interpreted and compiled code occurs when it comes time to execute that code.

Interpreted Code

When you use *interpreted code*, the computer reads the actual instructions written by the developer as it executes the code. The computer does this by using software called an interpreter that is designed to understand a specific language. We'll talk about two subcategories of interpreted languages: scripting languages and markup languages.

Scripting Languages

Scripting languages (or scripted languages) are often used by administrators to automate actions on a computer and for a variety of general programming tasks. Here are some examples of scripting languages:

- ▶ Perl
- ▶ R
- ▶ Python
- ▶ Ruby
- ▶ JavaScript
- ▶ VBScript

Markup Languages

The second category of interpreted language is the *markup language*. These are languages that provide tags that you can use to mark up text documents. The two most common examples of these are the *Hypertext Markup Language (HTML)*, which is used to create web pages, and the *Extensible Markup Language (XML)*, which is used to exchange structured data between systems.

Figure 26.2 shows an example of a web page written in HTML. If you notice all of the text highlighted in blue, these are the tags that represent different types of formatting that should be applied to the text. These tags usually appear in pairs. The first tag includes the instruction inside less-than and greater-than brackets, and the second tag is exactly the same, except there is a forward slash after the less-than symbol. Any text that appears between the two tags is given the formatting indicated by the tag.

```
<HTML>
<BODY>

This is <B>bold text</B>.

For more certification
information, visit <A
HREF="https://www.certmike.com">
the CertMike website</A>

</BODY>
</HTML>
```

FIGURE 26.2 Web page written in HTML

Figure 26.3 shows an example of a document written in XML. This document provides a set of data elements that are going to be exchanged between systems. XML uses tags just like those in HTML to provide names for each of the data elements.

Remember that scripting and markup languages are both examples of interpreted languages.

```
<PERSON>
 <FIRSTNAME>George</FIRSTNAME>
 <LASTNAME>Parker</LASTNAME>
 <AGE>28</AGE>
 <SALARIED>true</SALARIED>
</PERSON>

<PERSON>
 <FIRSTNAME>Theresa</FIRSTNAME>
 <LASTNAME>Monaghan</LASTNAME>
 <AGE>32</AGE>
 <SALARIED>false</SALARIED>
</PERSON>
```

F I G U R E   2 6 . 3   Document written in XML

Compiled Code

In languages that use *compiled code,* the programmer runs a tool called a *compiler* on their program to produce an *executable file*. This executable file contains instructions in *machine language* that carry out the programmer's instructions. When a user wishes to run the program, they launch the executable file, rather than the programmer's original source code.

Examples of compiled languages are as follows:

- ► C and C++
- ► Java
- ► Go
- ► Julia
- ► FORTRAN

EXAM TIP

In an interpreted language, the computer directly executes the source code written by the developer using a program called an *interpreter*. In a compiled language, a program called a *compiler* must first be used to convert the source code into an executable file. Compiled code normally runs faster than interpreted code.

SPECIALIZED LANGUAGES

There are two other categories of language that we need to talk about, but they're for special use cases.

Assembly Languages

Assembly language allows programmers to write code that works directly with the hardware, bypassing the use of a compiled or interpreted language. Each type of processor you might use has a different assembly language, and it is fairly rare to actually write code in assembly language for this reason (and because it's pretty difficult to use). Assembly language isn't quite the same as machine language, but they're very close. Today, the only time you see people writing assembly language is when they're working with specialized hardware, such as embedded devices or Internet of Things devices.

Query Languages

Query languages are used to ask questions of databases, and the main language in this category is Structured Query Language (SQL). We're going to cover SQL in much more detail in Part V of this book, so I won't discuss it now.

IDENTIFYING LANGUAGES

I know we covered a lot of different categories and languages, and you do need to know which language fits in which category for the exam. The summary chart in Figure 26.4 will help you remember the major languages that you might see on the exam.

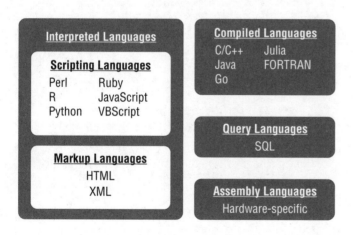

FIGURE 26.4 Language summary chart

CERTMIKE EXAM ESSENTIALS

▶ Interpreted languages are executed from source code using an interpreter. Interpreted languages may be either scripting languages (such as Perl, R, Python, Ruby, JavaScript, and VBScript) or markup languages (such as HTML and XML).

▶ Compiled languages use a compiler to convert source code into executable machine language. Compiled languages include C, C++, Java, Go, Julia, and FORTRAN.

▶ Structured Query Language (SQL) is used to interact with relational databases.

▶ Assembly language is written to work on a specific hardware processor.

Practice Question 1

Which one of the following languages requires a compiler to create executable code?

A. SQL
B. Python
C. C++
D. Perl

Practice Question 2

You are upgrading the hardware and operating system on a server that runs some custom code that was created by the software development team in your organization. Which one of the following types of code is most likely to need to be rewritten for the new server?

A. Interpreted language
B. Compiled language
C. Scripting language
D. Assembly language

Practice Question 1 Explanation

This question is asking you to recognize which category each programming language falls into. From the knowledge you gained in this chapter, you should know that C and C++ are compiled languages. In these languages, the developer writes source code in that language and then uses a compiler to create a machine language file that may be executed.

Python and Perl are interpreted scripting languages. In those languages, the code written by a software developer is directly executed by the language's interpreter. SQL is a query language used to send commands to a relational database.

Correct Answer: C. C++

Practice Question 2 Explanation

Code that is written in assembly language is written to work on a specific hardware processor. A server upgrade that changes the processor is likely to require new assembly language code that is designed to work on the new processor.

Software written in compiled languages does not need to be rewritten. Instead, the developer can take the original source code and recompile it to work on the new processor.

Similarly, interpreted languages do not need to be rewritten. The system administrator simply needs to ensure that an appropriate interpreter is installed on the new server.

Query languages, such as Structured Query Language (SQL), are not hardware specific, and as long as the same database server is installed on the server, existing SQL commands should continue to execute in the same way that they did on the old server.

Correct Answer: D. Assembly language

CHAPTER 27

Programming Organizational Techniques

Objective 4.2: Given a scenario, use programming organizational techniques and interpret logic

As software developers begin to create code, they use some standard tools to organize their work. These tools include pseudocode, which allows them to write code that is not yet in any specific programming language, and flowcharts, which show the general flow of software-based decision making.

In this chapter, you'll learn the first half of the material that you need to know about ITF+ objective 4.2. The remaining material for this objective is covered in Chapter 28, "Logic Components." The objectives covered in this chapter include:

▶ **Pseudocode concepts**
▶ **Flowchart concepts**

PSEUDOCODE

Software developers use a fairly consistent process for creating new pieces of software. The majority of their work is dedicated to creating what we call *algorithms*. Algorithms are just a fancy term for the step-by-step instructions that a computer should follow when it is executing the code.

Let's write a basic algorithm together that will convert temperatures from Fahrenheit into Celsius. First, I'll make sure that you understand the process for performing this conversion. Our algorithm will receive a single piece of input: a temperature in Fahrenheit. Then it will perform a series of calculations on that input. It will subtract 32 from the Fahrenheit temperature, then multiply that result by 5 and divide that result by 9. That produces the output as the equivalent temperature in Celsius.

The previous paragraph is an algorithm. It's written in text form, which isn't a standard way to write an algorithm, but it is an algorithm nonetheless because it describes the sequence of steps that we need to follow. If I gave you a temperature in Fahrenheit and asked you to convert it to Celsius, you could simply follow the process outlined here to perform that conversion. And I can also program a computer to do the same thing.

Pseudocode is a more common way to write an algorithm. Pseudocode is simply a plain English description of an algorithm that a software developer can take and use as the basis for a program written in any language. Here's an example of that same algorithm written in pseudocode:

```
Input: T (a temperature in Fahrenheit)

T = T - 32

T = T * 5

T = T / 9

Output: T (a temperature in Celsius)
```

This algorithm isn't written in any specific programming language. I could write code in Python, Java, C, or another programming language to execute this code, but I haven't done that yet. All I've done here is written the steps out in plain English using a programming style.

> **EXAM TIP**
> There aren't "correct" and "incorrect" ways to write pseudocode. Unlike code written in a programming language, there's no syntax to worry about. When you're writing pseudocode, you're just trying to document your ideas in a way that communicates clearly to yourself and others what you've done.

FLOWCHARTS

Flowcharts are another common design tool used by programmers to help them understand the steps that a program will follow when it has to make decisions.

For example, Figure 27.1 shows a flowchart that I might use to adjust the temperature in a building so that it stays within the range of 65 to 70 degrees. I enter at the top of the flowchart and then I get to the first decision: is the temperature greater than 70? If it is, I turn on the air conditioning and then end the program.

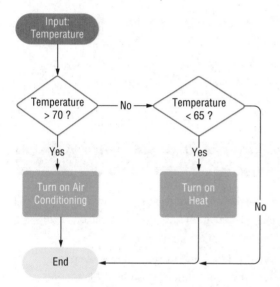

FIGURE 27.1 Temperature adjustment flowchart

If the temperature is not greater than 70 degrees, I get to the next decision: is the temperature less than 65 degrees? If it is, then I turn on the heat and end the program. If it is not, then the temperature is within the range of 65 to 70, so I don't take any action and just end the program.

When you're creating a flowchart, there are three basic symbols you can use (see Figure 27.2):

- ▶ Ovals, which are used as terminators. They mark either the beginning or the end of an algorithm.
- ▶ Rectangles, which are used as process steps. Rectangles are used to mark some type of action that is taking place.
- ▶ Diamonds, which are used as decision steps. Diamonds pose a question and then have outputs that are followed depending on the answer to the question. In most flowcharts, these questions are Yes/No questions that have only two possible answers, so there are two arrows leaving the diamond: one path to follow if the answer is yes, and another to follow if the answer is no.

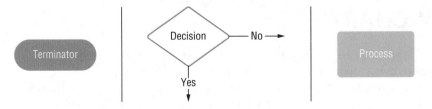

FIGURE 27.2   **Common flowchart shapes**

EXAM TIP

There are actually many other shapes used in flowcharts, and different programmers may have different styles when creating flowcharts. As you get ready for the ITF+ exam, however, you should only worry about these three shapes.

CERTMIKE EXAM ESSENTIALS

▶ Pseudocode allows software developers to write out the steps in an algorithm without using any specific programming language. It's a common way to organize work before beginning to write code.

▶ Flowcharts provide a method for visually describing the logical flow of code. In a flowchart, ovals represent the start or beginning of a flowchart. Rectangles represent process steps, and diamonds represent decision steps.

Practice Question 1

A software developer is beginning to design a new application and would like to develop a flowchart that will map out the process. They reach a step in the middle of the algorithm where the code will evaluate the number of items in inventory and either reduce the price of the item if the inventory is too high or order more of the item if the inventory is too low.

What shape would they use in a flowchart to represent the step where this evaluation is performed?

A. Rectangle
B. Diamond
C. Oval
D. Circle

Practice Question 2

A programmer recently completed the pseudocode for a new piece of software that they are writing, and they are ready to convert it into real code. What is responsible for converting the pseudocode into actual code?

A. Compiler
B. Interpreter
C. Assembler
D. Programmer

Practice Question 1 Explanation

This is clearly a decision step in the flowchart. The application must evaluate the current inventory level and then make a decision as to whether the inventory is too high or too low. Decision steps are represented in flowcharts using diamond shapes.

Once the software has made this decision, it may then move on to take the appropriate action. Those action steps are process steps and would be represented by rectangles. The portion of the flowchart that carries out this part of the code is shown here:

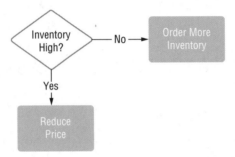

Ovals are used to represent the start and end of the flowchart, as they are terminator symbols. The scenario describes this as a step in the middle of the algorithm, so it would not be appropriate to use a terminator here.

Correct Answer: B. Diamond

Practice Question 2 Explanation

There is no automated tool that converts pseudocode into actual code. This is the work that programmers themselves must undertake. The purpose of pseudocode is to provide the programmer with a roadmap for creating actual code.

The other tools mentioned here play different roles in the software development process. Compilers are used to convert source code written in a compiled language into machine language. Assemblers convert assembly language into machine language. Interpreters are used to directly execute code written in an interpreted language.

Correct Answer: D. Programmer

CHAPTER 28

Logic Components
Objective 4.2: Given a scenario, use programming organizational techniques and interpret logic

When writing code, developers use special instructions to control the logical flow of the code's execution. Branching, or conditional execution, allows the developer to set the code up to perform different actions based on the circumstances. Looping allows the same code to be executed repeatedly until one or more conditions are met.

In this chapter, you'll learn the second half of the material that you need to know about ITF+ objective 4.2. The first half of the material for this objective was covered in Chapter 27, "Programming Organizational Techniques." The objectives covered in this chapter include:

▶ Branching
▶ Looping

BRANCHING

Conditional execution allows developers to write code that executes only when certain logical conditions are met. The most common conditional execution structure is the if..then..else statement. The general idea of the statement is summarized in this pseudocode:

```
if (logical_test1) then
  command1
else if (logical_test2) then
  command2
else if (logical_test3) then
  command3
else
  command4
```

Here's how this works. Each of the logical tests contained in this pseudocode is a question that can be answered with "yes" or "no" or, in logical terms, "true" or "false." For example, `logical_test1` might be the question "Is *x* greater than 3?" Each of the commands in the pseudocode is an action that the program should take if the preceding logical test is true.

When the program executes this code, it first checks to see if `logical_test1` is true. If it is, then it executes *command1* and the entire code statement is complete without performing any additional checks.

If `logical_test1` is false, then the program checks `logical_test2`. If that is true, then *command2* executes. If `logical_test2` is false, the program checks `logical_test3`. If that test is true, then *command3* executes.

If all of the logical tests are false, then *command4*, contained within the else clause, executes. This logical testing, working with values of true and false, is an example of performing *Boolean* operations.

An if..then..else statement may have one, many, or no else if clauses. The else clause is also optional. It's important to remember that, no matter how many clauses you have in your statement, only one can execute.

> **TIP**
> When executing an if..then..else statement, only one of the actions is executed. If multiple logical tests are true, then the code only executes the first true test that it encounters.

Let's look at an example of an if...then...else statement in action. Here's some code that prints different statements depending on the current temperature:

```
if (temperature > 90) then
  print "It's very hot!"
else if (temperature > 70) then
  print "It's somewhat hot."
else
  print "It's not hot."
```

If we run this code when the temperature is 95 degrees, the first test is true and the code prints "It's very hot!" and then exits.

If we run the code when the temperature is 75 degrees, the first test is false, so we move on to the next `else if` statement. That one is true, so we print "It's somewhat hot." and then exit.

If we run the code when the temperature is 30 degrees, the first test is false, so we move on to the second test, which is also false, and then we hit the `else` statement, which we execute and print "It's not hot." before exiting.

LOOPING

Looping operations allow you to repeat the same block of code more than one time. For example, you might want to run a certain piece of code 25 times, or once for each variable in a list.

for Loops

The *for loop* is one way that you can insert looping into your code. Here's a pseudocode example of how `for` loops are structured:

```
for variable = start to finish
    code statements
```

This `for` loop will create a new variable with the name `variable` and give it the starting value specified in `start`. It will then run the code statements the first time. After they complete, it will add 1 to the value of `variable` and execute the code statements again. This process will repeat until `variable` takes on the value of `finish`.

The exact behavior of this statement, including whether it executes the code one more time when the value of `variable` is equal to `finish`, depends on the programming language used.

Here's a more concrete example, still written in pseudocode:

```
for i = 0 to 10
    print i
```

This `for` loop would produce these results:

```
0
1
2
3
4
5
6
7
8
9
```

Again, it may print one more line containing the value 10, depending on the programming language.

while Loops

The *while loop* is another type of looping statement. Similar to `for` loops, `while` loops repeat a block of code multiple times. Instead of repeating a fixed number of times, they repeat until a condition is no longer true. They use the general format shown here:

```
while (condition)
    code statements
```

The code statements will perform some modification to the variable(s) checked in the `condition` statement. The `while` loop will then repeat continuously until `condition` evaluates as false.

For example, this `while` loop will execute as long as the value contained in the variable `i` is greater than 90:

```
i = 100
while (i > 90)
    print i
    i = i - 1
```

If we set `i` to 100 and then execute this code, the loop will run until `i` is not greater than 90, resulting in this output:

```
100
99
98
97
96
95
94
93
92
91
```

CERTMIKE EXAM ESSENTIALS

▶ Branching allows you to execute different code statements based on logical conditions. The primary mechanism for branching is the `if..then..else` statement.

▶ `for` loops allow you to execute the same code segment repeatedly a certain number of times. `while` loops work similarly but execute the code segment as long as a logical condition remains true.

Practice Question 1

Examine the pseudocode shown here:

```
if (x > 2) then

  print "We have enough inventory."
else if (x > 3) then
  print "We have too much inventory."
else if (x = 0) then
  print "We have no inventory."

else
  print "We do not have enough inventory."
```

If the value of x is set to 4 before this code executes, what will be the output?

A. We have enough inventory.
B. We have too much inventory.
C. We have no inventory.
D. We do not have enough inventory.

Practice Question 2

You are writing pseudocode for a new program and would like to check the temperature of a room. In your code, you would like to keep the air conditioning on until the room reaches 68 degrees Fahrenheit and then you would like to turn the air conditioning off.

Here is partial pseudocode to solve this problem:

```
COMMAND (temperature > 68)
     keep air conditioning on

     turn off air conditioning
```

What type of statement should you use where it currently says *COMMAND* to complete this code?

A. if
B. for
C. while
D. else

Practice Question 1 Explanation

When you encounter a question like this, you should walk through the pseudocode step by step, reading each line carefully without jumping to conclusions.

If you were to look at this code without following that process, you might quickly come to the conclusion that x is indeed greater than 3, so the code would print the statement "We have too much inventory." That, however, is not the correct answer.

The reason for this is that the conditions in an `if..then..else` statement are tested sequentially and the command corresponding to the first true condition is executed. In this case, the first test is asking if x > 2. The value of x is 4, which is greater than 2, so the code prints the line "We have enough inventory."

In this pseudocode, the reality is that the statement "We have too much inventory" will never print because any value of x that satisfies the test x > 3 will also satisfy the test x > 2 and will trigger the command to print "We have enough inventory."

Correct Answer: A. We have enough inventory.

Practice Question 2 Explanation

In this code, you would like to keep the air conditioning on until the temperature is lowered to 68 degrees. The command to complete this code is a `while` statement, as shown here:

```
while (temperature > 68)
    keep air conditioning on

turn off air conditioning
```

The code will remain in the `while` loop until the temperature reaches 68 degrees. Then it will exit the `while` loop and turn off the air conditioning.

A `for` loop would execute the command a certain number of times, instead of waiting until a logical condition is met, so it would not be appropriate here. The use of an `if` statement would test the logical condition, but it would only do so once, so it would turn the air conditioning on and then immediately turn it off. An `else` statement cannot be used here because it may only be used as a component of an `if..then..else` statement.

Correct Answer: C. while

CHAPTER 29

Programming Concepts

Objective 4.3: Explain the purpose and use of programming concepts

As you prepare for the ITF+ exam, you won't need to know how to write code, but you will need to be familiar with the basic concepts of programming. You'll encounter questions that ask you to understand and interpret pseudocode, and that requires understanding the use of variables, arrays, vectors, functions, and objects.

In this chapter, you'll learn the material that you need to know about ITF+ objective 4.3. The objectives covered in this chapter include:

▶ **Identifiers**
▶ **Containers**
▶ **Functions**
▶ **Objects**

VARIABLES AND ARRAYS

Variables and arrays are the basic constructs that we use to store data in memory. They're crucial to the understanding and execution of code written in any programming language.

Variables

Variables are one of the core concepts in any programming language. They allow developers to store information in memory using a descriptive name and then later reference that information in their script. Variables can store integers, decimal numbers, Boolean (true/false) values, dates and times, character strings, and virtually any other type of information that you might need.

Let's take a look at how we might use a variable in some pseudocode. Imagine that we have a small store that normally sells cupcakes for $2 but offers a 50 percent discount on Tuesdays. We might need a script that calculates Tuesday's price, like this one:

```
cupcake_price = 2

cupcake_price = cupcake_price / 2

print "The price of a cupcake is ", cupcake_price
```

In this script, `cupcake_price` is a variable. The first line of the script sets the value of that variable equal to 2.00. The next line changes the price to one-half of its current value. The last line prints the price of the cupcake, which will be $1 on Tuesday.

That's a simple example of a variable in action. Remember, when we execute a script containing a variable, the script interpreter performs a substitution, using the value stored in that variable's memory location in place of the variable name.

Arrays

In some cases, we need to keep track of many related variables at the same time. For example, we might have the ages of all students in a high school programming class. We might create a separate variable to keep track of each student's age, but that would make things very complicated. We'd have to remember the names of all those variables. *Arrays* offer a helpful way to store that information together. For example, we might create an array called `ages` using this code:

```
ages = [16,15,18,15,16,14,13,17,13,14]
```

This creates an array with 10 elements, each one corresponding to the age of a single student. We can pull out individual values from the array and inspect or manipulate them. For example, if we want to access the first element in the array, we can use this code, which would give us the value 16:

```
ages[0]
```

Now you might be wondering why I used the number 0 to reference the first element of the array. When programmers count elements in an array, they usually begin with 0 instead of 1. This means that a 10-element array has elements numbered 0 through 9.

If our first student has a birthday, we could increment that student's age with this command:

```
ages[0] = 17
```

That changes a single element of the array. Alternatively, if we wanted to add 1 to all of the students' ages, we could use this command to create the array and then perform a simple arithmetic operation:

```
ages = [16,15,18,15,16,14,13,17,13,14]
```

```
ages = ages + 1
```

This would result in an array with the values shown here:

```
ages [17,16,19,16,17,15,14,18,14,15]
```

DATA TYPES

In most programming languages, each variable has an associated data type that tells the computer how to handle it. This is how we tell the difference between numeric values, character strings, and other types of data that we might have stored in memory or on disk.

Numeric Data

Numeric data is, as the name implies, data that uses numbers. You might use a numeric data type to store the number of products you have remaining in stock, the weight of a person in pounds or kilograms, the length of a boat, or any other value that we can measure quantitatively.

There are two major subtypes of numeric data:

▶ *Integers* are values that do not have decimal or fractional values. They are whole numbers, such as 1, 2, and 3. They may also take on negative values, such as −145.

▶ *Floating point numbers*, or floats, are numbers that do have decimal places associated with them. They're decimal numbers. The precision of a floating point number indicates how many decimal places may be used with that number. The more precision we use, the more memory a floating point number consumes because the computer has to store the values in all those extra decimal places.

We sometimes have numeric values that will never change. In those cases, we don't have to put them in a variable, but we can use a similar data structure called the *constant*. Constants are values that don't ever change in our code. Otherwise, we can use them basically the same way that we use a variable.

Text Data

We also commonly work with *text data*—that is, data made up of characters. We use text for so many different purposes, ranging from small fields such as people's names or addresses, to large blocks of text that might make up a paragraph, an article, or even an entire book. Computers store text using a data type known as a *character string*. This simply means that it is a sequence, or string, of one or more characters put together to create a block of text. You can create strings of different lengths in databases, spreadsheets, and programming languages.

Character strings may contain either plain text, consisting only of letters and symbols, or they may contain alphanumeric text that mixes together numeric digits with letters and symbols. One important thing to understand is that if you have numeric data stored in a string, you can't perform mathematical operations on that data. The data might look like a number to us, but to the computer it's simply the text characters that make up those numbers.

ZIP CODES

One really interesting and tricky example of data types are the ZIP codes that we use as postal codes in the United States. These are five-digit or nine-digit numbers that uniquely identify a town or an area of a city for the delivery of mail. Since these are numbers, you might be tempted to store them using a numeric data type.

However, the problem is that many ZIP codes start with the digit zero. If you store those in a numeric data type, the computer will ignore the leading zero and truncate the ZIP code to be only four digits! For that reason, you should always store ZIP codes as text.

Boolean Data

The final data type that you should be familiar with for the exam is the *Boolean* data type. This is just a fancy way of saying that a variable can only contain one of two values: True or False. We might have a Boolean value stored in a database of employees indicating whether or not an employee is salaried. If the value is set to True, the employee is salaried. If the value is set to False, the employee is not salaried.

EXAM TIP

As you prepare for the exam, it's really important that you understand these different data types and that you're able to select the most appropriate data type for a given situation. That's a common topic that might appear on the test.

FUNCTIONS

In software development, we often wind up needing to use the same code over and over again. *Functions* provide us with an opportunity to create reusable pieces of code that can be easily called multiple times.

For example, in Chapter 27, "Programming Organizational Techniques," we looked at an algorithm for converting temperatures from Fahrenheit to Celsius. Here's that algorithm written in pseudocode:

```
Input: T (a temperature in Fahrenheit)

T = T - 32

T = T * 5

T = T / 9

Output: T (a temperature in Celsius)
```

If I had to do this conversion many times in my code, I could just copy and paste these steps over and over again, but that's not very efficient. It's a lot of typing for me, and if I made a mistake in my algorithm, I'd have to go correct it in many different places.

Instead, I might create a function that performs the conversion. I just name my function and provide the code that should be executed and the names of any variables it will take as input. This function takes a Fahrenheit temperature as input and returns the Celsius equivalent:

```
Function FahrenheitToCelsius(T)
{
T = T - 32

T = T * 5

T = T / 9

return T
}
```

Then whenever I want to use this code, I can just call the function with the Fahrenheit temperature. For example, if I call this function:

```
FahrenheitToCelsius(50)
```

it will go through the math and subtract 32 from 50, multiply it by 5, and divide it by 9 to get this result:

```
10
```

Similarly, if I call

```
FahrenheitToCelsius(90)
```

I get the result:

```
32.2
```

Functions can be used any time we want to have reusable code, and they may be used by a single developer, shared within a team or company, or even included in public libraries, where anyone can download them.

OBJECTS

Some programming languages are *object-oriented*. In this model, we don't write all our code in a step-by-step fashion, giving the computer a series of actions to take in order. Instead, we create a series of *objects* that each have some common components.

Objects have two major components:

▶ *Attributes* are the properties or variables associated with an object.
▶ *Methods* are the functions or procedures that can be taken on the object. They're similar to the functions that exist in other programming languages, but they are tied to an object rather than being generally available.

So let's think about this in a concrete example. Suppose we are writing code that deals with the different products sold in a store. We might create an object called Product that looks something like the one shown in Figure 29.1. Product has some attributes associated with it—things like the name of the product, the weight of the product, the price, a description, and so on.

```
┌─────────────────────────┐
│       Product           │
├─────────────────────────┤
│ Name:                   │
│ Weight:                 │
│ Price:                  │
│                         │
│ GetPrice()              │
│ SetPrice()              │
└─────────────────────────┘
```

FIGURE 29.1 The **Product** object

We can then interact with the object through methods. We'd have methods for anything someone might want to do to a product. For our purposes, let's just focus on price. There are two main things someone might want to do with the price: check the price of the product and change the price of the product. So, we'd write two methods that contain that code:

▶ A GetPrice() method that returns the current price of a product
▶ A SetPrice() method that changes the price of the product to a specific value

When we use this code, we would create copies of this object for each product that we sell. Each of these copies is called an *instance* of the object. Then we could reference each of them by name and call the methods of the object. For example, we might create instances of the Product object for a bicycle and a television, as shown in Figure 29.2.

Bicycle
Name: Bicycle
Weight: 50 lbs
Price: $142
GetPrice()
SetPrice()

TV
Name: TV
Weight: 92 lbs
Price: $700
GetPrice()
SetPrice()

FIGURE 29.2 Instances of the **Product** object for a bicycle and a TV

If we wanted to get the price of a bicycle, we'd reference the Bicycle object and call the getPrice() method to get the result $142:

```
Bicycle -> getPrice()
$142
```

If we wanted to change the price of the television to $800, we'd call the setPrice() method on TV and pass the value $800:

```
TV -> setPrice($800)
```

which would change the underlying price in that instance, as shown in Figure 29.3.

Bicycle
Name: Bicycle
Weight: 50 lbs
Price: $142
GetPrice()
SetPrice()

TV
Name: TV
Weight: 92 lbs
Price: $800
GetPrice()
SetPrice()

FIGURE 29.3 Updated instances of the **Product** object for a bicycle and a TV

EXAM TIP

When you take the exam, you should be familiar with the concept of an object and know that the characteristics of an object are stored in attributes and that we can take actions on objects using methods.

CERTMIKE EXAM ESSENTIALS

▶ Variables are used to hold data in memory during a program's execution. They may contain numeric data, text data, or Boolean values. Arrays are collections of multiple variables of the same type stored together.

▶ Functions contain reusable code that may be called multiple times from within a program and may be shared across programs.

▶ Object-oriented programming uses instances of objects that contain two components. Attributes are variables stored within the object, and methods are functions that may be used to manipulate and retrieve those attributes.

Practice Question 1

You are creating a variable for use within a program. The variable will contain the number of children that a person has. What data type would be most appropriate for this variable?

A. Floating point number
B. String
C. Boolean
D. Integer

Practice Question 2

You are looking at the source code for a program written in an object-oriented language and find an object class used to represent an employee in that program. The object contains the employee's pay rate in a variable called salary and has the ability to give the person a raise and increase their salary using a function called GrantRaise(). Which one of the following statements is correct?

A. Both salary and GrantRaise() are attributes.
B. Salary is an attribute and GrantRaise() is a method.
C. Salary is a method and GrantRaise() is an attribute.
D. Both salary and GrantRaise() are methods.

Practice Question 1 Explanation

The number of children that an individual has is a whole number and should, therefore, be stored as an integer value.

Floating point numbers contain decimal places. It would not make sense to store a fractional number of children, such as 1.5, so it would not be logical to use a floating point number for this purpose, since doing so could lead to nonsensical values being stored.

While you could use a text string to store the number of children, in the form "1" or "2", this is not the best way to store the data. It would not be possible to manipulate that number mathematically, such as incrementing it to mark the birth of a new child or adding several values together to find the combined number of children among a group of people.

Boolean values can only be True or False, so it would not be possible to store the number of children that an individual has in a Boolean. A Boolean value could be used for a field named HasChildren that is only used to record the fact that a person does or does not have children.

Correct Answer: D. Integer

Practice Question 2 Explanation

There are two important facts about objects that you need to know to answer this question. First, objects have attributes that are the properties or variables associated with an object. Second, objects have methods that are the functions or procedures that can be taken on the object.

In this case, `salary` is a property of the employee, so it is an attribute. `GrantRaise()` is a function that may be used to manipulate `salary`, so it is a method.

Correct Answer: B. Salary is an attribute and GrantRaise() is a method.

PART V

Domain 5.0: Database Fundamentals

Chapter 30   Database Concepts
Chapter 31   Database Structures
Chapter 32   Database Interfaces

Database Fundamentals is the fifth domain of CompTIA's ITF+ exam. In this domain, you'll learn about the purpose of databases and the techniques available to users who need to create, read, update, and delete (CRUD) database information. This domain has three objectives:

5.1 Explain database concepts and the purpose of a database

5.2 Compare and contrast various database structures

5.3 Summarize methods used to interface with databases

   Questions from this domain make up 11% of the questions on the ITF+ exam, so you should expect to see approximately 8 questions on your test covering the material in this part.

CHAPTER 30

Database Concepts

Objective 5.1: Explain database concepts and the purpose of a database

Organizations use databases to maintain centralized stores of data that are available to all users who need them and are protected against unauthorized access and accidental damage.

In this chapter, you'll learn everything you need to know about ITF+ objective 5.1, including the following topics:

▶ **Usage of database**
▶ **Flat file vs. database**
▶ **Records**
▶ **Storage**

DATABASES

Databases provide organizations with a way to store their data centrally in organized tables so that many people can access it at the same time. Popular database platforms include Microsoft SQL Server, Oracle, and MySQL.

> **EXAM TIP**
>
> Expect to see exam questions that ask you to decide the best way to store data in a given situation. If the question references any of the core advantages of a database over a flat file (i.e., multiple concurrent users, scalability, speed, and variety of data), you'll want to store the data in a database. If the data does not seem like it would easily be organized into tables, a database is probably not the best choice.

Databases vs. Flat Files

Databases offer an excellent alternative to *flat files*, which are files created in other applications that are stored on a hard disk without the benefit of a database server to help organize them. This approach works well for data used by a single person and in small quantities, but databases work better in many situations. The four key characteristics of databases are:

Databases allow multiple concurrent users to store and retrieve data.   If you've ever tried to access a file stored on a hard drive or server and edit it at the same time as other people, you know that this can be really challenging. Databases manage all of that for us, allowing everyone to share concurrent access.

Databases are very scalable.   That means that they can grow with our data. You can have a small database supporting just your department or an enormous database that serves thousands of people at the same time.

Databases have a speed advantage over flat files.   They're designed to help you find and retrieve the data that you need very quickly. There's no need to hunt through many files looking for the right data—databases allow you to search for the information you want using Structured Query Language (SQL).

Databases store a variety of data elements.   You can put text, numeric data, and even photos, videos, and other binary files into a database.

Structuring Data into Tables

It's important to remember that databases structure data into *tables*. If you have a situation where data is not organized into tables, it might fit better into a flat file format. For example, if you have a list of courses offered by a university, you can design a table that contains the key characteristics of each course. It might look something like Table 30.1.

TABLE 30.1

Department	CourseNumber	CourseName	Semester	Credits	Professor
CHEM	101	Introduction to Chemistry	Fall 2022	3.0	Smith
ECON	220	Macroeconomics	Spring 2023	4.0	Hutchinson
PHIL	220	Modern Philosophy	Spring 2023	3.0	Kolessar

That course data is easily organized into a table. On the other hand, imagine that you had driving directions between the White House and the U.S. Capitol in Washington, D.C. Those directions are step-by-step and would not easily fit into a table. It would better fit into a word processing document as a list, such as this one:

1. Head east on H Street NW.
2. Turn right onto 14th St NW.
3. Turn left onto Independence Ave SW.
4. Turn slight left onto Maryland Ave SW.
5. At the traffic circle, take the first exit onto First St SW.
6. Arrive at the United States Capitol.

Imagine if you tried to organize that information into a table. It would be quite difficult. You might try to create a table with six columns—one for each step of the directions. But what would happen if you tried to add another set of directions that had seven or eight steps? This type of information is just better suited for a flat file than a database.

USING A DATABASE

There are four major stages to configuring and working with the data stored in a database.

1. First, you need to create the database. This involves getting a computer to act as the database server. That computer will do all the processing for your database. The server will also contain one or more hard drives that will physically store the data that's maintained in the database. The use of hard drives is what makes database storage permanent. In IT terminology, we call that permanent storage *data persistence*.
2. Next, you need to get data into your database. This might be accomplished by *importing* existing datasets, such as loading data stored in CSV files or spreadsheets into database tables, or it may involve users *inputting* data directly into the database through a web application or other means.
3. Once your data is in the database, users can run queries and reports against the data. *Queries* are questions that users ask of the database. They're written in SQL, a special programming language.
4. *Reports* are predefined queries that you execute on a regular basis. For example, you might write a query that returns all the sales made by your organization in the last 24 hours. You could then set up a report that runs every night, producing a PDF file or spreadsheet of all those sales, and automatically send that report to sales managers.

CERTMIKE EXAM ESSENTIALS

▶ Database software allows the centralized storage and retrieval of information that is organized into tables.

▶ You should use a database instead of a flat file when you will have multiple concurrent users, when you require scalability or speed, and/or when you have a variety of data to store.

Practice Question 1

You are the IT manager for a midsized company and are helping the sales team develop a new solution for managing customer contacts. They would like a system that allows many different salespeople to access records at the same time and for changes made by one salesperson to be immediately visible to other salespeople.

What type of software would *best* meet this need?

A. Spreadsheet software
B. Accounting software
C. Database software
D. Instant messaging software

Practice Question 2

You are helping a chain of restaurants design a data management strategy. As the first stage of that project, you are identifying the types of information that would best fit into a database and those that would be better suited by other storage mechanisms.

Of the categories of data listed, which would be *least* well suited for storage in a database?

A. Customer contact information
B. Recipes used in the kitchen
C. Restaurant locations
D. Product inventory

Practice Question 1 Explanation

This question is asking us to identify the software that would *best* meet the described need. This is a common format for CompTIA exam questions, and you should be prepared to evaluate all the possible answer choices and find the one that is better than the others.

Let's evaluate these choices one at a time.

First, we have the possibility of using spreadsheet software. This is a possible solution. The sales team could create a spreadsheet of all customer contacts and have each team member update that spreadsheet when they have new information. We can't eliminate this choice up front, so we'll keep it alive for now.

Next, we have accounting software. That doesn't seem like a very good fit. Accounting software is designed to support accounting departments, so it's not going to be designed for supporting a sales team. We can eliminate that possibility.

Database software sounds like a very good fit for this situation. Databases are good at storing information that is organized into tables, and we could organize customer information into a set of tables. A spreadsheet could also handle that information, but databases are also great for applications where multiple users need concurrent access to data. So that makes a database a better solution than a spreadsheet. We'll keep databases alive and eliminate spreadsheets as a possible answer.

Finally, we have instant messaging software. That software is helpful for communicating among the team, but instant messaging software doesn't store data, so it's not a great choice here.

Correct Answer: C. Database software

Practice Question 2 Explanation

This question is asking you to identify which type of information is not well suited for storage in a database. Let's approach this by asking the opposite question for each data element: is this element well suited for storage in a database? We can answer that question by determining how easy it would be to store that information in a table as opposed to a flat file.

The first item is customer contact information. We could easily imagine storing this information in a table. That table might look something like Table 30.2.

TABLE 30.2 Customer contact information stored in a database table

FirstName	LastName	Email	Phone
Mike	Chapple	mike@certmike.com	574-555-1212
Jane	Adams	jadams@yahoo.com	212-555-1212
Mary	Smith	msmith@gmail.com	516-555-1212

So it seems that customer contact information can be stored in a table, and we can eliminate that as a possible answer.

Next, imagine recipes used in the kitchen. These are a series of ingredients and sequential steps, such as the one shown in Figure 30.1.

Gingerbread

75g butter
3 1/2tbsp golden syrup
60g light soft brown sugar
175g plain flour
1/4 tsp bicarbonate of soda
2tsp ground ginger

• Add butter, golden syrup and light brown sugar to a pan. Stir on a low heat until sugar has dissolved.

• Add flour, bicarbonate of soda and ginger to a mixing bowl then stir together. Make a well in the centre and pour in the sugar and butter mixture.

• Stir together to form a dough (it might be easiest to use your hands).

• Wrap in clingfilm and let chill for 30mins to firm up.

• Lay the dough between two sheets of baking parchment. Press dough lightly with a rolling pin. Give a quarter turn than repeat.

• Give it a final quarter turn, then start to roll backwards and forwards, giving regular quarter turns. until dough is roughly thickness of a £1 coin.

• Using a biscuit cutter cut out the shapes. Bake at 190°C (170°C fan) mark 5 for 10 to 12min, until lightly golden brown.

• The biscuits won't be firm but will harden when left to cool outside the oven.

FIGURE 30.1 Recipe example

This recipe presents a very different situation. It's not easy to imagine how you might structure this in a database table. For that reason, we're going to suspect that this might be the correct answer, but let's continue ruling out the other options.

The third data item is restaurant locations. As with our customer data, we can imagine storing that data in a table like Table 30.3.

T A B L E   3 0 . 3   Restaurant location information stored in a database table

RestaurantID	City	State	ZIP
102	Sea Cliff	NY	11579
103	Miami	FL	33131
104	Chicago	IL	60604

Finally, we have product inventory. Table 30.4 shows how a product inventory table might be stored in a database.

T A B L E   3 0 . 4   Product inventory information stored in a database table

ProductName	Quantity	Last Restocked
Chickens	12	1/14/2023
Cucumbers	9	1/16/2023
Eggs	102	1/19/2023

Evaluating all of these options, it seems that the recipes are the least well suited for storage in a database table, so we will choose that as our correct answer.

Correct Answer: B. Recipes used in the kitchen

CHAPTER 31

Database Structures

Objective 5.2: Compare and contrast various database structures

The data we work with every day comes in varying degrees of structure and may be in different formats as we store and process it. All data resides on a spectrum, ranging from highly structured tables to very unstructured, poorly organized data. We store this data in different types of databases, both relational and nonrelational systems.

In this chapter, you'll learn the material that you need to know about ITF+ objective 5.2. The objectives covered in this chapter include:

▶ Structured vs. semi-structured vs. nonstructured
▶ Relational databases
▶ Non-relational databases

STRUCTURING DATA

When you think of data, chances are that spreadsheets come to mind, such as the Microsoft Excel spreadsheet shown in Figure 31.1. Spreadsheets are valuable tools that allow us to organize our data in tabular form. That's an easy way for us to think about our data, and it's the most common way that we store data for use in analytics.

This approach, in which we organize our data into well-defined tables, describes a category of data known as *structured data*. Not only do we find this structured approach to data in spreadsheets, but we also find it in relational databases.

Relational databases allow us to create many different tables of data, each containing information about a single type of person, object, event, or other data subject. Database designers then create relationships between those different tables that describe how the data interacts.

	A	B	C	D	E
1	service_date	day_type	bus	rail_boardings	total_rides
2	1/1/01	U	297192	126455	423647
3	1/2/01	W	780827	501952	1282779
4	1/3/01	W	824923	536432	1361355
5	1/4/01	W	870021	550011	1420032
6	1/5/01	W	890426	557917	1448343
7	1/6/01	A	577401	255356	832757
8	1/7/01	U	375831	169825	545656
9	1/8/01	W	985221	590706	1575927
10	1/9/01	W	978377	599905	1578282
11	1/10/01	W	984884	602052	1586936
12	1/11/01	W	995561	607503	1603064
13	1/12/01	W	1018985	605252	1624237
14	1/13/01	A	591791	270056	861847
15	1/14/01	U	373091	174842	547933
16	1/15/01	W	675845	412149	1087994
17	1/16/01	W	1024367	622163	1646530
18	1/17/01	W	1018690	620343	1639033
19	1/18/01	W	1006996	618832	1625828
20	1/19/01	W	909964	583851	1493815
21	1/20/01	A	582348	263815	846163
22	1/21/01	U	378381	172107	550488
23	1/22/01	W	1005936	598777	1604713
24	1/23/01	W	1019983	610352	1630335

FIGURE 31.1 Microsoft Excel spreadsheet

Figure 31.2 shows an example of a very complex *database schema*. This is the schema for the AdventureWorks database, a database designed by Microsoft to mimic the operations of a bicycle manufacturing company. Each one of the boxes on this diagram represents a different table of data, and each one of the arrows represents a relationship between two tables. You don't need to worry about the complexity of this diagram. I just want you to understand that the data we use in our day-to-day business operations is highly structured.

At the other end of the spectrum, we have *unstructured data*. This is data that doesn't fit neatly into the table model. For example, we might have a collection of photographs, video recordings, word processing documents, and other data sources where users simply enter or collect data without the highly structured framework of a table. While it's true that most of the data that we use in analytics is structured data that lives in spreadsheets and databases, most of the data that exists in the world today is unstructured. It lacks the defined fields of more structured datasets.

Unstructured data often comes from machine data sources. Internet of Things devices, smartphones, tablets, personal computers, and servers all create digital footprints of their activity and often do so in unstructured form. This data can be a treasure trove for analysts seeking to find new data sources for use in their analysis, and organizations that take advantage of their unstructured data may achieve a real competitive edge.

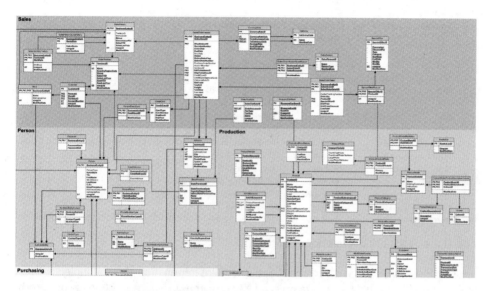

FIGURE 31.2   AdventureWorks database schema

> **NOTE**
>
> We like to put things into clear categories, and it's tempting for data profes-
> sionals to try to describe any data source as either structured or unstructured.
> However, the reality is that data resides on a spectrum, where it can range from
> highly structured, such as a database table, to highly unstructured, such as an
> audio recording. There's also plenty of room in between for data that has ele-
> ments of structure but that retains some unstructured elements.

RELATIONAL DATABASES

Databases use a *relational model* in which we organize our data into tables and each table
contains information about a single subject or topic.

Figure 31.3 shows an example of a table that we might use to track information about
the customers of a business. The subject of this table is customers, and you don't see any
information in the table that doesn't relate to a customer. There's no inventory information,
weather data, store phone numbers, or anything else that doesn't relate to our customers. If
we need to track that type of information, we put it in a different table.

	CustomerID	Cust First Name	Cust Last Name	Cust Street Address
1	1001	Suzanne	Viescas	15127 NE 24th, #383
2	1002	William	Thompson	122 Spring River Drive
3	1003	Gary	Hallmark	Route 2, Box 203B
4	1004	Robert	Brown	672 Lamont Ave
5	1005	Dean	McCrae	4110 Old Redmond Rd.
6	1006	John	Viescas	15127 NE 24th, #383
7	1007	Mariya	Sergienko	901 Pine Avenue
8	1008	Neil	Patterson	233 West Valley Hwy
9	1009	Andrew	Cencini	507 - 20th Ave. E. Apt. 2A
10	1010	Angel	Kennedy	667 Red River Road
11	1011	Alaina	Hallmark	Route 2, Box 203B
12	1012	Liz	Keyser	13920 S.E. 40th Street
13	1013	Rachel	Patterson	2114 Longview Lane
14	1014	Sam	Abolrous	611 Alpine Drive

FIGURE 31.3 Customers database table

Each column in a table is called a *field*, and it contains information about a single characteristic of the subject. For example, we have columns in Figure 31.3 for the customer's first name, last name, street address, and other attributes that we'd like to track about customers.

Each row in the table is called a *record* and it contains information about a single instance of the table subject. In Figure 31.3, our table subject is customers, so each row corresponds to an individual customer. The first row is about Suzanne Viescas, the second row is about William Thompson, and so on.

The rows and columns in a database table are very well defined. That's how databases extend the relational model used by spreadsheets. Data is still organized into single-subject tables, with each column representing a characteristic of the subject and each row representing an instance of the subject.

Database Keys

Every database table contains at least one *key*. Keys are special-purpose database fields that play important roles in the relational model. They help to organize the information in tables and also define the relationships between tables. You need to know about two different types of keys as you prepare for the ITF+ exam: primary keys and foreign keys.

Primary Keys

The *primary key* is the most important field in a database table. Its purpose is to allow the database to uniquely identify the records in a table. When we define a primary key field for a table, we must choose something that will always be unique. Every row in a table must have a unique value for the primary key.

The database enforces a business rule, called a *constraint*, that prevents us from inserting two rows into a table that have the same primary key value. Constraints are technical and business rules that define what values we can enter in a column, and the rule that says primary keys have only unique values is an example of a database constraint. We could create another constraint, for example, that limits us to entering reasonable birthdates for living people. For example, we might say that someone living today must have been born within the last 120 years.

Foreign Keys

The second type of key we need to discuss is the *foreign key*. Foreign keys define the relationships between tables. For example, Figure 31.4 shows a table, Orders, that contains information about orders placed at a company. It has a primary key called OrderID. It also has fields that contain references to other tables.

	OrderNumber	OrderDate	ShipDate	CustomerID	EmployeeID
1	1	2012-09-01 00:00:00.000	2012-09-04 00:00:00.000	1018	707
2	2	2012-09-01 00:00:00.000	2012-09-03 00:00:00.000	1001	703
3	3	2012-09-01 00:00:00.000	2012-09-04 00:00:00.000	1002	707
4	4	2012-09-01 00:00:00.000	2012-09-03 00:00:00.000	1009	703
5	5	2012-09-01 00:00:00.000	2012-09-01 00:00:00.000	1024	708
6	6	2012-09-01 00:00:00.000	2012-09-05 00:00:00.000	1014	702
7	7	2012-09-01 00:00:00.000	2012-09-04 00:00:00.000	1001	708
8	8	2012-09-01 00:00:00.000	2012-09-01 00:00:00.000	1003	703
9	9	2012-09-01 00:00:00.000	2012-09-04 00:00:00.000	1007	708
10	10	2012-09-01 00:00:00.000	2012-09-04 00:00:00.000	1012	701
11	11	2012-09-02 00:00:00.000	2012-09-04 00:00:00.000	1020	706

F I G U R E   3 1 . 4   Orders database table

For example, CustomerID in the Orders table is a reference to the customer ID field in the Customers table. The second record in the Orders table indicates that the order was placed by customer number 1001. That's Suzanne Viescas. We can use this field to combine information from related tables. We already know that CustomerID is the primary key for the Customers table. When we use it in this way in the Orders table, we call it a foreign key. So CustomerID is the primary key of the Customers table and it is a foreign key from the Orders table to the Customers table, as shown in Figure 31.5.

	CustomerID	CustFirstName	CustLastName	CustStreetAddress
	1001	Suzanne	Viescas	15127 NE 24th,#383
2	1002	William	Thompson	122 Spring River Drive
3	1003	Gary	Hallmark	Route 2, Box 203B
4	1004	Robert	Brown	672 Lamont Ave
5	1005	Dean	McCrae	4110 Old Redmond Rd.
6	1006	John	Viescas	15127 NE 24th, #383
7	1007	Mariya	Sergienko	901 Pine Avenue
8	1008	Neil	Patterson	233 West Valley Hwy
9	1009	Andrew	Cencini	507 - 20th Ave. E. Apt. 2A
10	1010	Angel	Kennedy	667 Red River Road
11	1011	Alaina	Hallmark	Route 2, Box 203B
12	1012	Liz	Keyser	13920 S.E. 40th Street
13	1013	Rachel	Petterson	2114 Longview Lane
14	1014	Sam	Abolrous	611 Alpine Drive

	OrderNumber	OrderDate	ShipDate	CustomerID	EmployeeID
1	1	2012-09-01 00:00:00.000	2012-09-04 00:00:00.000	1018	707
	2	2012-09-01 00:00:00.000	2012-09-03 00:00:00.000	1001	703
3	3	2012-09-01 00:00:00.000	2012-09-04 00:00:00.000	1002	707
4	4	2012-09-01 00:00:00.000	2012-09-03 00:00:00.000	1009	703
5	5	2012-09-01 00:00:00.000	2012-09-01 00:00:00.000	1024	708
6	6	2012-09-01 00:00:00.000	2012-09-05 00:00:00.000	1014	702
7	7	2012-09-01 00:00:00.000	2012-09-04 00:00:00.000	1001	708
8	8	2012-09-01 00:00:00.000	2012-09-01 00:00:00.000	1003	703
9	9	2012-09-01 00:00:00.000	2012-09-04 00:00:00.000	1007	708
10	10	2012-09-01 00:00:00.000	2012-09-04 00:00:00.000	1012	701
11	11	2012-09-02 00:00:00.000	2012-09-04 00:00:00.000	1020	706

FIGURE 31.5 CustomerID is a foreign key from the Orders table to the Customers table.

NONRELATIONAL DATABASES

Most databases are relational databases, but there are other types of databases that don't rely on the relational model. These *nonrelational databases* help us with some specialized data storage needs.

Key-value pairs are an example of a semi-structured approach to data storage. They provide a very lightweight way to store data that throws away many of the rules of relational databases. They don't have to be organized into tables. The only requirement is that we have a key that can be used to index the data and one or more values that we wish to store in the database. Each record can have different values and even different numbers of values.

Key-value stores are databases designed specifically to provide efficient storage and very fast retrieval of key-value pairs. They're often used in applications where the data is simple and the most important feature of the database is being able to get at that information quickly.

Figure 31.6 shows a simple example of a table created in DynamoDB, a key-value store from Amazon Web Services. This table contains some simple information about individuals and their skills. Notice that different people have different numbers of skills. When you first look at this table, you might think that it simply has fields labeled skill1, skill2, and skill3 and that the last field is blank for people who have only two skills. However, if you look at the two records that I've excerpted below the table, you'll notice that Hercules Mulligan only has two skill items associated with his record. There is no skill3 item. In this simple example of a key-value store, the employee ID is the key, and all the other fields are values.

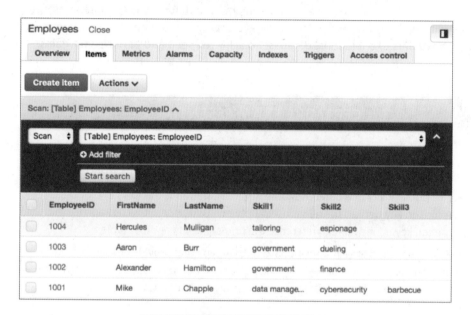

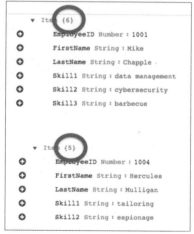

FIGURE 31.6 Table from a key-value store

Document databases (or document stores) are specialized databases designed to store larger documents, such as data in HTML, JSON, or XML format, and index them using a key. They are structured similarly to a key-value store but are optimized for storing extensive documents.

EXAM TIP

Those are just a few examples of nonrelational databases. As you prepare for the exam, you won't need to know the implementation details of these databases, but you should be aware that they exist and that they primarily give up some of the constraints of a relational database to achieve speed and performance gains.

CERTMIKE EXAM ESSENTIALS

▶ Relational databases structure data into tables of related data. Each column in a table represents an attribute and each row in a table represents an instance.

▶ The primary key of a database table uniquely identifies the rows in that table. A foreign key defines the relationship between two tables. It is common for the foreign key in one table to reference the primary key in another table.

▶ Key-value stores are a nonrelational database type that provide efficient storage and very fast retrieval of key-value pairs. Document databases work similarly to key-value stores but are optimized to store large documents.

Practice Question 1

Consider the two tables shown here.

Books

BookID	Title	PublicationYear	AuthorID	Price
1	ITF+ Essentials	2022	101	$40.00
2	CISSP Study Guide	2021	101	$70.00
3	Practical Machine Learning in R	2020	103	$40.00

Authors

AuthorID	FirstName	LastName
101	Mike	Chapple
102	David	Seidl
103	Fred	Nwanganga

Which one of the following statements most likely describes the relationship between these tables?

A. BookID is a foreign key from Books to Authors.
B. BookID is a foreign key from Authors to Books.
C. AuthorID is a foreign key from Books to Authors.
D. AuthorID Is a foreign key from Authors to Books.

Practice Question 2

You are examining the database used by a concert promoter and find that there is a table in that database named Concerts. Examining the table, you see that it contains information about all of the different events run by that promoter. Where would you expect to find the information about a single event?

A. In one column of the Concerts table
B. In several columns of the Concerts table
C. In one row of the Concerts table
D. In several rows of the Concerts table

Practice Question 1 Explanation

These tables aren't labeled with information about which fields are primary keys and foreign keys, so we must attempt to figure that out on our own. We know that every table should have a primary key and that the primary key must be unique for each row. Looking at these tables, it seems as if BookID is the primary key for the Books table and AuthorID is the primary key for the Authors table.

The question is asking us to identify the relationship between the two tables. We see that AuthorID appears in both of these tables, and it would be a natural relationship for a book to have an author.

We can describe this relationship in terms of keys by saying that AuthorID is a foreign key from the Books table (where it is the foreign key) to the Authors table (where it is the primary key).

Correct Answer: C. AuthorID is a foreign key from Books to Authors

Practice Question 2 Explanation

In a relational database table, columns represent attributes of the subject of the table. For example, in a Concerts table, you would expect to find columns with names such as Artist, Date, Time, Venue, and City.

Each row in a relational database table contains information about a single instance of the table subject. Therefore, each row in a Concerts table should contain all the information about one concert.

Correct Answer: C. In one row of the Concerts table

CHAPTER 32

Database Interfaces
Objective 5.3: Summarize methods used to interface with databases

Databases are an incredibly powerful tool that can transform the way an organization works. They play a crucial role in managing our data so that we can easily retrieve the data we need at the moment we need it. We have many different options for interacting with databases, but they are all based on a single standard: Structured Query Language (SQL).

In this chapter, you'll learn the material that you need to know about ITF+ objective 5.3. The objectives covered in this chapter include:

▶ **Relational methods**
▶ **Database access methods**
▶ **Export/import**

STRUCTURED QUERY LANGUAGE (SQL)

Structured Query Language (SQL) is the language of databases. Any time a developer, administrator, or end user interacts with a database, that interaction happens through the use of a SQL command. SQL is divided into two major sublanguages: *data definition language (DDL)* and *data manipulation language (DML)*.

Data Definition Language (DDL)

DDL is used mainly by developers and administrators. It's used to define the structure of the database itself. It doesn't work with the data inside a database, but it sets the ground rules for the database to function.

EXAM TIP

As you prepare for the exam, you'll need to be familiar with the major commands used in SQL. It's important to understand that you're not responsible for writing or reading SQL commands. You just need to know what the major commands are and when you would use them.

You need to know three specific SQL commands that are part of DDL:

- ▶ The CREATE command is used to create a new table within your database or a new database on your server.
- ▶ The ALTER command is used to change the structure of a table that you've already created. If you want to modify your database or table, the ALTER command lets you make those modifications.
- ▶ The DROP command deletes an entire table or database from your server. It's definitely a command that you'll want to use with caution!

The data definition language also contains a series of commands that allow you to change the permissions on a database. The exact commands that you'll use to do this depend on what database software you're using, but each has commands that allow you to grant and revoke permissions for users to access and modify your database.

EXAM TIP

DDL allows administrators to perform four types of action: CREATE, ALTER, DROP, and change permissions. You'll need to understand that these commands are part of the data definition language, that they're used to modify the database itself, and that they're generally used only by administrators and developers.

Data Manipulation Language (DML)

DML is a subset of SQL commands. They don't change the database structure, but they add, remove, and change the data *inside* a database. There are four DML commands that you need to know:

- ▶ The SELECT command is used to retrieve information from a database. It's the most commonly used command in SQL because it is used to pose queries to the database and retrieve the data that you're interested in working with.
- ▶ The INSERT command is used to add new records to a database table. If you're adding a new employee, customer order, or marketing activity, the INSERT command allows you to add one or more rows to your database.
- ▶ The DELETE command is used to delete rows from a database table. It's important not to confuse this command with the DROP command. The DROP command deletes an entire database table, whereas the DELETE command just deletes certain rows from the table.

▶ The UPDATE command is used to modify rows in the database. If you need to change something that is already stored in your database, the UPDATE command will do that.

Figure 32.1 provides a summary chart to help you keep these commands straight. You'll want to memorize these commands as you prepare for the ITF+ exam.

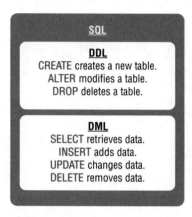

SQL

DDL
CREATE creates a new table.
ALTER modifies a table.
DROP deletes a table.

DML
SELECT retrieves data.
INSERT adds data.
UPDATE changes data.
DELETE removes data.

FIGURE 32.1 SQL command summary

DATABASE ACCESS METHODS

As we wrap up our coverage of relational databases, we need to cover a little bit more about how users, administrators, and developers access databases. You read earlier that everything that happens in a relational database happens as the result of a SQL command, but there are different ways those SQL commands might be written.

Writing SQL Commands

Sometimes people write SQL commands themselves. A developer, administrator, or power user who knows SQL might directly access the database server and send it a SQL command for execution. This often happens through a graphical user interface, such as Microsoft Azure Data Studio, shown in Figure 32.2. This tool allows you to type a database query into the top window pane, click the Run button, and then send your SQL command to the database server. The database server executes the command and then sends the results back to Azure Data Studio, which displays them in the bottom pane.

Utilities like Azure Data Studio can do more than just retrieve data. They also offer a graphical way for database administrators to reconfigure a database. You can click through

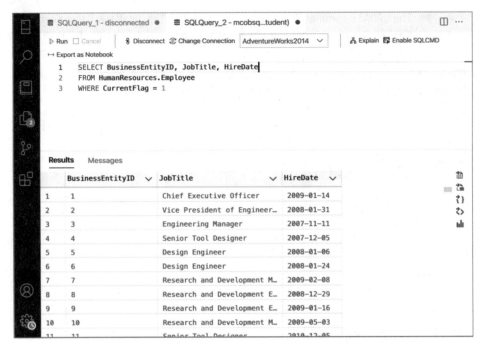

FIGURE 32.2 Executing a SQL command in Azure Data Studio

a series of menus to choose the changes you'd like to make to the database, and the utility writes SQL commands that carry out your requests and sends them to the database.

Query and Report Builders

Similarly, there are many query and report builder tools available that simplify database access for end users, allowing them to click through a series of menus and drag objects around on the screen to retrieve data from a database. The tools then translate those actions into SELECT statements that retrieve the desired information from the database.

Exporting Data

We also sometimes need to export data from a database for different purposes. We might perform a database dump to export large amounts of data from our database to another system. We also should regularly back up our database in full. This ensures that we have an extra copy of our database in case the database server fails or someone makes a mistake and we need to restore our data from those backups.

Programmatic Interactions

Finally, computer software can interact with databases programmatically. This just means that software can send SQL commands to the database as part of its activity. For example, when you fill out a form on a company's website, chances are that software is processing that form and then storing a record of your activity in a database.

CERTMIKE EXAM ESSENTIALS

▶ Structured Query Language (SQL) has two components. Data definition language (DDL) is used to modify the structure of the database, whereas data manipulation language (DML) is used to retrieve and manipulate the information in a database.

▶ In DDL, the CREATE command is used to create a new table or database. The ALTER command is used to modify an existing table or database. The DROP command is used to remove an entire table or database.

▶ In DML, the SELECT command is used to retrieve information from a database. The INSERT command is used to add information to a database. The UPDATE command is used to modify information in a database, and the DELETE command is used to remove information from a database table.

Practice Question 1

Your organization is changing the way that it conducts part of its business, and there is a database table that you no longer need. What command can you use to remove that table from the database?

A. ALTER
B. DELETE
C. UPDATE
D. DROP

Practice Question 2

You have been asked to retrieve information from a database. Your supervisor would like you to find the names of all customers who have not placed an order within the last year so that they can be sent a mailing with a special promotional offer. What SQL command would you use to obtain the required data?

A. SELECT
B. QUERY
C. RETRIEVE
D. UPDATE

Practice Question 1 Explanation

The DROP command is used to delete entire tables and databases from a database server. That is the appropriate command to use in this case.

This command is often confused with the DELETE command, which is used to remove some or all rows from a database table. The DELETE command removes these rows but cannot remove an entire database table.

The UPDATE command is used to modify the contents of existing rows, and the ALTER command is used to change the structure or configuration of a database or table.

Correct Answer: D. DROP

Practice Question 2 Explanation

The SELECT command is used to retrieve information from a database. You may use the SELECT command with a WHERE clause to search for database records that match certain criteria. (But don't worry, you don't need to know about WHERE clauses on the ITF+ exam!)

The UPDATE command is used to modify information contained in a database. This scenario does not ask you to change any information, so you should not use the UPDATE command.

RETRIEVE and QUERY are not valid SQL commands.

Correct Answer: A. SELECT

Domain 6.0: Security

Security is the sixth domain of CompTIA's ITF+ exam. In this domain, you'll learn the tools and techniques that IT professionals use to protect the confidentiality, integrity, and availability of information and systems under their care. This domain has seven objectives:

6.1 Summarize confidentiality, integrity, and availability concerns

6.2 Explain methods to secure devices and best practices

6.3 Summarize behavioral security concepts

6.4 Compare and contrast authentication, authorization, accounting, and nonrepudiation concepts

6.5 Explain password best practices

6.6 Explain common uses of encryption

6.7 Explain business continuity concepts

Questions from this domain make up 20% of the questions on the ITF+ exam, so you should expect to see approximately 15 questions on your test covering the material in this part.

CHAPTER 33

Confidentiality, Integrity, and Availability

Objective 6.1: Summarize confidentiality, integrity, and availability concerns

Information plays a vital role in the operations of the modern business, and we find ourselves entrusted with sensitive information about our customers, employees, internal operations, and other critical matters. As IT professionals, we must work with information security teams, other technology professionals, and business leaders to protect the security of that information.

In this chapter, you'll learn the material that you need to know about ITF+ objective 6.1. The objectives covered in this chapter include:

▶ **Confidentiality concerns**
▶ **Integrity concerns**
▶ **Availability concerns**

THE CIA TRIAD

When we talk about cybersecurity, we're referring to three main concerns: the confidentiality of information, the integrity of information, and the availability of information. You can remember these three main goals by thinking of the CIA triad shown in Figure 33.1. Each side covers one of the three main goals. The remainder of this chapter explores each of these concerns in detail.

F I G U R E   3 3 . 1   **The CIA triad summarizes the three main concerns of cybersecurity: confidentiality, integrity, and availability.**

CONFIDENTIALITY

Confidentiality ensures that only authorized individuals have access to information and resources. This is what most people think of when they think about information security—keeping secrets away from prying eyes. And it is, in fact, how security professionals spend the majority of their time.

> **EXAM TIP**
>
> As you prepare for the exam, you'll need to understand the main threats against each of the cybersecurity objectives. For confidentiality, we have five main concerns: snooping, dumpster diving, eavesdropping, wiretapping, and social engineering.

Snooping

Snooping is exactly what the name implies. The individual engaging in snooping wanders around your office or other facility and simply looks to see what information they can gather. When people leave sensitive papers on their desks or in a public area, it creates an opportunity for snooping.

Organizations can protect against snooping by enforcing a *clean desk policy*. Employees should maintain a clean workspace and put away any sensitive materials whenever they step away, even if it's just for a moment.

Dumpster Diving

Dumpster diving attacks also look for sensitive materials, but the attacker doesn't walk around the office. Instead they look through the trash, trying to find sensitive documents that an employee threw in the garbage or recycling bin.

You can protect your organization against dumpster diving attacks using a pretty simple piece of technology: a paper shredder! If you destroy documents before discarding them, you'll protect against a dumpster diver pulling them out of the trash.

Eavesdropping

Eavesdropping attacks come in both physical and electronic types. In a physical eavesdropping attack, the attacker simply positions themself where they can overhear conversations, such as in a cafeteria or hallway, and then listens for sensitive information.

We can protect against eavesdropping attacks by putting rules in place limiting where sensitive conversations may take place. For example, sensitive conversations should generally take place in a closed office or conference room.

Wiretapping

Electronic eavesdropping attacks are also known as *wiretapping*. They occur when an attacker gains access to a network and monitors the data being sent electronically within an office.

The best way to protect against electronic eavesdropping attacks is to use encryption to protect information being sent over the network. If data is encrypted, an attacker who intercepts that data won't be able to make any sense of it. You'll learn more about encryption in Chapter 38, "Encryption."

Social Engineering

The last type of confidentiality attack you need to know about is *social engineering*. In a social engineering attack, the attacker uses psychological tricks to persuade an employee to give them sensitive information or access to internal systems. They might pretend that they're on an urgent assignment from a senior leader, impersonate an IT technician, or send a phishing email.

It's difficult to protect against social engineering attacks. The best defense against these attacks is educating users to recognize the dangers of social engineering and empower them to intervene when they suspect an attack is taking place.

INTEGRITY

Security professionals are also responsible for protecting the *integrity* of an organization's information. This means that there aren't any unauthorized changes to information. These unauthorized changes may come in the form of a hacker seeking to intentionally alter information or a service disruption accidentally affecting data stored in a system. In either case, it's the information security professional's responsibility to prevent these lapses in integrity.

> **EXAM TIP**
>
> As you prepare for the exam, you'll need to know about four different types of integrity attacks: the unauthorized modification of information, impersonation attacks, man-in-the-middle attacks, and replay attacks.

Unauthorized Information Alteration

The unauthorized modification of information occurs when an attacker gains access to a system and makes changes that violate a security policy. This might be an external attacker, such as an intruder breaking into a financial system and issuing themselves checks, or it might be an internal attack, such as an employee increasing their own salary in the payroll system.

Following the principle of *least privilege* is the best way to protect against integrity attacks. Organizations should carefully consider the permissions that each employee needs to perform their job and then limit employees to the smallest set of permissions possible.

Impersonation

In an *impersonation* attack, the attacker pretends to be someone other than who they actually are. They might impersonate a manager, an executive, or an IT technician in order to convince someone to change data in a system. This is an extension of the social engineering attacks discussed earlier, and the best defense against these attacks is strong user education.

Man-in-the-Middle Attacks

Sometimes impersonation attacks are electronic. In a *man-in-the-middle* (MITM) attack (also known as an on-path attack), the attacker intercepts network traffic as a user is logging into a system and pretends to be that system. They then sit in the middle of the communication, relaying information between the user and the system while they monitor everything that is occurring. In this type of attack, the attacker might be able to steal a user's password and use it later to log into the system themself. These attacks can also be used to tamper with data before it reaches its intended destination.

Replay Attacks

In a *replay attack*, the attacker doesn't get in the middle of the communication but finds a way to observe a legitimate user logging into a system. They then capture the information used to log into the system and later replay it on the network to gain access themself.

The best defense against both replay and man-in-the-middle attacks is the use of encryption to protect communications. For example, web traffic might use the Transport Layer Security (TLS) protocol to prevent an eavesdropper from observing network traffic.

AVAILABILITY

As a security professional, you must also understand how to apply security controls that protect the *availability* of information and systems. As the third leg of the CIA triad, availability controls ensure that information and systems remain available to authorized users when needed. They protect against disruptions to normal system operation or data availability.

> **EXAM TIP**
>
> As you prepare for the ITF+ exam, you'll need to know about five different types of events that can disrupt the availability of systems: denial-of-service attacks, power outages, hardware failures, destruction of equipment, and service outages.

Denial-of-Service Attacks

Denial-of-service (DoS) attacks occur when a malicious individual bombards a system with an overwhelming amount of traffic. The idea is to send so many requests to a server that it is unable to answer any requests from legitimate users.

We can protect our systems against DoS attacks by using firewalls that block illegitimate requests and by partnering with our Internet service providers to block DoS attacks before they reach our networks.

Power Outages

Power outages can occur on a local or regional level for many different reasons. Increased demand can overwhelm the power grid, natural disasters can disrupt service, and other factors can cause power outages that disrupt access to systems.

We can protect against power outages by having redundant power sources and backup generators that supply power to our systems when commercial power is not available.

Hardware Failures

Hardware failures can and do occur. Servers, hard drives, network gear, and other equipment all fail occasionally and can disrupt access to information. That's an availability problem.

We can protect against hardware failures by building systems that have built-in redundancy so that if one component fails, another is ready to pick up the slack.

Destruction of Equipment

Sometimes equipment is just outright destroyed. This might be the result of intentional or accidental physical damage, or it may be the result of a larger disaster, such as a fire or a hurricane.

We can protect against small-scale destruction with redundant systems. If we want to protect against larger-scale disasters, we may need to have backup data centers in remote locations or in the cloud that can keep running when our primary data center is disrupted.

Service Outages

Finally, sometimes *service outages* occur. This might be due to programming errors, the failure of underlying equipment, or many other reasons. These outages disrupt user access to systems and information and are, therefore, an availability concern.

We can protect against service outages by building systems that are resilient in the face of errors and hardware failures.

CERTMIKE EXAM ESSENTIALS

▶ Confidentiality ensures that only authorized individuals have access to information and resources. As you prepare for the ITF+ exam, you should be aware of five major confidentiality threats: snooping, eavesdropping, wiretapping, social engineering, and dumpster diving.

▶ Integrity protects information from unauthorized changes. As you prepare for the ITF+ exam, you should be aware of four major threats to integrity: man-in-the-middle attacks, replay attacks, impersonation, and unauthorized information alteration.

▶ Availability ensures that information and systems are available for authorized use. As you prepare for the ITF+ exam, you should be aware of five major threats to availability: denial-of-service attacks, power outages, hardware failure, destruction, and service outages.

Practice Question 1

Which one of the following security risks would most likely be considered an availability issue?

A. Replay attack
B. Power outage
C. Social engineering
D. Snooping

Practice Question 2

What are the three major objectives of cybersecurity programs?

A. Confidentiality, integrity, and availability
B. Confidentiality, integrity, and authorization
C. Confidentiality, infrastructure, and authorization
D. Communications, infrastructure, and authorization

Practice Question 1 Explanation

Availability issues affect the ability of authorized users to gain access to information, systems, or other resources that they need. All of the issues listed here are cybersecurity risks that you need to be aware of when you take the ITF+ exam, but only power outages are classified as an availability risk. This is because a power outage can easily disrupt access to systems and information by causing those systems to be offline.

Replay attacks allow an unauthorized individual to impersonate a legitimate user and are primarily considered integrity risks.

Social engineering and snooping attacks may allow an attacker to gain access to sensitive information, and they are primarily considered confidentiality risks.

Correct Answer: B. Power outage

Practice Question 2 Explanation

The three major objectives of any cybersecurity program are protecting the confidentiality, integrity, and availability of systems and information.

Confidentiality ensures that only authorized individuals have access to information and resources. Integrity protects information from unauthorized changes. Availability ensures that information and systems are available for authorized use.

Correct Answer: A. Confidentiality, integrity, and availability

CHAPTER 34

Securing Devices
Objective 6.2: Explain methods to secure devices and best practices

We make use of many different types of computing devices in our businesses. From laptops and desktops to smartphones and tablets, organizations have hundreds or thousands of different devices connected to their networks and handling sensitive information. IT professionals must work to keep these devices secure because a single insecure device can open a network up to attack.

In this chapter, you'll learn the material that you need to know about ITF+ objective 6.2. The objectives covered in this chapter include:

▶ Securing devices (mobile/workstation)
▶ Device use best practices

DEVICE SECURITY

Security professionals have a variety of tools at their disposal to protect devices from common security threats. These include antivirus software, host firewalls, passwords, safe web browsing practices, and regular patching and updates.

Antivirus Software

Every device should have *antivirus software* installed that protects it from malicious software, or malware. Viruses, worms, ransomware, Trojan horses, and many other threats roam the Internet and threaten to compromise devices. Antivirus software scans files stored on computers or downloaded from the Internet for common threats and blocks malicious files from running on computers. It's one of the cornerstones of cybersecurity.

> **EXAM TIP**
> Modern security packages protect against many more threats than just viruses, so they are also called antimalware software. For our purposes, we can consider these two terms to mean the same thing.

Host Firewalls

Devices should also have *host firewalls* that block unwanted inbound connections from elsewhere on the network. The "host" in host firewall simply means that the firewall runs on a specific device and protects only that device, as opposed to a network firewall that protects an entire network. Organizations should use a combination of both host and network firewalls to provide strong protections.

Host firewalls work by restricting the systems and ports that may communicate with a device. The typical end user computer doesn't need to accept any inbound connections at all—there's simply no need for connections that aren't started by the end user. The most common exception to this is when remote management tools designed to allow remote IT support are installed on systems. In those cases, you may need to configure the host firewall to allow this type of network traffic, but you should limit the access to computers that are part of the help desk and to the specific port used for that remote access. Your networking team can help you figure this out.

Passwords

Passwords are the most basic form of authentication used to restrict access to a computer. You'll learn about more secure authentication mechanisms in Chapter 36, "Authentication, Authorization, Accounting, and Nonrepudiation," but at the very least, computers and other devices should have passwords enabled. Administrators should also remove any default passwords that came configured on the device to prevent anyone who knows that default password from gaining access.

Updates and Patching

Devices frequently need security updates to continue to protect themselves against new threats. Software and operating system vendors release *patches* that fix security vulnerabilities and protect systems from many types of malware and hacking techniques that exploit old vulnerabilities that remain on systems.

Safe Web Browsing Practices

Finally, systems should be configured to enforce safe web browsing practices. Users should be prompted to confirm that they wish to download software any time a remote website tries to install software on their systems, and any software they accept should be run through a malware scan. Administrators should also use content filtering technology to block users from accidentally visiting malicious websites.

SOFTWARE SECURITY

We also face some security risks from the software that we install and run on our systems. Software may contain errors, or even intentional flaws that jeopardize the security of the systems that run them. And if a system runs insecure software and becomes compromised, that could jeopardize the security of the entire network.

For this reason, IT professionals should carefully monitor what types of software run on their systems. When a user wants to use a new software package, it's important to analyze that software for potential security risks and make sure that it's safe before moving forward with the installation.

Software Sources

One of the most important things that you can do when evaluating new software is validate that it came from a legitimate source. This may require some research on your part, investigating what company or developer created the software and what it's intended to do. You can be much more trusting of software that comes from a major developer, such as Microsoft, Apple, or SAP, than you might be of software from a company that you've never heard of before.

Also, make sure that you're obtaining software from a trustworthy source. If you're downloading software from the Internet, be certain that you're downloading a copy from the vendor's website and not from a third-party site. If you download software from any source other than the original equipment manufacturer (OEM), then it's possible that a third party modified the software and created a security vulnerability.

Removal of Software

Finally, you should continue to monitor the software installed on your systems and remove software that is suspected to be malicious, that is unwanted, or that is no longer necessary to meet business requirements. The more software packages you have installed on a system, the greater the possibility that the system will have some serious security flaws. This concept of reducing the amount of software on a system to the smallest possible amount is known as reducing the attack surface.

CERTMIKE EXAM ESSENTIALS

▶ Security professionals are responsible for adopting security controls that protect devices in their organizations. Common device security controls include antivirus software, host firewalls, passwords, safe browsing practices, and patching/updates.

▶ Verify the sources of software used in your organization to validate that it comes from a legitimate source. These sources may include the original equipment manufacturer (OEM) or third-party software vendors.

▶ Monitor the software installed on systems in your organization and promptly remove any software that is unwanted, unnecessary, or potentially malicious.

Practice Question 1

Which one of the following security controls is *least* likely to prevent the installation of malware on a computer?

A. Antivirus software
B. Safe browsing practices
C. Strong passwords
D. Patching

Practice Question 2

You are working with a user at a branch office and are trying to connect to their system by Remote Desktop. You are unable to make the connection even though the user verified that the software is running on their computer. You are able to connect to the systems belonging to other users in the same office. What component should you check first as the likely source of the problem?

A. Network firewall
B. Antivirus software
C. Content filters
D. Host firewall

Practice Question 1 Explanation

Antivirus software is designed specifically to detect and block malware, so it would definitely be of assistance here. Applying security patches protects systems against common vulnerabilities used to install malware, so it would also be an effective control. Malware often infects systems when users visit malicious websites and unintentionally install it, so safe web browsing practices would also be effective.

While strong passwords are an important security control, they are less likely to protect against malware infections than other types of attack.

Correct Answer: C. Strong passwords

Practice Question 2 Explanation

The immediate conclusion you should come to is that some component is blocking the network connection, and this is the work normally performed by firewalls. Neither antivirus software nor content filters typically interfere with network connection attempts, so we can rule out both of those answer choices from the start.

This leaves us with the possibility that the connection is being blocked by either a network firewall or a host firewall, both of which are reasonable possibilities. However, we also know that you are able to connect to the systems belonging to other users in the same office. All users in an office would be protected by the same network firewall, so it is unlikely that the network firewall is the problem. It is far more likely that this individual computer's host firewall is incorrectly configured and needs to be adjusted to allow remote access.

Correct Answer: D. Host firewall

CHAPTER 35

Behavioral Security

Objective 6.3: Summarize behavioral security concepts

IT professionals spend much of their time working with end users, and it is important to understand how the behavior of those users affects security. As you prepare for the ITF+ exam, you must have a strong understanding of when users should have an expectation of privacy and the security controls you can use to protect confidential information.

In this chapter, you'll learn the material that you need to know about ITF+ objective 6.3. The objectives covered in this chapter include:

▶ **Expectations of privacy**
▶ **Written policies and procedures**
▶ **Handling of confidential information**

PRIVACY

In the digital era, the organizations we deal with collect a lot of information about individual people and their actions. From credit card transactions to educational records, each of us generates a significant trail of data behind us, and we are rightfully concerned about the *privacy* of that information.

As IT professionals, we have a few interests in how organizations collect and use personal information:

> ▶ We're obviously concerned about the privacy of our own personal information.
> ▶ We have a responsibility to educate the users in our organization about how they can protect their own personal information.
> ▶ We have a responsibility to assist the privacy officials within our organization with the work they need to do to protect the personal information entrusted to our organization.

Types of Private Information

Private information may come in many forms. Two of the most common elements of private information are personally identifiable information and protected health information:

> ▶ *Personally identifiable information (PII)* includes all information that can be tied back to a specific individual.
> ▶ *Protected health information (PHI)* includes health care records that are regulated under the Health Insurance Portability and Accountability Act (HIPAA).

Expectation of Privacy

Privacy programs are based on a legal principle known as the *reasonable expectation of privacy*. Many laws that govern whether information must be protected are based on whether the person disclosing the information had a reasonable expectation of privacy when they did so and whether the disclosure would violate that reasonable expectation of privacy.

When you put content on social media, whether it be a post on a social networking site or a comment on a shared video, you generally have no reasonable expectation of privacy. You're posting that content publicly or to a large group of people, and a reasonable person would assume that is not a private conversation.

However, when you send a message to someone over email or instant messaging, or share a file through a file sharing site with a specific person or small group, you do have an expectation of privacy. If you don't encrypt the message, you do run the risk that others will eavesdrop on the message, but you have a more reasonable expectation of privacy.

At the other end of the spectrum, when you provide private information to a government agency through their website, such as completing your taxes or registering for a medical insurance program, you have a much greater expectation of privacy. In those cases, you expect that the agency collecting information from you will treat that information with care and not share it without your permission. And, in fact, most countries have laws that require this information be kept private.

When you're using a computer or network that belongs to your employer, you generally do not have a reasonable expectation of privacy. The employer owns that equipment and is normally legally entitled to monitor the use of their systems. If you're using software on your employer's desktop computer, accessing business information over a corporate network, or even using the Internet at work for personal use, you generally should not expect to have privacy for your communication.

As an IT professional, you should communicate to users clearly and accurately about their privacy expectations. It's important to reinforce that when employees of your organization are using systems or networks that belong to the organization, they should not have an expectation of privacy.

You also need to ensure that you and your organization are appropriately handling confidential information. In addition to personal information about employees and customers, you should take steps to safeguard other sensitive information, including passwords and company confidential information.

SECURITY POLICIES AND PROCEDURES

Security professionals do a lot of writing! We need clearly written guidance to help communicate to business leaders, end users, and each other about security expectations and responsibilities. In some cases, we're setting forth mandatory rules that everyone in the organization must follow, whereas in other cases we're simply giving advice. Each of these roles requires communicating a bit differently.

That's where the security policy framework comes into play. Most security professionals recognize a framework consisting of four different types of documents: policies, standards, guidelines, and procedures.

Security Policies

Security policies are the bedrock documents that provide the foundation for an organization's information security program. They are often developed over a long period of time and carefully written to describe an organization's security expectations.

Compliance with policies is mandatory and policies are often approved at the very highest levels of an organization. Because of the rigor involved in developing security policies, authors should strive to write them in a way that will stand the test of time.

For example, statements like "All sensitive information must be encrypted with AES-256 encryption" or "Store all employee records in Room 225" are not good policy statements. What happens if the organization switches encryption technologies or moves its records room?

Instead, a policy might make statements like "Sensitive information must be encrypted both at rest and in transit using technology approved by the IT department" and "Employee records must be stored in a location approved by Human Resources." Those statements are much more likely to stand the test of time.

Security Standards

Security standards prescribe the specific details of security controls that the organization must follow. Standards derive their authority from policy. In fact, it's likely that an organization's security policy would include specific statements giving the IT department authority to create and enforce standards. They're the place to include things like the company's approved encryption protocols, record storage locations, configuration parameters, and other technical and operational details.

Even though standards might not go through as rigorous a process as policies, compliance with them is still mandatory.

Security Guidelines

Security professionals use *guidelines* to provide advice to the rest of the organization, including best practices for information security. For example, a guideline might suggest that employees use encrypted wireless networks whenever they are available. There might be situations where a traveling employee does not have access to an encrypted network, so they can compensate for that by using a VPN connection. Remember, guidelines are advice. Compliance with guidelines is not mandatory.

Security Procedures

Procedures are step-by-step instructions that employees may follow when performing a specific security task. For example, the organization might have a procedure for activating the incident response team that involves sending an urgent SMS alert to team members, activating a videoconference, and informing senior management.

Depending on the organization and the type of procedure, compliance may be mandatory or optional.

EXAM TIP

When you take the exam, be sure that you keep the differences between policies, standards, guidelines, and procedures straight. Specifically, remember that compliance with policies and standards is always mandatory. Complying with guidelines is always optional, and compliance with procedures can go either way depending on the organization and the specific procedure in question.

CERTMIKE EXAM ESSENTIALS

▶ IT professionals have an obligation to protect the privacy of personal information, particularly when the individuals involved have a reasonable expectation of privacy.

▶ The types of personal information that must be safeguarded include personally identifiable information (PII), which is any personal information that may be tied to an individual, and protected health information (PHI), which includes medical records.

▶ The common types of security documents include policies, standards, guidelines, and procedures. Compliance with policies and standards is always mandatory.

Practice Question 1

Of the people described below, who would have the least expectation of privacy?

A. Patient discussing medical records with a nurse
B. Employee sending an email to a friend in the office
C. Student discussing grades with a teacher
D. Two people having a private conversation

Practice Question 2

You are writing a document that explains the step-by-step process that your organization's help desk should follow when helping a user reset a forgotten password. What type of document are you creating?

A. Policy
B. Standard
C. Procedure
D. Guideline

Practice Question 1 Explanation

A patient discussing medical records with a nurse is in a situation where there is a strong expectation of privacy. These records are protected health information (PHI) and should be treated very carefully. Of the situations listed, this is likely the one with the greatest expectation of privacy.

A student discussing grades with a teacher and two people having a private conversation are also in situations where they should have some expectation of privacy.

An employee of an organization sending an email at work has no expectation of privacy. The employer is entitled to inspect any information sent or received using a work computer, even if that information is of a personal nature.

Correct Answer: B. Employee sending an email to a friend in the office

Practice Question 2 Explanation

The key to answering this question correctly is noticing that the document is a step-by-step process. This type of process should be documented in a procedure.

Security policies are high-level documents that would not contain technical details and certainly would not include the specific steps followed by a help desk. Standards normally describe technical requirements for information and systems. Guidelines are optional processes that provide best practice advice.

Correct Answer: C. Procedure

Authentication, Authorization, Accounting, and Nonrepudiation

Objective 6.4: Compare and contrast authentication, authorization, accounting, and nonrepudiation concepts

Protecting access to systems and other resources requires that we allow authorized individuals to access that data while blocking any unauthorized access attempts. In order to do this, we must have confidence that a user is who they claim to be and know what they are allowed to do. The authentication and authorization processes provide us with this confidence.

In this chapter, you'll learn the material that you need to know about ITF+ objective 6.4. The objectives covered in this chapter include:

► **Authentication**
► **Authorization**
► **Accounting**
► **Nonrepudiation**

ACCESS CONTROL

As IT professionals, one of the most important things that we do is ensure that only authorized individuals gain access to information, systems, and networks under our protection. The *access control* process consists of three steps that you must understand: identification, authentication, and authorization.

Identification

During the first step of the process, *identification*, an individual makes a claim about their identity. The person trying to gain access doesn't present any proof at this point; they simply make an assertion. It's important to remember that the identification step is only a claim and the user could certainly be making a false claim! Imagine a physical world scenario in which you want to enter a secure office building where you have an appointment. During the identification step of the process, I would walk up to the security desk and say, "Hi, I'm Mike Chapple."

Authentication

Proof comes into play during the second step of the process: *authentication*. During the authentication step, the individual proves their identity to the satisfaction of the access control system. In our office building example, the guard would likely wish to see my driver's license to confirm my identity.

Authorization

Just proving your identity isn't enough to gain access to a system, however. The access control system also needs to be satisfied that you are *allowed* to access the system. That's the third step of the access control process: *authorization*. In our office building example, the security guard might check a list of that day's appointments to see if it includes my name.

Digital Authentication and Authorization

So far, we've talked about identification, authentication, and authorization in the context of gaining access to a building. Let's talk about how they work in the electronic world.

When we go to log in to a system, we most often identify ourselves using a username, most likely composed of some combination of the letters from our names. When we reach the authentication phase, we're commonly asked to enter a password.

Finally, in the electronic world, authorization often takes the form of *access control lists (ACLs)* that itemize the specific filesystem permissions granted to an individual user or group of users. Users proceed through the identification, authentication, and authorization processes when they request access to a resource.

Accounting

In addition to this process, access control systems provide accounting functionality that allows administrators to track user activity and reconstruct it from logs. This may include tracking user activity on systems and even logging user web browsing history. Any tracking that takes place as part of an organization's monitoring program should fit within the boundaries set by the law and the organization's privacy policy.

> **NOTE**
> Together, the activities of authentication, authorization, and accounting are commonly described as AAA, or "triple A."

As you design access control systems, you need to think about the mechanisms that you use to perform each of these tasks. You also want to consider the environments supported by identity and access management mechanisms. In a modern computing environment, where organizations combine resources from both cloud and on-premises systems, you'll want an *identity and access management (IAM)* system that can work across both environments.

AUTHENTICATION FACTORS

Computer systems offer many different authentication techniques that allow users to prove their identity. Let's take a look at three different authentication factors:

▶ Something you know
▶ Something you are
▶ Something you have

Something You Know

By far, the most common authentication factor is *something you know*. We've already talked about how passwords are the most commonly used authentication technique. This is a "something you know" factor because the password is something that the user remembers and enters into a system during the authentication process. Personal identification numbers (PINs) and the answers to security questions are also examples of something you know.

Something You Are

The second authentication factor is *something you are*. *Biometric* authentication techniques measure one of your physical characteristics, such as a fingerprint, eye pattern, face, or voice. Figure 36.1 shows an example of a smartphone fingerprint reader performing biometric authentication.

FIGURE 36.1 **Fingerprint authentication on a smartphone**

Figure 36.2 shows a more complex eye scan being performed as a biometric access control for entering a facility.

Something You Have

The third authentication factor, *something you have*, requires the user to have physical possession of a device, such as a smartphone running a software token application or a hardware authentication token keyfob. These devices generate one-time passwords that are displayed to the user and allow them to prove that they have access to a physical device.

FIGURE 36.2 Eye scan authentication entering a facility

EXAM TIP

The exam objectives also mention that a user's presence in a specific geographic location can be used as part of the authentication process. Location data may indeed be used to strengthen an authentication process, but it does not provide authentication itself. The fact that I am located inside a secure office building may make a system more confident that I am an employee, but it doesn't make the system more confident that I am a specific employee, since many different people have access to the building.

A common way to use location-based authentication is to reduce the authentication requirements if a user is physically present in a secure location. For example, a company might only require password authentication for users located in a secure facility while requiring the use of a second factor for those outside the secure location.

Multifactor Authentication

When used alone, any one of these techniques provides some security for systems. However, they each have their own drawbacks. For example, an attacker might steal a user's password through a phishing attack. Once they have the password, they can then use that password to assume the user's identity. Other authentication factors aren't foolproof either. If you use smartcard authentication to implement something you have, the user may lose the smartcard. Someone coming across it may then impersonate the user.

The solution to this problem is to combine authentication techniques from multiple factors, such as combining something you know with something you have. This approach is known as *multifactor authentication (MFA)*.

Take the two techniques we just discussed: passwords and smartcards. When used alone, either one is subject to hackers gaining knowledge of the password or stealing a smartcard. However, if an authentication system requires both a password (something you know) and a smartcard (something you have), it brings added security. If the hacker steals the password, they don't have the required smartcard, and vice versa. It suddenly becomes much more difficult for the attacker to gain access to the account. Because something you know and something you have are different factors—this is multifactor authentication.

We can combine other factors as well. For example, a fingerprint reader (something you are) might also require the entry of a PIN (something you know). That's another example of multifactor authentication.

When evaluating multifactor authentication, it's important to remember that the techniques must be *different* factors. An approach that combines a password with the answer to a security question is *not* multifactor authentication because both factors are something you know.

> **EXAM TIP**
> When you take the exam, you'll likely find a question about multifactor authentication. Be careful to ensure that the authentication techniques come from two different factors. Mistaking two "something you know" techniques for multifactor authentication is a common exam mistake!

Single Sign-On

The last authentication concept we need to discuss is *single sign-on (SSO)*. This technology shares authenticated sessions across systems. Many organizations create SSO solutions within their organizations to help users avoid the burden of repeatedly authenticating. In an SSO approach, users log on to the first SSO-enabled system they encounter and then that login session persists across other systems until it reaches its expiration. If the organization sets the expiration period to be the length of a business day, it means that users only need to log in once per day and then their single sign-on will last the entire day.

AUTHORIZATION

Authorization is the final step in the access control process. Once an individual successfully authenticates to a system, authorization determines the privileges that individual has to access resources and information.

Least Privilege

Before we discuss the different ways that you can implement authorization, let's cover an important underlying principle: the principle of *least privilege*. This principle states that an individual should only have the minimum set of permissions necessary to accomplish their job duties.

   Least privilege is important for two reasons:

▶ Least privilege minimizes the potential damage from an insider attack. If an employee turns malicious, the damage they can cause will be limited by the privileges assigned to them by job role. It's unlikely, for example, that an accountant would be able to deface the company website because an accountant's job responsibilities have nothing to do with updating web content.

▶ Least privilege limits the ability of an external attacker to quickly gain privileged access when compromising an employee's account. Unless they happen to compromise a system administrator's account, they will find themselves limited by the privileges of the account that they steal.

Authorization Models

We use the principle of least privilege when we design the access control systems that enforce authorization requirements. We have several different authorization models that we can use when designing these systems.

Mandatory Access Control

Mandatory access control (MAC) systems are the most stringent type of access control. In MAC systems, the operating system itself restricts the permissions that may be granted to users and processes on system resources. Users themselves cannot modify permissions. For this reason, MAC is rarely fully implemented on production systems outside of highly secure environments. MAC is normally implemented as a rule-based access control system where users and resources have labels and the operating system makes access control decisions by comparing those labels.

Discretionary Access Control

Discretionary access control (DAC) systems offer a flexible approach to authorization, allowing users to assign access permissions to other users—the owners of files, computers, and other resources have the *discretion* to configure permissions as they see fit. Discretionary access control systems are the most common form of access control because they provide organizations with needed flexibility. Imagine if users in your organization didn't have the ability to assign file rights to other users as needed and IT had to be involved in every request. That would certainly make life difficult, wouldn't it?

Most organizations use DAC systems to restrict access to their data. Users who own files can grant permission to access those files to other users. They do this by changing the permissions on an access control list (ACL) for that file, such as the one shown in Figure 36.3.

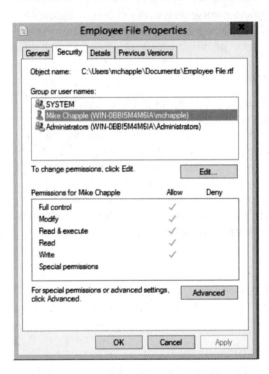

FIGURE 36.3 Microsoft Windows access control list

Role-Based Access Control

Role-based access control (RBAC) systems simplify some of the work of managing authorizations. Instead of trying to manage all the permissions for an individual user, administrators create job-based roles and then assign permissions to those roles. They can then assign users to roles. This is a little more work up-front, but it makes life much easier down the road.

When a new user arrives, the administrator doesn't need to figure out all the explicit permissions that user requires—the user just needs to be assigned to the appropriate roles and all the permissions will follow. Similarly, when a group of users needs a new permission, the administrator doesn't have to apply it to each user individually. It can be assigned to the role, and all users with that role will receive the permission automatically.

> **NOTE**
>
> When we're designing an access control system, we need to select the approach that best balances security requirements and business needs in our organization. If we choose a system that is not strict enough, we might unintentionally jeopardize our security. On the other hand, if we choose a system that is too strict, we might make it too difficult for people to get their work done.

ACCOUNT TYPES

Access control systems contain several different types of accounts, and each category requires different types of controls.

User Accounts

Most of the accounts that we manage are standard user accounts. They're assigned to an individual user and grant routine access to resources. Everyone from the receptionist to the CEO in an organization typically has a standard user account, even though those accounts may have dramatically different privileges. User accounts should be subject to routine monitoring for compromise and should follow a life cycle management process for creation and removal.

Administrator Accounts

Some accounts belong to system administrators and have extensive privileges to modify system configurations. These accounts are highly sensitive and should be carefully guarded using a process known as *privileged account management*. Generally speaking, you should log every action performed by a privileged account and treat any suspicious activity occurring on a privileged account as a high priority for investigation.

It's easy for users with privileged access to make mistakes and cause unintended but drastic consequences. Also, the more that you use an account, the higher the likelihood of compromise. Therefore, administrative users who require privileged access typically have standard user accounts that they use for most of their routine activity and then manually elevate their account to privileged status when they need to issue an administrative command. The exact mechanism for this elevation will vary depending on the access control system, but it may consist of logging in with a different account or assuming an administrative role.

Guest Accounts

Guest accounts provide users with temporary access to resources. For example, you might use guest accounts to grant a visitor access to your wireless network. Guest accounts should be tied to unique individuals and should expire after a reasonable period of time.

Shared/Generic Accounts

Shared or generic accounts are accounts where more than one individual has access to use the account. Generally speaking, these accounts are a bad idea. It is difficult to trace who performed an action with a shared account, and every user has plausible deniability when several people have access to an account.

Service Accounts

Service accounts are a special type of account used internally by a system to run a process or perform other actions. These accounts typically have privileged access and should be carefully controlled. You should configure service accounts so that they may not be used to log on to the system interactively and their passwords should not be known by anyone.

NONREPUDIATION

Another important focus of some security controls is providing *nonrepudiation*. Repudiation is a term that means denying that something is true. Nonrepudiation is a security goal that prevents someone from falsely denying that something is true.

For example, you might agree to pay someone $10,000 in exchange for a car. If you just had a handshake agreement, it might be possible for you to later repudiate your actions. You might claim that you never agreed to purchase the car or that you agreed to pay a lower price.

We solve this issue by using signed contracts when we sell a car. Your signature on the document is the proof that you agreed to the terms, and if you later go to court, the person selling you the car can prove that you agreed by showing the judge the signed document. Physical signatures provide nonrepudiation on contracts, receipts, and other paper documents.

There's also an electronic form of the physical signature. *Digital signatures* use encryption technology to provide nonrepudiation for electronic documents. You won't need to know the details of how digital signatures work on the ITF+ exam, but you should know that digital signatures provide nonrepudiation for electronic documents.

There are other ways that you can provide nonrepudiation as well. You might use biometric security controls, such as a fingerprint or facial recognition, to prove that someone was in a facility or performed an action. You might also use video surveillance for that same purpose. All of these controls allow you to prove that someone was in a particular location or performed an action, offering some degree of nonrepudiation.

CERTMIKE EXAM ESSENTIALS

▶ The access control process consists of three major steps. Identification is when a user makes a claim of identity. Authentication is when the user proves that identity claim. Authorization is when the system determines that the user is allowed to perform a requested action.

▶ Accounting processes create a record of who performed which actions on a system and are useful when investigating security incidents.

▶ Multifactor authentication combines authentication techniques using at least two of the three factors: something you know, something you have, and something you are.

▶ Nonrepudiation uses technical measures to ensure that a user is not able to later deny that they took some action.

Practice Question 1

You are considering deploying a multifactor authentication system to protect access to your organization's virtual private network (VPN). Which one of the following combinations of controls would meet this requirement?

A. Password and PIN
B. Fingerprint and eye scan
C. Smartcard and fingerprint
D. Keyfob and smartcard

Practice Question 2

You are working with a home loan provider who needs a system that will ensure they can prove in court that a user signed a contract. What type of requirement are they most directly trying to achieve?

A. Authentication
B. Authorization
C. Accounting
D. Nonrepudiation

Practice Question 1 Explanation

Before we can answer this question, we must identify the authentication factors in use here.

Passwords and PINs are both examples of something you know.

Fingerprint and eye scans are both examples of something you are.

Keyfobs and smartcards are both examples of something you have.

The only answer option that combines techniques from two different factors is the use of a smartcard (something you have) with a fingerprint (something you are).

Correct Answer: C. Smartcard and fingerprint

Practice Question 2 Explanation

This is a tricky question because the user is technically performing all of these actions. Before allowing a user to sign a contract, the system must be confident in their identity, and it gains this confidence through the authentication process. It must also be sure that the user is allowed to enter into the contract, which it does through the authorization process. And the lender will definitely want to keep a record of the action, which is done through the accounting process.

However, this question is about proving to a third party that the user signed the contract. This is preventing the user from denying the action and is a nonrepudiation requirement.

Correct Answer: D. Nonrepudiation

CHAPTER 37

Password Best Practices
Objective 6.5: Explain password best practices

Passwords remain the most common authentication technique used by modern organizations. IT professionals often work with passwords as they assist users in navigating the authentication process.

In this chapter, you'll learn the material that you need to know about ITF+ objective 6.5. The objectives covered in this chapter include:

▶ **Password length**
▶ **Password complexity**
▶ **Password history**
▶ **Password expiration**
▶ **Password reuse across sites**
▶ **Password managers**
▶ **Password reset process**

PASSWORD POLICIES

When you set a password policy for your organization, you have a number of technical controls available that allow you to set requirements for how users choose and maintain their passwords. Let's discuss a few of those mechanisms.

Password Length

The simplest and most common control on passwords is setting the *password length*. This is simply the minimum number of characters that must be included in a password.

It's good practice to require that passwords be at least eight characters, but some organizations require even longer passwords. The longer a password, the harder it is to guess.

Password Complexity

Organizations may also set *password complexity* requirements. These requirements force users to include different types of characters in their passwords, such as uppercase and lowercase letters, digits, and special characters. Just as with password length, the more character types in a password, the harder it is to guess.

Password Expiration

Password expiration requirements force users to change their passwords periodically. For example, an organization might set a password expiration period of 180 days, forcing users to change their passwords every six months. These days, many organizations no longer have password expiration requirements, allowing users to keep the same password for as long as they'd like and only requiring that they change it if the password is compromised.

Password History

Password history requirements are designed to prevent users from reusing old passwords. Organizations with password history requirements configure their systems to remember the previous passwords used by each user and prevent them from reusing that password in the future. Password history controls allow the administrator to identify how many old passwords are remembered for each user.

Password Resets

Every organization should allow users to change their passwords quickly and easily. You want users to be able to privately select their own passwords and do so whenever they are concerned that their password may be compromised.

One point of caution is that organizations should carefully evaluate their password reset process for users who forget their passwords. If they're not designed well, these processes can provide an opportunity for attackers to gain access to a system by performing an unauthorized password reset.

Password Reuse

IT teams should also strongly encourage users not to reuse the same password across multiple sites. This is difficult to enforce, but it does provide a strong measure of security. If a user reuses the same password on many different sites and one of those sites is compromised, an attacker might test that password on other sites, hoping that the password owner reuses the same password.

Password Managers

It's difficult for users to manage unique passwords for every site they visit. That's where password managers play a crucial role. These valuable tools are secure password vaults, often protected by biometric security mechanisms that create and store unique passwords. They then automatically fill those passwords into websites when the user visits them. That way users can have unique, strong passwords for every site they visit without having to remember them all.

Figure 37.1 shows an example of LastPass, a popular password manager, being used to create a new, strong password.

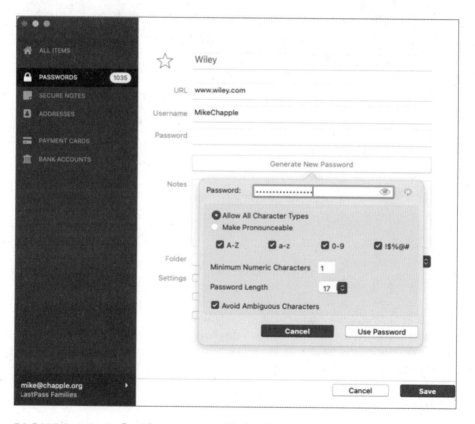

FIGURE 37.1 Creating a password in LastPass

CERTMIKE EXAM ESSENTIALS

▶ Password length requirements set a minimum number of characters that must be in a user's password, and password complexity requirements mandate the use of different character types.

▶ Password history requirements prevent the reuse of old passwords, and password expiration requirements force the periodic reset of existing passwords. Users should be permitted to reset their passwords whenever they wish.

▶ Users should be encouraged not to reuse passwords across multiple sites because this increases the risk of compromise. Password managers provide a convenient tool for managing many unique, strong passwords.

Practice Question 1

Andy is attempting to change his password and has created the following long password:

p7djkqnr2LAD

He receives an error message that he must use a symbol in his password. What password policy is he failing to meet?

A. Password length
B. Password history
C. Password complexity
D. Password reuse

Practice Question 2

You recently learned that a website belonging to one of your competitors was breached, and you are concerned that users with accounts on both sites will have their passwords compromised on your site as well. Which one of the following password policies would best protect against this risk?

A. Password reuse
B. Password complexity
C. Password length
D. Password history

Practice Question 1 Explanation

This is an example of a password complexity requirement. The message is requiring that Andy use a symbol in his password, and password complexity requirements require the use of different character types.

There is no indication that Andy is attempting to reuse an old password that would violate a password history requirement. Nor is he trying to use a password from another site that would violate a password reuse requirement. There is also no indication that his password is too short and does not meet the password length requirements.

Correct Answer: C. Password complexity

Practice Question 2 Explanation

The primary risk here is that some of your customers are using the same password on your competitor's site and your site. If the breach compromised passwords, the attacker would be able to use credentials from the other site to access accounts on your site. A password reuse policy would protect against this risk.

Password length and complexity requirements ensure that users create strong passwords, but the strength of the password is not in question here. If the attacker is able to obtain the passwords from another site, it does not matter how strong they are.

Password history requirements may be of some use in this situation because they would prevent a user from reusing the compromised password at a later date, but that is not the primary threat here. The major risk is that an account will be compromised now because it shares a password with an account on the compromised site.

Correct Answer: A. Password reuse

Encryption
Objective 6.6: Explain common uses of encryption

Encryption protects information from prying eyes by making it unreadable to anyone who does not have the required decryption key. We use encryption to protect data that is at rest on a storage device or in motion over a network.

In this chapter, you'll learn the material that you need to know about ITF+ objective 6.6. The objectives covered in this chapter include:

▶ **Plain text vs. cipher text**
▶ **Data at rest**
▶ **Data in transit**

CRYPTOGRAPHY

Encryption is one of the most important security controls that we can use to protect the confidentiality of our data. Encryption uses mathematical operations to transform information into a format where it is unreadable by anyone other than the authorized user.

EXAM TIP

The math behind encryption is pretty complex, but the good news is that you won't be responsible for any of that math on the ITF+ exam. You just need to know the basics of what encryption does and how you can use it to protect your organization.

Encrypting Data

When we are encrypting data, we start with some *plain text* information. Plain text is just a fancy way of saying that we have information in normal form. Anyone who looks at that data can read it. Figure 38.1 shows an example of a file containing plain text—the first paragraph from this chapter.

```
● ● ●                    Chapter 38 — vi plaintext.txt — 58×11
Encryption protects information from prying eyes by making
 it unreadable to anyone who does not have the required de
cryption key.  We use encryption to protect data that is a
t rest on a storage device or in motion over a network.
▌

~

~

~

~

~
```

FIGURE 38.1 Plain text message

We then take that information and use an encryption algorithm in combination with an encryption key to encrypt the data. The algorithm is the mathematical formula for the encryption, and the key is basically the password to the data. Once we've taken plain text data and encrypted it, we then call the data *ciphertext*. Figure 38.2 shows the ciphertext obtained by encrypting the plain text message shown in Figure 38.1.

```
● ● ●                    Chapter 38 — vi ciphertext.txt — 58×11
69E26EAEE650B3DF894A95206D7DC8752D803A38412D8144E49CD50ECF
4BFF4172DCF5F294786279BEEE5082098F308436122C6481681443A87B
7BD61F397CD5CAE73A91B6B750C64A7C46FC05266662045F003237AE12
3CB977AEFC770ABB9476756D9D070874F7DF0947E9B535259974168078
840F73C54D53D6AA77D88C73CC81510A8573E4D3FFDA2EE4735F981876
4E4598FAE2FAC4F9307B3033B221DAF2A63803672DCE4F1DB401E2C649
D13D995FFADE7FB8B15658FC82962AB38867F205C62826F0D44D9EA6C6
BA58834CB947807A5AB87EFE14F9FD3C4BD9AAEA1B8A71E811109422E9
E36C333C69260456
▌
```

FIGURE 38.2 Ciphertext message obtained by encrypting the plain text in Figure 38.1

That ciphertext data is completely unreadable to anyone who examines it. It just looks like nonsense, and we can't make heads or tails of it. That stays true until we decrypt the data.

Decrypting Data

When someone wants to *decrypt* the ciphertext and turn it back into plain text, they use the decryption algorithm and the decryption key to perform that transformation. If they don't know the correct decryption key, the decryption simply won't work. So protecting the key is vital. As long as unauthorized users don't have access to the decryption key, they won't have access to the data.

USES OF ENCRYPTION

We use encryption in two different environments. We use it to protect data at rest and we use it to protect data that is in transit.

Data at Rest

Data at rest is simply stored data. We can encrypt individual files, entire disks, or the contents of a mobile device. If someone gains access to one of those encrypted files, disks, or mobile devices, we don't need to worry about the encrypted data because they won't have access to the decryption key.

Full-disk encryption (FDE) is a technology built into some operating systems that automatically encrypts all of the data stored on a device. FDE technology is particularly useful for laptops, tablets, smartphones, and other devices that may be lost or stolen. Someone who steals the device will not be able to access the data it contains if that data is protected by full-disk encryption.

Data in Transit

Data in transit is data that's moving over a network. We can protect this data as well by using encryption.

When we access a website using the standard *HTTP* protocol, that data is unencrypted and anyone who observes our network activity can eavesdrop on our web use. However, if we use the secure *HTTPS* protocol, that connection is encrypted and the data being sent over the network is safe from prying eyes.

We can use the same encryption technology to protect the data being sent in email messages, from mobile applications to their servers, or even to protect entire network connections with encryption using a *virtual private network (VPN)*.

EXAM TIP

When you take the exam, you should understand that encryption is used to transform plain text into ciphertext and that it protects both data at rest—stored in files or on devices—and data in transit as it is being sent over a network.

CERTMIKE EXAM ESSENTIALS

▶ Encryption is the process of transforming plain text information into ciphertext that can't be read by unauthorized individuals. Decryption uses a decryption key to convert ciphertext back into plain text.

▶ Encryption may be used to protect data at rest by encrypting individual files or folders. Full-disk encryption (FDE) uses encryption to protect the entire contents of a device.

▶ Encryption may be used to protect data in motion by encrypting it as it travels over a network. The HTTPS protocol encrypts web traffic and is a secure alternative to the unencrypted HTTP protocol. Virtual private networks (VPNs) encrypt entire network connections.

Practice Question 1

You are concerned that users traveling with laptops will have those devices stolen while in transit. What encryption technology would best protect the data stored on those laptops?

A. HTTPS

B. HTTP

C. VPN

D. FDE

Practice Question 2

You have a group of remote users who need to access the corporate network from their homes. You would like to protect the information that they send back and forth to the corporate network, regardless of the application that they use. What encryption technology would best meet this need?

A. HTTPS

B. HTTP

C. VPN

D. FDE

Practice Question 1 Explanation

This question is asking us to identify an encryption technology that will protect data at rest and, in particular, the entire contents of a laptop. Full-disk encryption (FDE) is designed for this use case. FDE encrypts an entire hard drive, rendering the contents inaccessible to an unauthorized individual who steals or finds the device.

HTTP is not an encrypted protocol. HTTPS is a secure, encrypted alternative to HTTP but it is used to protect web traffic, which is an example of data in motion, and would not be effective in protecting a lost or stolen laptop.

Similarly, virtual private networks (VPNs) protect network communications and would not be effective in protecting a lost or stolen laptop.

Correct Answer: D. FDE

Practice Question 2 Explanation

We can begin here by eliminating full-disk encryption (FDE) as an answer choice because FDE is designed to protect the contents of a disk—data at rest. It does not protect data in transit over a network.

The HTTP protocol is unencrypted, so it does not provide any protection. HTTPS is a secure, encrypted alternative to HTTP, but it is used only to protect web traffic. It would protect any web communications from the remote users but would not protect other applications.

Virtual private networks (VPNs) create secure network connections between two locations and would be an effective means of protecting the communications of these remote users.

Correct Answer: C. VPN

CHAPTER 39

Business Continuity and Disaster Recovery

Objective 6.7: Explain business continuity concepts

Business continuity planning is one of the core responsibilities of the information security profession. We face many potential disruptions in our business operations, ranging from natural disasters to human-created threats. Business continuity programs seek to make our businesses resilient against these threats.

In this chapter, you'll learn the material that you need to know about ITF+ objective 6.7. The objectives covered in this chapter include:

▶ **Fault tolerance**
▶ **Disaster recovery**

BUSINESS CONTINUITY

Business continuity efforts are a collection of activities designed to keep a business running in the face of adversity. This may come in the form of a small-scale incident, such as a single system failure, or a catastrophic incident, such as an earthquake or a tornado. Business continuity plans may also be activated by human-made disasters, such as a terrorist attack or hacker intrusion.

While many organizations place responsibility for business continuity with operational engineering teams, business continuity is a core security concept because it is the primary control that supports the security objective of availability. Remember, that's one of the CIA triad objectives of information security: confidentiality, integrity, and availability.

Developing a Business Continuity Plan

When an organization begins a business continuity effort, it's easy to quickly become over-whelmed by the many possible scenarios and controls that the project might consider. For this reason, the team developing a business continuity contingency plan should take time up-front to carefully define their scope. Answer the following questions:

> ▶ Which business activities will be covered by the plan?
> ▶ What types of systems will it cover?
> ▶ What types of controls will it consider?

The answers to these questions will help you make critical prioritization decisions down the road.

Business Continuity Controls

With the answers to our scope questions in mind, business continuity professionals have a number of tools at their disposal to help remediate potential availability issues.

Redundancy

One of the critical ways that IT professionals protect the availability of systems is ensuring that they are *redundant*. That simply means that they are designed in such a way that the failure of a single component doesn't bring the entire system down—business can continue in the face of a single predictable failure. Redundancy should include having redundant servers, redundant disks, redundant power sources, and redundant network connections. That will help protect your business against many different types of failure by building systems that are protected against small failures. Increasing the redundancy of systems is one way of making them *fault tolerant*. This means that they are likely to be able to continue operating even after experiencing some type of failure.

EXAM TIP

Uninterruptible power supplies (UPSs) play an important role in providing fault-tolerant power to systems. They have large batteries that are capable of keeping equipment running in the face of a brief power outage. UPS batteries typically only last for minutes, so longer-term outages require alternative sources of power, such as those offered by a diesel-powered generator.

Another example of fault tolerance is the use of a technology called *redundant arrays of inexpensive disks (RAID)*. RAID technology places multiple hard drives in a single server and stores copies of data in multiple locations. This protects the system so that no data is lost, even if one of the hard drives fails.

Replication

Organizations should also perform *replication* of their data to alternate locations. This provides redundancy for that data. Ideally, organizations will conduct regular backups of their critical data files, operating systems, and databases and place those backups in secure locations. While organizations may keep some of their backups locally at their main data center for convenience, it's also important to have backups stored offsite, either at another location or in the cloud. These off-site backups provide redundancy in the event that a catastrophic disaster destroys an entire building.

Redundancy and replication play a crucial role in building an organization's business continuity plan and protecting the organization against many different contingencies.

DISASTER RECOVERY

Business continuity programs are designed to keep a business up and running in the face of a disaster, but unfortunately, they don't always work. Sometimes continuity controls fail or the sheer magnitude of a disaster overwhelms the organization's capacity to continue operations. That's where disaster recovery begins.

Disaster recovery is a subset of business continuity activities designed to restore a business to normal operations as quickly as possible following a disruption. The disaster recovery plan may include immediate measures that get operations working again temporarily, but the disaster recovery effort is not finished until the organization is completely back to normal.

The initial response following an emergency disruption is designed to contain the damage to the organization and recover whatever capacity may be immediately restored. The activities during this initial response will vary widely depending on the nature of the disaster and may include activating an alternate processing facility, containing physical damage, and calling in contractors to begin an emergency response.

During a disaster recovery effort, the focus of most of the organization shifts from normal business activity to a concentrated effort to restore operations as quickly as possible. From a staffing perspective, this means that many employees will be working in temporary jobs that may be completely different from their normally assigned duties. Flexibility is key during a disaster response. Also, the organization should plan disaster responsibilities as much as possible in advance and provide employees with training that prepares them to do their part during disaster recovery.

Disaster Communications

Communication is crucial to disaster recovery efforts. Responders must have secure, reliable means to communicate with each other and the organization's leadership. This includes the initial communication required to activate the disaster recovery process, even if the disaster occurs after hours; regular status updates for both employees in the field and leadership; and ad hoc communications to meet tactical needs.

Assessing Damage and Recovering

After the immediate danger to the organization clears, the disaster recovery team shifts from immediate response mode into assessment mode. The goal of this phase is simple: to triage the damage to the organization and develop a plan to recover operations on a permanent basis.

This plan must be prioritized to ensure that the most important data and systems are restored first. In some circumstances, it may also include intermediate steps that restore operations temporarily on the way to permanent recovery. After developing a plan, responders then execute it, restoring operations and access to systems and data in an orderly fashion.

EXAM TIP

The disaster recovery effort only concludes when the organization is back to normal operations in their primary operating environment.

CERTMIKE EXAM ESSENTIALS

▶ Business continuity controls are designed to keep business operations running in the face of an emergency. Redundancy and replication are common business continuity controls. Redundancy uses multiple components to protect against the failure of a single component. Replication makes copies of data elsewhere.

▶ Disaster recovery controls are designed to restore normal operations after an event disrupts those normal operations. Disaster recovery picks up the pieces when business continuity efforts fail.

▶ Disaster recovery efforts end only when the organization is operating in its primary operating environment.

Practice Question 1

Which one of the following technologies is a redundancy control that protects against the failure of a single disk?

A. RAID
B. Firewall
C. VPN
D. Dual-power supplies

Practice Question 2

You are helping your organization recover from a server crash. Your supervisor asks you to ensure that your largest customer's data is restored first. What term best describes the nature of this request?

A. Communication
B. Prioritization
C. Redundancy
D. Continuity

Practice Question 1 Explanation

Firewalls and VPNs are security controls, but they are not redundancy controls. Firewalls block unwanted network connections and VPNs secure network traffic. Therefore, we can eliminate both of those answer choices.

Dual-power supplies are a redundancy control, but they protect against the failure of a power supply, not the failure of a disk.

Redundant arrays of inexpensive disks (RAID) arrays are designed to create redundancy for disks, protecting against the failure of a single disk.

Correct Answer: A. RAID

Practice Question 2 Explanation

This is an example of a prioritization request. In the aftermath of a disaster, it is common to identify the most important systems and data to restore and then restore those first. This prioritization helps guide the recovery efforts.

While this is also an example of a communication, that is a very general term, so prioritization better describes the request.

Redundancy is the use of multiple systems or components to protect against a failure. That is not happening in this scenario. Continuity is the set of actions designed to keep operations running during an emergency. Continuity has failed in this scenario, and you are in the disaster recovery process.

Correct Answer: B. Prioritization

Index

ONLINE TEST BANK

To help you study for your CompTIA ITF+ certification exam, register to gain one year of FREE access after activation to the online interactive test bank—included with your purchase of this book! All of the chapter review questions and the practice tests in this book are included in the online test bank so you can practice in a timed and graded setting.

REGISTER AND ACCESS THE ONLINE TEST BANK

To register your book and get access to the online test bank, follow these steps:

1. Go to www.wiley.com/go/sybextestprep. You'll see the "**How to Register Your Book for Online Access**" instructions.
2. Click "here to register" and then select your book from the list.
3. Complete the required registration information, including answering the security verification to prove book ownership. You will be emailed a pin code.
4. Follow the directions in the email or go to www.wiley.com/go/sybextestprep.
5. Find your book on that page and click the "Register or Login" link with it. Then enter the pin code you received and click the "Activate PIN" button.
6. On the Create an Account or Login page, enter your username and password, and click Login or, if you don't have an account already, create a new account.
7. At this point, you should be in the test bank site with your new test bank listed at the top of the page. If you do not see it there, please refresh the page or log out and log back in.